Praise for *Cultural Agility*

"By any standard, cultural agility—in a mosaic of contexts and roles—is critical to compete and win in global markets. Caligiuri delivers valuable talent-management practices that complete the mosaic and accelerate cultural agility."

—Wayne F. Cascio, Ph.D., Robert H. Reynolds Distinguished Chair in Global Leadership, University of Colorado—Denver; senior editor, *Journal of World Business*; and author, *Investing in People: Financial Impact of Human Resource Initiatives*

"In the new global economy, organizations win with talent—and global competence and agility are key drivers of workforce success. Based on more than two decades of academic research and consulting experience, Caligiuri provides a practical how-to guide for building a pipeline of culturally agile talent. Executives, business leaders, HR professionals—anyone who needs to build cross-cultural competence in the workforce—will benefit from reading *Cultural Agility*."

—Mark Huselid, Ph.D., Distinguished Professor of HR Strategy, Rutgers University; author, *The HR Scorecard, The Workforce Scorecard*, and *The Differentiated Workforce*

"Ideal for managers, leaders, and HR professionals who understand the complex challenges of globalization—and know the important role cross-culturally competent professionals can play to help their organizations overcome them."

—Dan Cable, Ph.D., Professor of Organizational Behavior, London Business School; author, *Change to Strange: Create a Great Organization by Building a Strange Workforce*

CULTURAL AGILITY

CULTURAL AGILITY

Building a Pipeline of Successful
Global Professionals

PAULA CALIGIURI

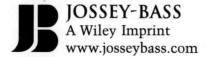

JOSSEY-BASS
A Wiley Imprint
www.josseybass.com

Published by Jossey-Bass
A Wiley Imprint
One Montgomery Street, Suite 1200, San Francisco, CA 94104-4594—www.josseybass.com

Cover image by Veer. Cover design by Mary Pomerantz Advertising.

Jossey-Bass books and products are available through most bookstores. To contact Jossey-Bass directly call our Customer Care Department within the U.S. at 800-956-7739, outside the U.S. at 317-572-3986, or fax 317-572-4002.

Wiley publishes in a variety of print and electronic formats and by print-on-demand. Some material included with standard print versions of this book may not be included in e-books or in print-on-demand. If this book refers to media such as a CD or DVD that is not included in the version you purchased, you may download this material at http://booksupport.wiley.com. For more information about Wiley products, visit www.wiley.com.

Library of Congress Cataloging-in-Publication Data

Caligiuri, Paula.
  Cultural agility : building a pipeline of successful global professionals / Paula Caligiuri.
    p.   cm. —(Jossey-Bass business and management series)
  Includes bibliographical references and index.
  ISBN 978-1-118-27507-8 (cloth); ISBN 978-1-118-33337-2 (ebk);
  ISBN 978-1-118-33127-9 (ebk); ISBN 978-1-118-33054-8 (ebk)
    1. International business enterprises—Cross-cultural studies. 2. International business enterprises—Management. 3. Management—Cross-cultural studies. I. Title.
  HD2755.5.C365   2012
  658.3008—dc23

                                                                      2012022628

Printed in the United States of America
FIRST EDITION

HB Printing   10 9 8 7 6 5 4 3 2 1

With love and appreciation, I dedicate this book to my parents, John and Angie.

CONTENTS

PART 3: Attract and Select the Most Culturally Agile Talent   67

PART 4: Train and Develop Culturally Agile Talent   117

PREFACE

If cultural agility could be traded as a commodity, it would be white-hot right now. The current supply of culturally agile professionals is meager compared to the burgeoning organizational demand. In survey after survey, business leaders from CEOs to CHROs express the need to compete aggressively for cross-culturally competent global business professionals.

As a person who has chosen to read this book, you are probably aware of the challenges posed by the global environment. Drawing from your own experiences, you can probably provide some illustrative examples of why a more robust pipeline of culturally agile professionals is needed in your organization. You might tell me about a business unit that has been stalled trying to enter an emerging market, mired in bureaucracy and draining valuable resources. You might cite a costly example of a high-profile global innovation team whose members cannot catch a collaborative stride and are missing critical performance goals. You might share stories of international assignees who were brilliant in their functional roles domestically but unsuccessful when living or working internationally. You might also have a story about a bungled global technological implementation, a misguided attempt at offshoring, or a high-profile foreign acquisition that ultimately fell far below its expected return on investment.

If any of these challenges sound familiar, you are not alone. They are playing in an almost continuous loop in organizations around the world. This book is for managers and leaders who understand all these challenges and know that building a pipeline of culturally agile professionals within their organizations will help address them. The book is also for HR professionals tasked with delivering talent with increased cross-cultural competencies and cultural agility to their organizations, but concerned about their lack of available developmental options. These HR professionals understand that cross-cultural training and international assignments cannot build cross-cultural competencies effectively or efficiently enough to provide a workable solution.

These concerns are justified, because cultural agility is not developed in the way most people believe it is. Employees cannot "take the training course" or "go to the residential program" to gain it. It is just not that simple. At the same time, it really isn't all that complicated. You can build practices into organizations to increase cultural agility at a much faster rate than you have been doing. By fully understanding how cultural agility is attained, you can identify those who will experience accelerated development through their work in international and multicultural environments. You can help your organization win the future by effectively building the best possible pipeline of cross-culturally competent and culturally agile professionals. I am certain that we can do much better in fostering cultural agility, because we now have a significant knowledge base on the best practices. We know who will gain cultural agility—and how.

WHY I WROTE *CULTURAL AGILITY*

In a world that is easily interconnected through cyberspace and international airports, it is easy to forget that global success takes more than a passport and a plane ticket. I wrote *Cultural Agility* because in the two decades since the Berlin Wall fell—the symbolic start of the era of globalization—individuals, teams, and companies continue to struggle with the human resource challenges related to globalization. The many technological, communications, and transportation advances have masked the fact that success in global endeavors remains, more often than not, dependent on individual professionals with an ability to operate effectively in intercultural situations. These professionals have cultural agility.

I wrote *Cultural Agility* to share the insights I have gleaned from two decades of research and consulting dedicated to helping students, individuals, companies, teams, and executives become effective in today's complex global environment. Since the late 1980s, I have been studying what it takes to succeed globally—identifying the qualities that characterize those with cross-cultural competence and helping organizations build cultural agility in their respective workforces. The time has come to share what I've learned.

HOW THIS BOOK IS ORGANIZED

Part One, Introduction: The Basics of Cultural Agility, comprises Chapter One (What Is Cultural Agility—and Why Is It So Crucial Today?), which defines cultural agility and underscores the immediate need for organizations to build a pipeline of culturally agile professionals. It outlines several erroneous assumptions that can create barriers to the development of cultural agility in organizations.

In Part Two, Who Is Culturally Agile? Chapters Two and Three examine that question through the lens of the *Cultural Agility Competency Framework*, a model of twelve cross-cultural competencies that sets the foundation for strategic talent management to build a pipeline of culturally agile professionals.

Chapter Two (Three Cross-Cultural Competencies Affecting Culturally Agile Responses) delves deeply into the first three of these competencies, citing supporting research and practical examples to demonstrate their importance. Chapter Three (Nine Cross-Cultural Competencies Affecting Success of Culturally Agile Professionals) discusses the remaining nine competencies of the Cultural Agility

Competency Framework. It presents validity evidence for the competencies and offers illustrations of culturally agile professionals operating with these competencies.

In Part Three, Attract and Select the Most Culturally Agile Talent, Chapters Four and Five focus on strategies for staffing the organization with the needed culturally agile professionals.

Chapter Four (Attracting and Recruiting for Cultural Agility) describes how organizations can attract the culturally agile professionals they need. Beyond attraction, we also need these professionals to say yes to the job offers we extend. This chapter describes ways to create a compelling employee value proposition for culturally agile professionals. Chapter Five (Assessing and Selecting for Cultural Agility) delves into the attributes of those with the greatest propensity to readily develop cultural agility. To assist you in your role as a business leader, HR professional, or team leader, this chapter will offer tools to help you assess and select those who belong in your organization's pipeline of culturally agile professionals.

The chapters of Part Four, Train and Develop Culturally Agile Talent, focus on developing a learning system for building cultural agility in the workforce through organizational intervention. Chapters Six, Seven, and Eight describe how organizations can use experiential assignments to develop cultural agility in their workforce.

Chapter Six (Building the Foundation for Cultural Agility with Cross-Cultural Training) highlights the most important learning goals for cross-cultural training and the best way to design and deliver these programs. This chapter illustrates ways to increase the value and efficacy of cross-cultural training programs. Chapter Seven (Crafting Developmental Cross-Cultural Experiences to Increase Cultural Agility) presents compelling evidence for other developmental interventions that will result in the greatest gains in cultural agility for your employees. This chapter presents the contingencies under which cross-cultural experiences can be developmental. It also provides details about specific interventions that have worked for leading organizations in accelerating the development of cultural agility. Chapter Eight (Developing Cultural Agility Through International Assignments) focuses on the most common method for developing cultural agility: international assignments. Although this practice is indeed common, it has proven to be only partially effective. This chapter explains why and offers specific recommendations for designing truly developmental international assignments.

Part Five, Conclusion: Leadership and Organizational Factors, comprises Chapter Nine (Managing and Leading to Build Cultural Agility in the Workforce), which illustrates how business leaders can motivate and equip their workers to become more culturally agile. Even the best recruitment, selection, training, and development practices will not result in a culturally agile workforce unless the organization's culture and leadership also support this goal. This concluding chapter guides organizational leaders in leading by example and building a corporate culture that embodies cultural agility. It also discusses the integration of the functional areas within HR necessary to implement the practices supporting the development of workforce cultural agility, namely, global mobility, talent development, and recruiting. The chapter ends by encouraging you, the reader, to turn inward, to develop your own cultural agility as you build your organization's pipeline of culturally agile professionals.

A WORD ABOUT WORDS

In my vocabulary for this book, I opted for common usage over academic parlance. The umbrella terms I've adopted are consistent with the phrases used by the organizations and professionals with whom I've worked. Although I do not expect my use of terms to be controversial, I do believe they deserve some clarification.

I use *global professional* to describe any individual who is working with, for, or alongside those of different nationalities, whether in a domestic or international context. As such, a call center operator who has never left India but serves U.S. clients is as much of a global professional as the CEO of a leading Dutch organization with subsidiaries in forty countries. I use *development* and related terms like *developmental* and *developmental experience* to refer to the building of cross-cultural competencies, whereas in general HR usage these may refer to job competencies of any kind. This book is about creating a pipeline of those who can succeed in cross-cultural contexts; clearly, there is a wide range of situations that might be defined this way. In this book, I am taking the broadest possible view of the term *cross-cultural* to include multicultural, intercultural, or international tasks, jobs, roles, and assignments. These tasks, jobs, roles, and assignments might involve a business trip or a longer relocation to another country, or they might occur domestically, with coworker interactions creating the cross-cultural context. Any experience that involves working with, for, or alongside individuals from different cultures is considered cross-cultural for the purposes of this book.

Considering these examples, you can also see that I am using *organization* broadly to refer to the various firms, businesses, associations, and institutions that employ professionals in cross-cultural contexts. Although most of this book is written with private sector business organizations in mind, its advice applies to a wide range of organizations striving to build cultural agility. Over the past decade, I have worked with organizations ranging from Fortune 100 firms to small entrepreneurial ventures, from the U.S. military and civilian government agencies to nongovernmental humanitarian organizations. These organizations share the desire to build a pipeline of individuals who can be effective in a cross-cultural context.

Without splitting hairs too much on terminology, you get the picture: this book is for all professionals who operate in situations where culture might influence the outcome of their work.

ACKNOWLEDGMENTS

This book would have been impossible to write without the generous assistance of many wonderful people. I especially thank those who agreed to be interviewed and granted permission for their stories to be told: Marcelo Baudino, Christina Biedny, Randall Bradford, Sean Dubberke, Udo Fichtner, Rachele Focardi-Ferri, Chris Houghtaling, Jim Kupczyk, Jason Newman, James Piecowye, Jake Shannon, Otis Shepard, Chris Steinmetz, Sudhey Taveras, Theo van der Smeede, Zsolt Vincze, Jyoti Yagnik, and Asif Zulfiqar. Truly among the most cultural agile professionals on the planet, they are each worthy of deep admiration.

There are many talented practitioners and researchers who have advanced our knowledge of international HRM and have shaped my thinking on this subject. I have been fortunate to collaborate with them in research and practice—and feel truly blessed to also call them friends. I thank Nataliya Baytalskaya, Dick Beatty, Jaime Bonache, Wayne Cascio, Bill Castellano, Jean-Luc Cerdin, Saba Colakoglu, Jeff Conte, Andrea David, Dave Day, Victoria DiSanto, Michael Elia and the Team at TraQs Consulting, Jim Farr, Su Chuen Foo, Stan Gully, Hilary Harris, Thomas Hippler, Mark Huselid, Rick Jacobs, Kaifeng Jiang, Johanna Johnson, Mila Lazarova, Dave Lepak, Robert Lesser, Ahsiya Mencin, Ray Noe, Riall Nolan, Jean Phillips, Kat Ringenbach, Mike Schell and the Team at RW³ LLC, Jim Sesil, Laura Shankster-Cawley, Guenter Stahl, Linda Stroh, Vesa Suutari, Ibraiz Tarique, and Rosalie Tung.

For their support and guidance, heartfelt appreciation is extended to my senior editor at Jossey-Bass, Kathe Sweeny, and to my literary agent, Joe Veltre. Two individuals fall into the category of "godsends" in the last few months before *Cultural Agility* went into production: Elsa Peterson and Sari Maneotis. I thank them both for their tremendous contributions to this book.

I owe my deepest gratitude to my husband, George D'Annunzio. He generously cleared the decks for me on many days so that I could be alone to write. I love and appreciate George for many reasons, not the least of which is his willingness to join me in life's global adventure.

PART

1

INTRODUCTION: THE BASICS OF CULTURAL AGILITY

For the past two decades, I've worked with leaders from many global organizations who, without hesitation, can easily identify the global stars among their workforce. Equally without hesitation, they lament the need for more such stars. Business leaders are concerned about a shortage of the human talent required to meet the demands of future global business needs, such as expanding through innovations in mature markets, competing in emerging markets, collaborating with cross-border supply chain partners, integrating offshored support systems, and the like. The platform, if you will, is on fire. There is no time to lose.

CHAPTER

1

WHAT IS CULTURAL AGILITY—AND WHY IS IT SO CRUCIAL TODAY?

Within any global organization, it is the people—the human talent—who are actively engaged in assessing global risk, interacting with government regulators, and responding to unexpected shocks to the market, as well as handling mergers and acquisitions and the day-to-day management of global subsidiaries, teams, joint-venture relationships, and the like. The organization's human talent is building credibility and trust with foreign partners, vendors, clients, contractors, subordinates, and peers. It is through global professionals that the organization builds its knowledge of customs, norms, languages, legal systems, and other cultural capital. Ultimately, the organization depends on its global professionals to make it increasingly more competitive in the global economy.

With that in mind, take a moment to think about the global professionals in your own organization. Even though they are critical to your organization's global competitive advantage, they might also be at the heart of your business problems. When over one thousand CEOs in more than fifty countries were surveyed, "managing diverse cultures" was one of the top concerns they cited for the future.[1] A significant number of the CEOs in this survey indicated that their organizations' ability to be effective in this increasingly complex global environment is challenged by cultural barriers, such as cultural issues and conflicts, conflicting regulatory requirements, unexpected costs, stakeholder opposition, and—most central for this book—inadequate supply of talent to compete. Global business professionals—with responsibilities as diverse as market expansion, product innovation, and postacquisition integration—are technically and functionally gifted, but may lack the cultural agility needed for the task at hand.

Expansion abounds for organizations in every sector as global growth becomes the key to their future success. Across organizations, the time is right for investing in cultural agility. Global business growth is the way to win the future, and this growth depends on the strategic management of human talent. A 2011 survey of more than seven hundred CEOs found that talent management is one of the most critical vehicles for implementing global business growth strategies for the future.[2] Business leaders know that they need to invest in their strategies for managing talent if they are to win in more complex global environments, such as emerging markets.[3] There is widespread agreement among CEOs and other senior executives that talent management is critically important in formulating successful global growth strategies. It is time to deliver the talent management practices to empower your organization to win the future.

Talent management is one of the most critical vehicles for implementing global business growth strategies for the future.

CULTURAL AGILITY: A MEGA-COMPETENCY WITH THREE LEVELS

Cultural agility is the mega-competency that enables professionals to perform successfully in cross-cultural situations. All of us possess some level of cultural agility even before working in another culture or with people from different cultures. The idea of cultural agility follows from the common understanding of physical agility. Fitness experts describe agility as the ability to change the position of one's body rapidly and accurately without losing balance. Think about the natural differences among beginners in a yoga class: some are more naturally nimble, coordinated, and athletic. Depending on their natural abilities, these individuals will have different experiences in the class—some will feel exhilarated, some encouraged, and others very discouraged. If they continue with subsequent classes, all will improve their agility over time, though they will develop at different rates. Cultural agility works in the same manner. Professionals will develop their cultural agility differently depending on their international career orientation, personality characteristics, bio-data (including nonwork cross-cultural experiences), language skills, and cross-cultural competencies.

You have probably admired the agility of prima ballerinas, Cirque du Soleil performers, and professional football players making awe-inspiring goals in the final seconds of a game. Watching them in motion, you may be tempted to believe they were born with their godlike bodies and superhuman physical abilities. But you probably also know that years of training and unrelenting hours of practice have blazed clear neural pathways between their minds' commands and their bodies' movements. In truth, both nature and nurture play a part: these individuals' elite level of physical agility is a combination of natural abilities, motivation to succeed, guided training, coaching, and development over time. Cultural agility, as this book describes, is gained in the same manner—by combining individual skills and abilities, motivation, and experience.

Culturally agile professionals succeed in contexts where the successful outcome of their jobs, roles, positions, or tasks depends on dealing with an unfamiliar set of cultural norms—or multiple sets of them. These professionals might be aid workers operating in rural communities in developing nations, or professional athletes playing for teams located in a different country. They might be research scientists working in colocated multicultural research teams, or international assignees living and working in a different culture. They might be call center operators who are speaking with customers located in another part of the world, or professionals who are selling their products or services to clients from different cultures. Although a myriad of technical skills are necessary and will clearly affect performance, those technical skills are oftentimes not sufficient for success given the cross-cultural context of the role. For global professionals, performance depends on not only the *content* of their jobs but also on their ability to function in the cross-cultural *context* of their jobs. Cultural agility enables technically competent professionals to be successful irrespective of the multicultural or cross-cultural context.

For global professionals, performance depends on not only the content of their jobs but also on their ability to function in the cross-cultural context of their jobs.

Cultural agility is a practice, not an achievement, and building it is a process, not an event. For this reason, development is a concept closely related to cultural agility. The one is a route to the other. By ensuring that the cross-cultural experiences your professionals are exposed to are truly developmental, you can increase the cultural agility in your organization's talent pipeline.

Whatever their job titles or roles, culturally agile professionals are able to accurately read the cross-cultural or multicultural situation; assess the differences in behaviors, attitudes, and values; and respond successfully within the cross-cultural context. Success in a cross-cultural context is the most important indicator of a professional's cultural agility. Culturally agile professionals achieve success in multicultural, international, and cross-cultural situations by leveraging three different cultural responses:

1. Cultural adaptation

2. Cultural minimization

3. Cultural integration

Cultural adaptation is used at those times when adapting one's behavior to the norms of the context is critical. Cultural minimization, in contrast, is used at times when one's own cultural norms need to supersede the cultural expectations of others.

Cultural integration is used when finding a compromise is most important and well worth the effort. Successful culturally agile professionals are adept at toggling among these three responses.

The cross-cultural competencies that culturally agile professionals possess facilitate their effectiveness in three important ways:

1. Global professionals are able to manage their own response set in order to quickly, comfortably, and effectively work in different cultures and with people from different cultures.

2. Global professionals are able to connect with others from different cultures—to communicate appropriately, build trust, and gain the necessary credibility to work effectively in cross-cultural jobs, tasks, and roles.

3. Global professionals are able to make appropriate decisions by accurately reading and responding in the cultural context, while accounting for the business strategy and key elements of the cultural context (such as laws and regulations).

Collectively, cross-cultural competencies constitute the first-level indicator of cultural agility (depicted as the base of the pyramid in Figure 1.1), a foundation on which the higher-level competencies are developed.

FIGURE 1.1. *The Levels of Cultural Agility*

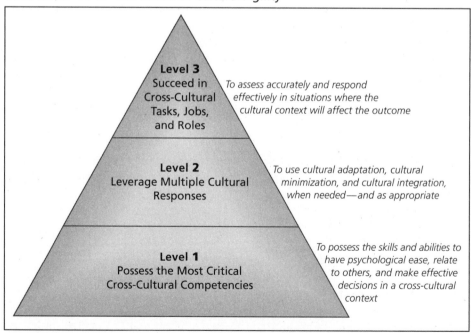

Level 3
Succeed in Cross-Cultural Tasks, Jobs, and Roles
To assess accurately and respond effectively in situations where the cultural context will affect the outcome

Level 2
Leverage Multiple Cultural Responses
To use cultural adaptation, cultural minimization, and cultural integration, when needed—and as appropriate

Level 1
Possess the Most Critical Cross-Cultural Competencies
To possess the skills and abilities to have psychological ease, relate to others, and make effective decisions in a cross-cultural context

THE NEED FOR SPEED IN BUILDING A PIPELINE OF CULTURALLY AGILE PROFESSIONALS

The demand for culturally agile professionals continues to accelerate in the twenty-first century as many organizations track a substantial increase in the percentage of profits generated outside their home countries. In the United States, despite its large domestic market, emblematic American companies such as Avon, Dow Chemical, and PepsiCo reported that 80 percent, 68 percent, and 45 percent of their revenues, respectively, were generated outside the United States.[4] This growth in international markets is resulting in an ever-increasing mix of people from different countries and cultures—partners, clients, customers, and colleagues.

A survey of global industry leaders found that expanding global customer reach to new emerging markets and engaging in successful mergers and acquisitions are among organizations' leading global business strategies.[5] This enthusiastic pursuit of global expansion, though clear and logical on paper, is not without problems and risks. Paul Clark, Ernst & Young's insurance sector leader for Asia-Pacific, aptly noted that when operating across countries, especially in emerging markets, business challenges become "compounded by the problems of working in foreign countries, including customs, culture, language, and different regulatory systems and working practices."[6] Such problems can also include unexpected changes in foreign government regulations, unstable political or economic conditions, currency fluctuations, insufficient collaborative technology, inadequate managerial control of a joint venture, or a much-needed associate's refusing a critical international assignment because his or her spouse is unwilling to relocate.

Expanding global customer reach to new emerging markets and engaging in successful mergers and acquisitions are among organizations' leading global business strategies.

But despite the challenges, risks, and ambiguities of global growth, its opportunities remain a powerful draw for organizations, which continue to expand their operations internationally at an unprecedented rate. To help navigate around or mitigate these potential challenges and risks, organizations rely on successful global professionals who can operate effectively in cross-cultural and international environments. I've not met a high-level leader in any industry who doesn't see cultural agility as a key factor for future success. On the contrary, I've found unanimous agreement that their organizations' global growing pains would ease if they had access to a robust pipeline of culturally agile professionals. The question is *how* to develop this pipeline—and how to do so *quickly*. In this book, I outline how to implement the most critical talent management practices to attract, recruit, select, train, and develop a culturally agile workforce.

The shortage of professionals with cross-cultural competencies is a concern shared by military leaders as well as corporate executives. The U.S. Army, for example, has been unambiguous in emphasizing the extent to which cross-cultural competence is needed now and in the future. The *Army Culture and Foreign Language Strategy* (released in December 2009) states that "Today's full spectrum operations require adaptable foreign language and cultural capabilities to be fully successful. Existing education and training programs and initiatives are helping to meet some needs, particularly for specialists, but do not meet the full needs of the Army. Closing the gaps in culture and foreign language capability requires addressing two major areas: building unit capability and expanding the scope of leader development."[7]

If you remove the words "the Army" from this passage and replace them with the name of your organization, you are likely to have an accurate summary of your organization's current state and future need for cultural agility. Although the professional roles of your associates are different from those of the soldiers and leaders in the U.S. Army, the need for cultural agility is the same. The global economy is also creating the need for companies to cast wider nets to source the best for their organizations, whether that means the best supply chain partners or the talent for the most critical roles. From professional sports leagues to executive suites, a global "best player" model is emerging. In the U.S.-based National Basketball Association, the number of foreign-born players has tripled since 1990; the number of international players in Major League Baseball is now roughly 30 percent.[8] In the boardrooms of major organizations, the same pattern emerges. Roughly two-thirds of organizations have members of their global management boards who originate from countries outside the organizations' home market.[9] The ranks of top management have also been opened to foreign-born nationals. This is a relatively new phenomenon, as global diversity in this realm was practically nonexistent as recently as the mid-1990s. Such CEOs as Howard Stringer (Sony), Indra Nooyi (PepsiCo), and Carlos Ghosn (Nissan and Renault) exemplify the trend toward having the global best players on executive teams.

In 2005, I published a study with Mila Lazarova and Stephan Zehetbauer examining whether the national diversity of top leaders (executive team and board of directors) was related to organizations' international financial performance and global reach—namely, their foreign assets ratio, foreign sales ratio, foreign subsidiaries ratio, and foreign employees ratio.[10] We found a strong positive relationship between leadership teams' national diversity and international performance. Of course, as with all studies interpreting correlations from a snapshot in time, we cannot say which came first—the national diversity of the leadership teams or the organizations' global performance. Frankly, for these purposes it does not matter. We know that in either case the trend is interesting, growing, and unlikely to reverse itself. The most likely explanation of our findings is that broadening global markets allow organizations to be more receptive to the presence of nonnational executives. Leaders today, now sharing the executive suite with leaders from diverse national backgrounds, will clearly need a greater amount of cultural agility than ever before.

Of course, it is not only corporate boards, top management teams, and professional athletes who are working with greater numbers of colleagues from different cultures. Globalization is affecting almost every worker today. According to a recent U.S. Census Bureau report, 12.3 percent of U.S. residents are foreign born—up from just 5 percent in 1970—and over 80 percent of these foreign-born individuals are of workforce age (eighteen to sixty-four).[11] This integration is not limited to the melting pot of the United States; the United Nations Global Commission on International Migration reported that 191 million people are living in a country other than where they were born. Comparing this figure with the world's population of 6.5 billion yields the global picture: worldwide, about one person in thirty-five is living and working in a foreign country.[12]

Today more than ever, professionals are not only working with people from different countries but also *relocating* to foreign countries as international assignees. More than 60 percent of global mobility professionals from companies headquartered all around the world expect their numbers of international assignments to increase in the coming year.[13] Twenty percent of these organizations reported having more than five hundred international assignees located around the world. And those are only the people who *reside* in foreign countries. We also need to consider the thousands who *travel* to other countries for business, whether to attend a meeting, conference, or training course for a few days or weeks, or who are in a position that requires substantial business travel or is colocated in multiple countries.

Many people assume that with the substantial investment in collaborative technology, such as multisite video and Web-enabled meetings, international business travel has been decreasing. In fact, international business travel is still on the upswing. Even though 79 percent of 350 global travel managers (those who manage corporate travel budgets) identified "cost control" and "reducing the overall level of spending on travel" as the greatest challenges facing business travel programs, 54 percent of them expect their business travel volumes to increase in the coming year as they have in the past.[14]

Without ever leaving their home countries, millions of professionals communicate across national borders in the daily course of their jobs. While their bodies are located in their home countries, their voices and words are heard and read all around the world, sometimes in many countries the same day. Combining this with the international migration statistics, we can clearly see that cultural agility is crucial not only for business travelers and international

Cultural agility is crucial not only for business travelers and international assignees but also for professionals working in their home countries.

assignees but also for professionals working in their home countries. The need for cultural agility is growing exponentially, touching more professionals today than ever before.

BARRIERS TO CREATING A PIPELINE OF CULTURALLY AGILE PROFESSIONALS

Before you can develop the practices to effectively build a pipeline of culturally agile professionals, you will need to first identify the barriers that could prevent their success within your organization. These barriers are the erroneous assumptions held by leaders and managers in your organization; they affect how cultural agility is created and developed. If not addressed, these barriers could prevent your organization from successfully investing in and ultimately building a pipeline of culturally agile professionals. The four greatest barriers are

- Assuming that one possesses cross-cultural competence after only limited exposure to countries or cultures. This assumption produces overconfidence in one's culture-specific knowledge when it is in fact merely superficial.

- Assuming that one success in a prior global or multicultural role means cross-cultural competence has been achieved. This assumption produces succession plans in which talent is "anointed" as having cross-cultural competencies when they might not exist.

- Assuming that observed or perceived similarities indicate deeper cultural similarities. This assumption produces an overestimation of commonalities and an underestimation of the influence of cultural differences among people, practices, and principles.

- Assuming that technology transcends cultural differences. This assumption produces an overreliance on technology to solve cultural challenges in communications and collaboration.

Before you can fully explore the best possible talent management practices for building a pipeline of culturally agile professionals in your organization (or convince others in your organizations to be part of this workforce solution), you will need to first diagnose whether your organization makes any of these erroneous assumptions or operates with any of the associated blinders, which can subtly and unintentionally stifle these efforts. In the remainder of this chapter, we'll examine these assumptions. The remainder of the book will provide ways to address them.

"Grab some lederhosen, Sutfin. We're about to climb aboard the globalization bandwagon."

Robert Weber/The New Yorker Collection/www.cartoonbank.com

Assumptions About Prior Cultural Exposure

You have probably heard at least one of the common metaphors for culture: culture as an iceberg, culture as an onion, culture as an ocean. Each of these metaphors portrays culture as having a deceptive outer surface, with the real interest, problems, and challenges hidden underneath. There is a great deal of truth in this concept. Consider the surface indicators of culture you experienced the last time you traveled to another country. In the hour or two it took to disembark from the plane, collect your luggage, ride in a taxi, check into the hotel, and go to your first meeting, you are likely to have noticed several things about the country's culture. Before you could finish your first jet lag–inspired cup of coffee, you probably observed the style of dress, the degree of friendliness, traffic patterns, hygiene, punctuality, meeting formality, and communication style prevalent in the country where you landed. These observable behaviors—the tip of the iceberg, the onion skin, the ocean's surface—are easy to see and feel, and relatively easy

> *The real challenges for global professionals are rarely found on the observable surface of cultures—and culturally agile professionals know this.*

to maneuver around. The depth of the culture most business travelers experience is often limited to these observable behaviors, viewed through the traveler's own cultural lens. The real challenges for global professionals are rarely found on the observable surface of cultures—and culturally agile professionals know this.

The cultural challenges are almost always a function of deeper differences than those that meet the eye. (To experience this point through your five senses, now is a good time to go into the kitchen and slice open a strong onion.) The inner or below-the-surface culture includes characteristics or principles that are often taken for granted by those living in that culture. These below-the-surface characteristics can be divided into two categories: cultural attitudes and cultural values.

- *Cultural attitudes* are unspoken opinions about what is considered beautiful or ugly, respectful or rude, appropriate or inappropriate, risky or safe, desirable or undesirable.

- *Cultural values* are embedded assumptions that sometimes cannot be articulated, even by those who know the culture well. At the national level, cultural values may include basic principles, such as the right of independence, the privileges of birth-right, the importance of the collective's interests over one's own, and the nature of virtues (courage, honor, integrity, and so on).

One derailing assumption among global professionals is that frequent business travel can be equated to increased country-specific understanding—more frequent travel is assumed to indicate a deeper understanding of the culture. This is incorrect. Taking multiple business trips to a given country does not necessarily make professionals proficient in that country's culture any more than their watching many hockey games would make them proficient hockey players. Both playing hockey and developing cultural agility require some basic skills and abilities. In both cases, some contact is needed. If you asked me how many times I've been to Singapore, I'd pause, gaze up toward some invisible mental calendar, and probably answer "about ten." If you ask me what I know about Singapore or Singaporeans, I'd confess that my knowledge is about as superficial as that of any typical business professional, despite my ability to maneuver around Changi Airport with the best of my fellow airport club members. Given the structure of the program for which I was a professor, my work in Singapore gave me only minimal contact with peer-level Singaporeans.

Professionals also make an assumption about the duration of time they spend in another country. International assignees in most organizations spend an average of two years in their host countries. Although two years may seem like a lot of time to benefit from what could be a developmental opportunity, many international assignees spend those two years in a cocooned environment, insulated from the host country's culture. They often live in expatriate communities alongside their fellow compatriots. They are given market-basket allowances to buy the foods most familiar to them, regardless of the expense. They join international clubs and send their children to international schools with others who are in the expatriate community. Their work context might have cultural elements, but the office environment tends to be a hybrid of the company's corporate culture and the national culture, swayed more heavily toward the corporate culture with the increased number of international assignees. The typical experience of a foreign assignment can do little to change or improve cross-cultural competencies or build cultural agility.

If you have learned to speak a second language as an adult, you'll appreciate the parallel assumption individuals make when they become overconfident in their language skills after advancing to an intermediate level in the new language. They know proper pronunciation and can form grammatically correct sentences. However, the minute they engage in conversation with a native speaker—especially over the phone—they are quickly overwhelmed. The native speaker talks too fast, uses sentence structure that is too complex, uses too many colloquialisms not found in the textbook, and may have an accent different from the pronunciation formally taught. After such a humbling experience, new language learners will recalibrate their perception of their level of fluency.

Frequent business travelers and cocooned international assignees might believe they have become "fluent" in the foreign culture when in fact they do not yet understand cultural nuances. A deeper understanding of the attitudes and values of the culture is developed through personal and professional peer-level contacts and far deeper experiential opportunities, which are not often present when one is on the typical business trip or international assignment. Unfortunately, the lesson in overconfidence comes more slowly than it does in our language example, and there are fewer opportunities for recalibrating humbling experiences.

Assumptions About Prior Success

This second assumption follows on the heels of the first, but focuses not on what individuals believe about themselves but on what leaders in organizations believe about their employees who are frequent business travelers and international assignees. To understand the root of this assumption, we need to recognize that organizations typically grow increasingly more global, not less so. As their operations and market share become more international and cross-cultural, the roles and positions occupied by their strategic talent require more global responsibilities. Talented professionals who are successful in their domestic context are assigned to spearhead the international expansion of their functional areas, business units, or global teams. This is the natural career progression in most organizations' talent management programs: highly capable associates within the organization, those outstanding in their respective technical or managerial functions in the domestic context, are invited to do what they do best—only this time they are expected to do it in an international or multicultural context.

Unfortunately, what unfolds next is central to the reason why, after decades of global growth, companies still lack the culturally agile professionals they desperately need today: associates' initial cross-national or multicultural assignments are generally considered developmental or "stretch" roles because of their expanded responsibilities. Some professionals are wildly successful in these roles. Others crash and burn. Most are somewhere in between. Those who are generally successful in those initial cross-cultural or multicultural roles are organizationally anointed, assumed to have cross-cultural competence, and moved into the global talent pool.

If these anointed professionals go on to be less successful in subsequent international or multicultural roles, their cross-cultural competence is usually not questioned. Instead, their professional shortcomings are addressed with a focus on functional or managerial competencies. Minimal, if any, attention is paid to the development of cross-cultural competencies because, according to conventional assumptions, they have already earned that merit badge. These professionals, in the name of development, are sent to university-based residential executive development programs, given coaches for additional functional or leadership improvement, or shifted to a different role, citing a "bad fit" with a given role.

Do you think this is an assumption made in your organization? Try this diagnostic: ask your colleagues to name professionals in your organization who they consider to be knowledgeable about a given country or culture. Once a few names have surfaced, ask "Why?" You are likely to hear such responses as, "He spent a lot of time flying to France to work out the bugs in the Big Technical Integration" and "She was in Australia for six months as part of the Really Big Merger deal last year." In today's corporate halls, business trips and international assignments accumulate like knowledge chips. Although international business travel and international assignments can be highly developmental (more on this in Chapters Seven and Eight), the talent management metric for judging cultural agility should not be frequency or duration of trips to a foreign country.

Assumptions About Cultural Similarities and Differences

A third barrier to creating a pipeline of culturally agile professionals is an assumption on the part of individuals who travel or live abroad: they are often blinded by (or comforted by) the similarities they experience around the world. More than twenty-five hundred years ago Socrates proclaimed, "I am not an Athenian or a Greek, but a citizen of the world." Today many business executives are "citizens of the world" in the most superficial sense. They know how to find a good sushi restaurant when traveling in Europe, order French champagne in South America, and have a European fitted shirt tailored in Asia. They know their way around airport clubs and duty-free shops. They share business-class cabins, English language fluency, affluence, and often a common educational background with their global professional peers.

Consider the common experience of education. Leading business schools offering International MBA degrees, such as the London Business School, Hong Kong UST Business School, and INSEAD, boast that over 90 percent of their students come from countries other than the country in which they are studying. In leading International MBA programs in the United States (Wharton, Harvard, Stanford, MIT, University of Chicago, and Columbia), about 50 percent of the students are not American.[15] The experience of attending a leading business school can be a powerful socializing agent, shaping attitudes as well as behaviors. For most, it is a bonding experience: classmates share meals, knowledge, and class notes. They collaborate in teams to complete class assignments, resolve interpersonal conflicts, and celebrate graduation with the same wide smiles and sense of accomplishment. For these students, the business school experience fosters the development of some cursory cross-cultural competencies in a controlled and institutionally supportive environment.

But are these International MBA graduates culturally agile? Victoria DiSanto and I conducted a study looking at newly minted International MBAs who were selected for global leadership rotational programs in three leading U.S.-based organizations.[16] In each of the programs, which represented three different industries (financial services, pharmaceuticals, and consumer products), one of the rotations would be an international assignment lasting six to twelve months. Across the three organizations, the groups were evenly staggered: one-third of the MBAs were on their international rotation, one-third had not yet started their international rotation, and one-third had completed their international rotation. These were graduates of the world's leading International MBA programs, with the heaviest representation from INSEAD, Wharton, and the London Business School. Approximately 35 percent of the participants in this study were from the United States; the remaining 65 percent were from eighteen other countries. Many were multilingual (60 percent were fluent in two languages) and rather well traveled (50 percent had lived in another country for longer than a year prior to accepting the position in the rotational program). As a group, the participants in our study were already cross-culturally competent business professionals—or so we thought. But when we analyzed the data, a different picture emerged.

We asked our participants to self-rate both their knowledge and their abilities to conduct business in another country. This was the surprise: the group who had not yet been on their international assignment rotation rated themselves significantly *higher* than the other two groups in terms of their abilities. As Figure 1.2 illustrates, the group

FIGURE 1.2. *Self-Ratings of Abilities and Knowledge from Global Rotational Programs*

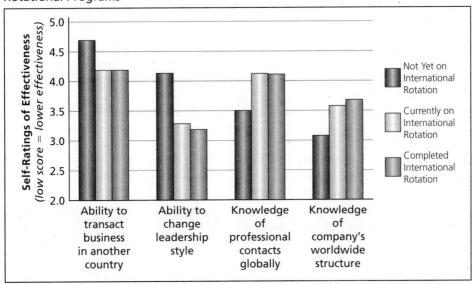

who were currently on the international rotation and the group who had already completed it both rated their cross-cultural abilities lower in comparison.

On the face of it, this might seem like a contrary finding—but this is hardly the case if you consider the first two assumptions. Our well-traveled International MBA graduates *assumed* that their combination of international travels and multicultural contacts with classmates had endowed them with a high level of cross-cultural abilities. Apparently, graduate school had lulled them into cross-cultural comfort. When the veil of the academic setting was lifted (that is, when they completed or were in the process of completing their international rotation), they were shocked to realize that their cross-cultural abilities were not as advanced as they had thought. Cultural bravado was replaced by cultural humility—and cultural humility is a highly valuable competency for global professionals to possess. This is a powerful lesson—both for their own development of cultural agility and as future advocates of programs to build cultural agility in the workforce.

Cultural bravado was replaced by cultural humility—and cultural humility is a highly valuable competency for global professionals to possess.

This is not to say that the experience of the International MBA program didn't start them at a more advanced level. It did. Graduates from elite business schools possess a deeper knowledge than most on issues of international business. As our study also illustrated, and as you can see from Figure 1.2, the participants built on their existing base of knowledge and gained additional international knowledge from having had the experience of the international rotation.

Like elite business schools, regional headquarters and foreign subsidiaries of global organizations often engender perceptions of cultural similarity. A study by Jan Selmer and Corinna de Leon illustrates this point.[17] These researchers studied the work values of middle-level Singaporean managers working for the Singaporean subsidiaries of Swedish organizations and compared them with Swedish managers in Sweden and Singaporeans working for non-Swedish organizations. They found that Singaporean managers working for Swedish organizations adopted some of the Swedish work values, including the preference for less tension and stress on the job, good physical working conditions, and cooperation between colleagues—and differed from their compatriot Singaporean colleagues working for other organizations. The Singaporeans had acculturated to the Swedish ways of working, making it rather easy for Swedish business travelers visiting their Singaporean subsidiaries to perceive cultural similarities. From the familiar logo on the wall to the shared corporate values, the workplace environment can be a strong socializing influence. Global business professionals who spend much of their time in their own company's subsidiary locations may erroneously perceive more similarities than actually exist between cultures. These cultural similarities are real; that's not the problem. The problem occurs when these perceptions of similarity are taken to another cultural context.

Among well-traveled and well-educated professionals, the need for cultural agility is masked by the common reality they share with their fellow cosmopolitan business executives. It is easy for them to overestimate the commonalities among people because their experience is, rather legitimately, one where differences are minimized. Although these commonalities help bridge the cross-national differences between these professionals within their own cultural microcosm, the greatest challenges for global business tend to exist in the "real world" outside that sheltered environment.

Assumptions About Technology

Consider all the communication, conferencing, and collaborative management and coordination tools your organization uses regularly, from the ubiquitous voice mail and email, texting and instant messaging, conference calls and videoconferencing to the highly sophisticated project management and knowledge management systems. Chances are high that the use of them in your organization is substantial—and that their use is increasing every year. When almost four thousand managers from all around the world were surveyed on their organizations' use of unified communication and collaboration technology, nearly 40 percent of them reported that their organizations will increase spending on these tools.[18] Of the organizations that have not yet deployed communication and collaboration tools, more than 80 percent plan to deploy them in the next two to three years. We are clearly becoming a more interconnected world.

Many of these elaborate communication and collaboration systems are sold with the promise of reducing travel costs, improving speed and effectiveness of collaboration among geographically dispersed associates, and dissolving national borders by creating a virtual meeting space. Are these claims true? Cristina Gibson and Jennifer Gibbs conducted an extensive study with 266 engineers who were members of fifty-six aerospace design project teams.[19] The teams each had between four and ten members, scattered around countries and various project sites. Collectively, the teams were part of an umbrella project worth about $200 billion; their innovations were clearly critical to the success of the organization. The teams varied in national diversity and geographic dispersion—but they also varied in their reliance on electronic communications (email, teleconferencing, and collaborative software).

The results were staggering. National diversity and geographic dispersion reduced the project teams' innovation. But what about the use of electronic communications? Surely that must have helped the team members catch their collaborative stride? On the contrary, the greater the cross-national teams' reliance on electronic communications, the *less* innovative they were.

What ultimately yielded the most innovative results in the work of these culturally diverse project teams? It was their interpersonal relationships. Specifically, the teams that

The greater the cross-national teams' reliance on electronic communications, the less *innovative they were.*

had created a psychologically safe communication climate were the ones with the highest product innovation. In a psychologically safe climate, team members trusted each other and believed they could express their ideas, talk through the problems they encountered, and be assertive about their thoughts and feelings.

This study clearly refutes the assumption that technology can eliminate the challenges of cultural differences. In fact, it indicates just the opposite: by building trust and establishing comfortable methods for communicating and collaborating, global professionals can mitigate the challenges of technology. Among those teams with a high use of electronic communications, having a psychologically safe communication climate produced a roughly 20 percent increase in the project teams' innovation ratings over those in a climate the members did not consider psychologically safe. It seems that overreliance on technology might be negative, but the negative effects are mitigated when team members feel good about their working relationships.

Using collaborative technology does not fully vanquish cultural differences any more than the use of English as a common business language does. When people use communication and collaboration technology, they bring with them their cultural norms for information sharing, communication, collaboration, and preferences for technology. This is evident in a study conducted by Pnina Shachaf examining the influence of information and communication technology on globally dispersed R&D teams from nine countries.[20] These technology-laden team members reported that both "cultural and language differences resulted in miscommunication, which jeopardized trust, cohesion, and team identity." It would be difficult to create psychologically safe communications with colleagues from different countries when the basic elements of trust and cohesion are missing.

The R&D team members in this study also spoke about the increased "cost of interactions": the slower pace of conference calls and other synchronous meetings, the greater effort to write emails in clear and simple phrases, and the extra time spent clarifying the accuracy of communications for those writing and speaking in a second language. However, Pnina did find several positives for technology use. For example, nonvisual asynchronous technology, such as email, was able to eliminate miscommunication resulting from cultural differences in nonverbal cues (because you cannot react to something you cannot see) and to reduce miscommunication resulting from cultural differences in verbal communication styles (because team members spent more time thinking through what they wanted to communicate in writing).

TAKE ACTION

Based on the information presented in this introductory chapter, the following is a list of specific actions you can take to begin building your organization's pipeline of culturally agile global professionals:

- Identify from a strategic standpoint the top five to ten ways your organization is becoming more globally integrated. For each of these, identify the key roles that will be required to operate with cultural agility. Now look at the professionals currently filling those roles in your organization. To what extent are these individuals culturally agile?

- Identify the organizational champions—in addition to yourself—who understand the importance of building a pipeline of cultural agile professionals. Have them do the same exercise described in the previous bullet point and see whether their conclusions concur with yours. As a group, can you identify your organization's cultural agility "pressure points" from a strategic perspective?

- Review the four erroneous assumptions that stand in the way of developing cultural agility. Use them to diagnose your organization's readiness and to identify (and remove) potential barriers to building a pipeline of culturally agile professionals.

PART

2

WHO IS CULTURALLY AGILE?

In Chapter One, we discussed erroneous assumptions about cultural agility, clarifying what cultural agility isn't and who doesn't have it. We needed to start there as a diagnostic, a test of your own assumptions about cultural agility. Now it is time to delve more deeply into what cultural agility is. The competencies that make up cultural agility include those that enable professionals to (1) manage themselves in international or multicultural situations, (2) interact effectively with people from different cultures, and (3) make effective business decisions. As a mega-competency, cultural agility represents the ability to toggle successfully among three possible responses in cross-cultural contexts: minimization, adaptation, and integration. Let's start here and discuss who culturally agile professionals are and how they do what they do.

CHAPTER

2

THREE CROSS-CULTURAL COMPETENCIES AFFECTING CULTURALLY AGILE RESPONSES

In 2001, the British-Dutch conglomerate Unilever bought the American Vermont-based ice cream manufacturer Ben & Jerry's. A key asset of Ben & Jerry's was its market niche among those customers who appreciated the premium ice cream with unusual flavor names like Karamel Sutra, Chocolate Therapy, and Imagine Whirled Peace. In the acquisition, Unilever needed to preserve this market niche, which was based in no small part on the corporate image of Ben & Jerry's social responsibility and left-leaning social activism. With an image honed by the founders Ben Cohen and Jerry Greenfield over almost twenty years, Ben & Jerry's worked with sustainable, Fair Trade certified and organic suppliers; used environmentally friendly packaging; paid premium prices to dairy farmers from Vermont who did not give their cows growth hormones; and created business opportunities for depressed areas and disadvantaged people. Giving 7.5 percent of their pretax revenues to charity, publicly traded Ben & Jerry's could not be accused of corporate greed. At the time of the acquisition, however, the Ben & Jerry's alternative management style lacked the fiscal and managerial discipline market analysts and investors demanded. The company's stock had fallen from almost $34 in 1993 to $17 in 1999.

Enter Unilever and Yves Couette, Unilever's choice to be the CEO of its new odd-ball acquisition.[1] As a longtime corporate Unilever executive, the French-born Couette had spent several years running businesses in Mexico and India. Couette needed to thread the proverbial needle as the CEO, to understand this alternative American organization enough to preserve the intangible assets of Unilever's new acquisition while at the same time introducing some parent-company fiscal and managerial controls.

Within his first few months as CEO (an acronym that at Ben and Jerry's means chief euphoria officer), Couette demonstrated his true cultural agility by adapting some—but not all—of his leadership style and business practices.[2] He began with symbolic gestures. He came to work dressed casually, and volunteered to mix mulch at a company-sponsored gardening project in the local community. These initial gestures helped build rapport and ease employees' concern that Couette was sent by Unilever to dissolve Ben & Jerry's small-town American (and anticorporate) culture. On a more tangible level, Couette also continued the corporate social responsibility approach of the founders, saying that he envisioned Ben & Jerry's to be "a grain of sand in the eye of Unilever" because these practices were more generous than those typically found in publicly traded companies.

Even after the Unilever takeover, the core of Ben & Jerry's values remain. The company continues to contribute about $1.1 million annually through employee-led corporate philanthropy and makes substantial product donations to community groups.[3] Today, Ben & Jerry's press releases reinforce this commitment to "doing good," stating that "the purpose of Ben & Jerry's philanthropy is to support the founding values of the company: economic and social justice, environmental restoration and peace through understanding, and to support our Vermont communities." Under Couette's leadership through the postacquisition transition, the Ben & Jerry's external mission continued.

However, Couette knew that some things needed to change at Ben & Jerry's to deliver a financial return to Unilever. In a very un–Ben & Jerry's act, he downsized the company—eliminating jobs and closing plants. He provided structure and introduced some basic organizational practices, and opened Ben & Jerry's positions to Unilever's global talent pool. Knowing that these moves would be unpopular with the employees, he justified them by saying that "the best way to spread Ben & Jerry's enlightened ethic throughout the business world was to make the company successful."[4]

There was also an integration of the Ben & Jerry's practices with those of Unilever. For example, Ben & Jerry's began using the Unilever performance management system—but added its own performance dimension of maintaining the company's social mission. Many would agree that in this critical postacquisition integration phase, Couette successfully led Ben & Jerry's both to maintain its corporate identity and brand image and, at the same time, to become profitable.

THE CULTURAL AGILITY COMPETENCY FRAMEWORK: TWELVE KEY COMPETENCIES

It was not by accident that Yves Couette, a highly culturally agile professional, was able to navigate the myriad of cultural challenges embedded in the Ben & Jerry's acquisition. Over years of working in different environments around the world, Couette has honed cross-cultural competencies enviable in many global organizations today. Unfortunately, there aren't enough culturally agile professionals who share his competencies. In a survey conducted by the Economist Intelligence Unit, more than four hundred global business executives were asked to name the primary shortcomings of management-level and other specialized workers in various markets around the world.[5] Three of the top four areas of concern were competencies related to cross-cultural agility: limited creativity in overcoming challenges, limited experience within a multinational organization, and culture-related issues. The report concluded that "many candidates do not yet possess the understanding and sensitivity to navigate the intricate internal politics of a global organization or deal with the very different cultural backgrounds of a diverse workforce." Karl-Heinz Oehler, vice president of global talent management at the Hertz Corporation, offered this insight on the findings in this report: "The rarest personality traits are resilience, adaptability, intellectual agility, versatility—in other words, the ability to deal with a changing situation and not get paralyzed by it."

Research and practice have identified certain cross-cultural competencies that enable professionals to assess cross-cultural situations accurately and operate effectively within them. The twelve most critical of these cross-cultural competencies

The Cultural Agility Competency Framework

Competencies Affecting Behavioral Responses

1. Cultural Minimization
2. Cultural Adaptation
3. Cultural Integration

Competencies Affecting Individuals' Psychological Ease Cross-Culturally

4. Tolerance of Ambiguity
5. Appropriate Self-Efficacy
6. Cultural Curiosity and Desire to Learn

Competencies Affecting Individuals' Cross-Cultural Interactions

7. Valuing Diversity
8. Ability to Form Relationships
9. Perspective-Taking

Competencies Affecting Decisions in a Cross-Cultural Context

10. Knowledge and Integration of Cross-National/Cultural Issues
11. Receptivity to Adopting Diverse Ideas
12. Divergent Thinking and Creativity

constitute the *Cultural Agility Competency Framework*. Although the framework is not an exhaustive list of cross-cultural competencies, these are the competencies I consider to be the most important because they are the ones with the greatest validity evidence—with demonstrated relationships to success in diverse international, cross-cultural, and multicultural roles. Please take a moment to review the Cultural Agility Competency Framework (see box on page 25) and judge for yourself which competencies make the greatest amount of sense for your organization's strategic needs.

HOW THE COMPETENCIES AFFECTING BEHAVIORAL RESPONSES ARE DIFFERENT

The three cross-cultural competencies affecting behavioral responses—cultural minimization, cultural adaptation, and cultural integration—are different from the other nine competencies in the Cultural Agility Competency Framework. Those other cross-cultural competencies (to be discussed in detail in Chapter Three) operate from a human talent approach which posits that their presence in global professionals is good and that a greater level of the competencies is related to a higher degree of cultural agility—in short, more is better. We have research and cases to show a direct relationship between their presence and subsequent professional successes in cross-cultural settings.

But in the case of cultural minimization, cultural adaptation, and cultural integration, the pattern for success changes: the presence of these three cross-cultural competencies is good *when they are leveraged at the appropriate times*. Unlike the other cross-cultural competencies, these three are not simply "nice-to-haves." Global professionals must be able to *use* these competencies correctly to increase their overall cultural agility. For example, cultural minimization is potentially derailing for global professionals in circumstances where some level of cultural sensitivity is needed; in those circumstances, inattention to the effect of culture will be detrimental to the outcome. Similarly, leveraging cultural adaptation at the wrong time can result in professionals' overinterpreting behaviors on the basis of cultural expectations or nationality. And using cultural integration at the wrong time can run the risk of taking too much time to build consensus, especially in situations where it would be appropriate to use either the organization's approach or the local approach.

COMPETENCIES AFFECTING BEHAVIORAL RESPONSES IN CROSS-CULTURAL CONTEXTS

Successful global professionals like Yves Couette know that cultural agility comprises more than just *cultural adaptation*; however, there are times when adapting to the norms and behaviors of the local context is essential. They know they cannot ignore cultural differences; however, there are times when *cultural minimization* is needed—when a higher-order professional demand will supersede cultural expectations and make it necessary to override a cultural norm. They know that merging multiple cultures to create a new set of behavioral norms can be time consuming and challenging—but there are times when *cultural integration* is most important and well worth the effort. Successful culturally agile professionals decide which approach or orientation to cultural differences is needed, and behave accordingly. Having these three competencies available as plausible responses is akin to having multiple tools in the proverbial toolbox. The most cultural agile professionals have a command of each of these orientations and can leverage them as needed, depending on the situation in which these professionals are operating.

James Piecowye, a Canadian culturally agile professional, has been an associate professor in the College of Communication and Media Sciences at Zayed University in Dubai, United Arab Emirates, since 2000. James knows exactly what it means to toggle among these three cultural orientations, something he had been doing long before he even left Canada. James, who is originally from Ajax, Ontario, an English-speaking part of Canada, pursued his doctoral degree at the University of Montreal, a French-language institution in Quebec.

James credits this experience living in French-speaking Quebec with laying the foundation for his cultural agility; he quickly learned that his French language acquisition, while challenging, was merely providing the means to deliver far deeper cultural challenges. Staying in Montreal for fifteen years, James learned to toggle effectively among the three cultural orientations. For example, he earned the trust of his French-speaking colleagues in the quintessentially French manner—slowly, over time. The more time he invested in building professional relationships and adapting to the French culture, the more his French-speaking colleagues accepted him, eventually even speaking with him in English. At the same time, he wrote in English and adopted the broader English-speaking Canadian norms for conducting his research, even though they were not typical among his French-speaking colleagues.

Now living and working in Dubai, James notes similarities between the United Arab Emirati and French Canadian cultures: "There is more of a community and communal aspect to the French Canadian culture that I don't think exists anywhere else in Canada. In a sense, the French Canadian culture is more like the tribal culture of the United Arab Emirates." As he is quick to add, however, "moving to the UAE was a huge cultural change—not just the Arab culture but also the expatriate culture with its mix of Indians, Pakistanis, Europeans, Australians, North Americans, and Asians. It was an extreme experience." James reconciled the cultural challenges and embraced the opportunities in the UAE, again negotiating with his multiple cultural orientations.

James is a male professor in an accredited university in Dubai that teaches only Arab women. He brings cultural minimization into the classroom by maintaining his standards and expectations for his students' learning. Suspending his judgments, James uses cultural adaptation and adjusts his behaviors to accommodate the more collectivist Emirati ways, which are rooted in their Arab culture and predominantly Islamic religion. He uses cultural integration also, starting with the ideas that he and his students share a common desire to learn and that the best way to learn is to collectively create an interactive environment where students can comfortably share their experiences. James calls it "meeting in the middle."

Over the past six years, James has also been a radio host on DubaiEye (103.8 FM), which describes itself as "Dubai's premier talk radio station" and offers broadcasting twenty-four hours a day in eight languages. Its listeners include expatriates from some forty countries. Again showing his cultural agility, James works with British, Australian, South African, and Filipino presenters at the station. "What makes the relationship work," he says, "is that we are all working toward the same goal to create informative, compelling, and enjoyable radio. The fact that each of our countries may have a different radio culture is of little consequence. What is important is that we all agree to work collaboratively in an environment different from our own—one that does not have legislated freedom of the press or even a long radio culture."

As a culturally agile professional, James selects a particular cultural orientation intentionally. For example, he does not have a maid or a gardener, opting to eschew the symbols of class status that his profession and income give him in the traditionally hierarchical culture of the UAE. James initially predicted that as a result of his counter-cultural behavior, he would receive less respect from the laborers in the neighborhood. (He thought, at the time, that it was a very small price to pay to maintain the pleasure he experiences when tending to his garden and washing his car.) In fact, the opposite occurred: the neighborhood gardeners and maids respect James tremendously because, as a person of status doing their jobs, he elevates their own positions through his actions, and they appreciate the respect James gives them. In reflecting on his own career and the careers of his colleagues with cultural agility, James shares that cultural agility "does not mean people either agree fully or give up their own cultural norms, but it does suggest that they are able to look beyond the differences and work toward common goals—goals which will invariably be influenced by and rooted in the local host culture." As his comment reflects, James operates with an authentic respect for other cultures while maintaining a healthy sense of self.

As a professor and popular radio host, James has achieved the success that accrues to culturally agile professionals who operate with multiple available behavioral responses, leveraged appropriately depending on the requirements of the professional situations. They will use cultural minimization when the situation demands that their behaviors supersede the local context. They will adapt their behaviors when the situation demands attention to the local context. They will also create a new behavioral set, taking elements from multiple cultural contexts.

In a study of more than two hundred global professionals and international assignees from more than forty countries, Ibraiz Tarique and I found that those who possessed a greater number of available cultural responses earned higher ratings from their supervisors on "how effectively they work with colleagues from different cultures." Figure 2.1 illustrates this result.

The given global context of the job, task, or professional role is what matters most when deciding which behaviors are the most appropriate for success, whether one should behave with *cultural adaptation, cultural minimization*, or *cultural integration*. As shown earlier, these three make up the behavioral responses in the Cultural Agility Competency Framework. Figure 2.2 provides a definition of each of these competencies.

FIGURE 2.1. *Number of Available Cultural Orientations and Ratings of Global Professionals' Ability to Work Effectively with Colleagues from Different Cultures*

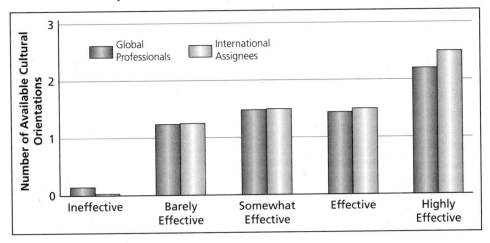

FIGURE 2.2. *Competencies Affecting Behavioral Responses*

Competency	Definition
Cultural Minimization	To standardize or control the cultural differences that exist in the environment and respond in a way that will create greater consistency, irrespective of culture. To effectively limit the effect of any cultural differences.
Cultural Adaptation	To adjust to the cultural differences and respond in a way that is the expected norm of the other culture. To effectively adapt to the other culture's norms and behaviors.
Cultural Integration	To create a new set of norms and respond with collaboration to find solutions acceptable to both (or all) cultures affected, but not overrepresenting either (or any one) culture. To be effective in creating new norms and behaviors.

In the remainder of this chapter, I will examine each of these three competencies with examples from various sectors of the business world. Although all three are essential for success as a global professional, each is especially crucial—and effective—in certain areas, including the following:

Jobs and roles most often requiring *cultural minimization* to be successful include

- Health and safety
- Quality assurance

- Strategic company-wide practices (especially those considered key to competitive advantage)
- Global image or brand

Jobs and roles most often requiring *cultural adaptation* to be successful include

- Sales and marketing
- Government relations
- Working with regulatory agencies
- Local-level manufacturing operations

Jobs and roles most often requiring *cultural integration* to be successful include

- Global teams
- Joint ventures
- Postacquisition or postmerger integration
- Negotiations

Cultural Adaptation

Culturally agile professionals are able to navigate the differences in cultural norms and behaviors and to adjust—when needed—to be successful. As a culturally agile business leader, Yves Couette adapted his management style and organizational decisions to fit with the alternative, antiestablishment norm of Ben & Jerry's to gain trust and build credibility with Ben & Jerry's employees. There are many roles, tasks, and positions where adaptation to the demands of the host culture or another individual's culture is needed in order for a professional to be successful. Activities where professionals need to work with influential national institutions, such as a country's government or regulatory agencies, require cultural adaption to accommodate a different set of rules, regulations, and laws. Activities involving product development and design, especially in such areas as fashion and food, also require cultural adaptation to understand and accommodate differences in taste and preferences. Activities in which the goal supersedes the process for achieving it might also require cultural adaptation, such as maintaining local preferences for production facilities in situations where doing so would not negatively affect the outcome. Likewise, sales, marketing, and customer service roles require cultural adaptation to develop the client relationship, build trust and credibility with the client, and meet the client's expectations.

There are many roles, tasks, and positions where adaptation to the demands of the host culture or another individual's culture is needed in order for a professional to be successful.

Cultural Adaptation and Client Development   In the case of sales and client development, the person who is selling will, most often, need to adapt to the buyer's culture in order to be perceived as credible and trustworthy—and, ultimately, to be successful. To illustrate this professional demand, researcher Chanthika Pornpitakpan assessed the reactions of Japanese and Thai "buyers" to American "sellers" in a sales context.[6] She found that in the scenarios where the Americans adapted their behaviors to be more consistent with the cultural expectations of their Japanese and Thai clients, they were perceived more favorably. The American sales team members were perceived as more attractive sellers (for example, likable, comfortable to deal with) and had better anticipated outcomes of their sales presentation (for example, being granted a sales contract or considered for future sales) when they exhibited at least some level of cultural adaptation. For example, the Thais perceived the American sales team members more favorably and anticipated a better sales outcome when the Americans wore Thai suits (for example, Chut Phra Rachatan), accepted invitations to lunch, addressed them as "Khun" followed by first names, and used less expressive gestures. The Japanese perceived the American sales team members more favorably and anticipated a better sales outcome when the Americans used the Japanese style of exchanging business cards, spent time building the relationship before doing business, and addressed them with the title "Buchoo." Figure 2.3 illustrates the differences among how the American sales teams were perceived under the different scenarios of adaptation.

Adaptation of even the most basic behaviors can feel awkward at first. It might even feel disingenuous or "phony" to use the behavioral norms of another culture. Chanthika tested this by asking the Thai and Japanese "buyers" whether they perceived the Americans' attempt to adapt to their cultural norms as derogatory. Overwhelmingly, the Thai and Japanese clients perceived the adapters as "not at all" derogating their cultural identity. In other words, in the sales setting, there was no downside—beyond feeling a bit awkward at first—for sales representatives trying to adapt their behaviors to be culturally consistent with those of the client.

Chris Houghtaling understands firsthand the benefit of some cultural adaptation to the sales situation. Chris is an American currently living in Vienna, Austria, where he lectures in sales for the University of Applied Sciences, Wiener Neustadt. Chris is a culturally agile sales and marketing professional who, in 1999, completed his International MBA through the University of South Carolina's Darla Moore School of Business with a joint degree from the Executive Academy at the Wirtschaftsuniversität Wien, one of Austria's leading business schools. According to *U.S. News & World Report*, this program has been ranked among the top three among International MBA programs for the past twenty-two years.[7] For the past twelve years, since graduating with his International MBA, Chris has been working in sales, leveraging his cross-cultural competencies to increase his success.

Prior to starting his International MBA, Chris recalls being attracted to an international career while working for USRobotics Corporation (USR). As part of USR's new U.S. government sales team, Chris established an Internet presence for U.S. government

FIGURE 2.3. *Level of Americans' Adaptation to Thai and Japanese Cultures and the Americans' Perceived Effectiveness by Their Thai and Japanese Clients*

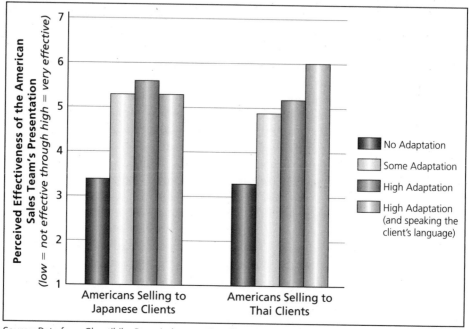

Source: Data from Chantihika Pornpitakpan, "The Effects of Cultural Adaptation on Business Relationships: Americans Selling to Japanese and Thais," *Journal of International Business Studies* 30, no. 2 (1999), pp. 317–337.

agencies located outside the United States to gather product information and obtain pricing from government-approved resellers. This required him to coordinate with internal and external partners worldwide. He enjoyed working with people from different cultures, observing different professional styles and approaches to business. After completing his International MBA, learning German, and working in Vienna for a couple of years, Chris relocated back to the United States and began a successful career in pharmaceutical sales. Within the first year, he turned around a territory that traditionally performed in the bottom 25 percent to become a top 20 percent territory.

In 2005, while working in northern Virginia, Chris tried a practical experiment with Ken Sharan, a colleague from India who was working in the Baltimore, Maryland, area. With the goal of improving their sales performance, they leveraged what they knew about cultural differences to develop better and deeper client relationships with foreign-born doctors by adapting their relationship-building styles to their clients' cultures.

Chris, who was doing frontline sales with clients ranging from general practitioners to infectious disease and pulmonary specialists to hospital administrators, found that subtle and sincere cultural adaptations were viewed positively. He developed relationships with his clients who were Chinese nationals by researching facts and ideas from

China's rich medical history and discussing them with the Chinese physicians. To connect with his physician clientele from India, he learned about the various regions and religions of their diverse country. With sincere interest, he was able to establish a more open dialogue, better accommodate his clients, and build deeper relationships. For example, he could suggest more appropriate regional or vegetarian restaurants for business meetings; he could also incorporate his clients' religious and national holidays into his sales planning and scheduling. Chris wished his Chinese physicians "Happy New Year" around the Chinese New Year and his Indian physicians "Happy Diwali" or "Happy Holi" at the appropriate times. These small gestures signaled to his customers that he cared about them and not just about making sales. His sincere interest in his clients' cultures and his small culturally adaptive gestures made a big difference. Chris saw his sales dramatically increase among his culturally diverse clients. Among this group of clients, Chris's market share jumped from 8.7 percent to 18.4 percent within six months, and the success was sustained over time. Ken enjoyed similar success.

Chris learned a lot from his and Ken's practical experiment on the power of cultural adaptation. As he observed,

> Sales professionals know that to be good at what you do, you need to approach each customer to learn what their needs, objections, and buying triggers are. However, with the strategy of standardizing marketing messages that is taking place in many organizations, there is pressure from companies to follow the standardized sales message and presentation, regardless of the customer. This causes sales professionals to become distracted from what they do best, building meaningful relationships that positively impact business . . . In the majority of the world, building relationships with your customers is much more important than in the U.S. Gaining trust and respect on a personal level before you can start to sell your product comes before making a smooth sales presentation.

The advice Chris offers resonates among culturally agile sales professionals. It is important to concurrently *standardize* marketing messages, *integrate* the various motivators for clients to purchase (that is, their buying triggers), and *adapt* the relationship to the clients' cultural differences. In the case of client development, the latter is particularly critical. With that in mind, Chris offers advice to other sales professionals and organizations working across cultures:

> First, organizations and sales professionals need to evaluate if they are open to adjusting themselves, their style, and their messaging for each customer and if they are willing to put this openness into practice. The second is that companies and sales professionals need to recognize the fact that people from another country do not leave their social norms and values behind when they move, and it is to everyone's benefit to incorporate some of your customer's social norms and values into your sales activities. Although this may feel unnatural to the salesperson, when done with

honesty toward the person to whom you are directing your cultural openness, and not the sale, the customer will, in most cases, appreciate the effort and recognition.

As Chris notes, this adaptation might feel unnatural or awkward at first, but it will be the key to success in the long run. Aside from the initial awkwardness, adapting one's surface-level cultural behaviors—mixing mulch or washing one's own car, wearing certain clothes, selecting appropriate restaurants, exchanging business cards, remembering to greet a customer on certain holidays—should be relatively straightforward for most global professionals. Most can make these cultural adaptations, muddling through those unfamiliar surface behaviors at first (the kisses, the firm handshakes, the bows) to feel less self-conscious and more comfortable with practice. The greater challenges for global professionals tend not to be in adapting to surface behaviors when needed; they lie in adapting to deeper aspects of a different culture, such as the differences in work practices, attitudes and values, and, at times, ethical norms.

My research concurs with the experiences Chris shared. When fifty global sales professionals were rated by their supervisors on their effectiveness in interacting with clients from different countries, those with a higher level of cultural adaptation were more effective compared to those with a lower level. As Figure 2.4 illustrates, adaptation is related to success with clients.

Cultural Adaptation in Manufacturing This is all very well for professionals in sales, where "the customer is always right." But what about cultural adaptation in other sectors of the business world? Let's consider the possible adaptations needed

FIGURE 2.4. *Effectiveness of Sales Professionals and Their Cultural Orientations*

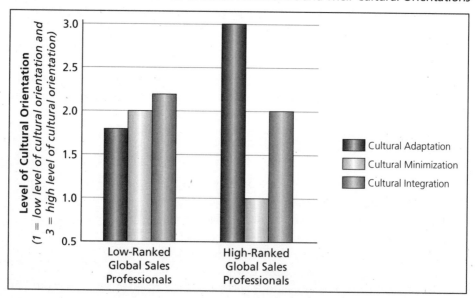

among professionals in the manufacturing industry. At first glance, these roles for operations professionals might seem culture-free because there are robust universal common goals for production facilities: everywhere, production facilities hope to increase productivity, quality, safety, and efficiency while reducing waste, time, inventory, and injury. The goals might be common, but *how* operations professionals motivate workers to achieve those goals will often need to be adapted to the local culture.

A study by the Australian researcher Giles Hirst and his colleagues compared predictors of productivity in manufacturing facilities in the United Kingdom and China.[8] Specifically, they examined the effect on workers' stress levels of the practice of empowering workers by giving them greater autonomy, discretion to make decisions, and control over their work. The production workers from the United Kingdom felt less stress as the result of being given greater autonomy. However, the experience for the production workers in China was the direct opposite: they experienced more stress from the same practice, given their cultural preference for directive leadership. This is relevant to productivity because Giles found in both countries that productivity decreased when workers felt that the demands on them were particularly high. Stress can exacerbate the problem of interpreting work demands. Figure 2.5 illustrates this finding.

In a study I conducted with Ibraiz Tarique, about ninety global manufacturing managers were rated by their supervisors on their effectiveness in supervising people from different countries. In further analysis of these data, I found that the manufacturing managers with higher levels of cultural adaptation and cultural integration were

FIGURE 2.5. *The Difference Between British and Chinese Workers' Reactions to Being Given Autonomy*

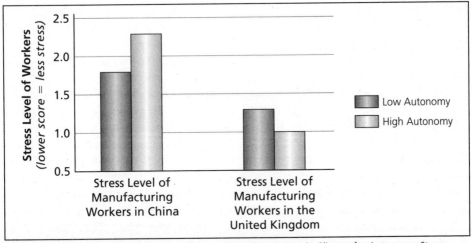

Source: Data from Giles Hirst and others, "Cross-Cultural Variations in Climate for Autonomy, Stress and Organizational Productivity Relationships: A Comparison of Chinese and UK Manufacturing Organizations," *Journal of International Business Studies* 39, no. 8 (2008): 1343–1358.

FIGURE 2.6. *Effectiveness of Manufacturing Professionals and Their Cultural Orientations*

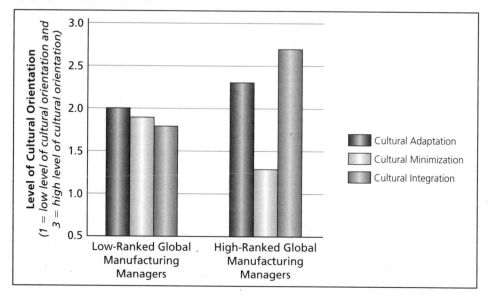

more effective than those with lower levels of these orientations.[9] As Figure 2.6 illustrates, being able to both adapt and compromise, when needed, is related to success when supervising subordinates in a cross-cultural manufacturing capacity.

Cultural Adaptation in Government Sales and manufacturing are not the only sectors where cultural differences will affect the outcome of professionals' activities. Shung Shin, Frederick Morgeson, and Michael Campion studied 910 midcareer American professionals who were working for an international agency of the U.S. government.[10] They worked in public relations, as economic analysts, as political analysts, and in other such positions and were expected to spend two-thirds of their tenure with the agency working in international posts. As a result, the professionals in the study were well-seasoned global professionals. Shung, Frederick, and Michael found that although the overall duties of these professionals did not change as a function of being relocated, the way in which they performed their duties did. For example, when these professionals were in more collectivist or group-oriented countries, they performed more relationship-oriented tasks, such as teaching; coaching others; and coordinating, developing, and building teams. They performed these tasks less frequently in more individualistic cultures.

Cultural Adaptation's Major Challenge: Ethical Dilemmas The government example we've just discussed illustrates how professionals might need *to adapt the way they* *work* in order to be effective in another culture. The previous examples illustrate how culturally agile professionals might need *to adapt certain practices* in order to be successful in their role. But what if we delve deeper into the interpretation of behaviors from the perspective of one's values—and how those interpretations might vary in different cultural contexts? I'm not saying that individuals' values themselves would change—but that the global professionals' *interpretations* of behaviors might vary with a broader understanding of the demands of the international or multicultural situation. Before working globally, a professional might judge a certain norm or practice as inappropriate, wrong, inefficient, or even unethical—but might revise that initial impression after fully understanding the context. For example, in some countries it is appropriate to hire one's family members to fill key positions in one's organization. In many Western cultures, this nepotism might be seen as a corrupt or inappropriate form of favoritism. But in many Eastern cultures, the person you can trust the most to work hard for you would be someone who is a family member.

In some situations there will be a (more or less) universally accepted interpretation of behaviors that are appropriate or inappropriate, right or wrong, efficient or inefficient, and ethical or unethical. Other times, the interpretation will need to pass through a culturally agile lens—one where the context is fully understood. Culturally agile professionals can more readily differentiate between situations where a local practice violates universally accepted norms, and situations where cultural adaptation is warranted.

Andrew Spicer, Thomas Dunfee, and Wendy Bailey compared seasoned global professionals—Americans who were living and working in Russia—with comparably placed American professionals who were working in America.[11] The two groups did *not* differ in their attitudes and intended behaviors in scenarios involving universally accepted ethical norms, such as failing to inform employees about the physical risk from exposure to hazardous materials, or investing money in capital equipment instead of paying wages. Personally, I was relieved to learn that all of the American professionals in their study—whether working in Russia or America—viewed these behaviors as immoral, unfair, and unjust.

When the scenarios turned to more situation-specific norms, however, the attitudes toward the situation and their intended behaviors in the situation changed depending on the group. The Americans working in Russia evaluated locally specific ethical dilemmas, such as paying small bribes to a government official or keeping two sets of books for different accounting purposes, less harshly than did their compatriot counterparts working in the United States. Although they still viewed these practices as generally unethical, those working in Russia exhibited attitudes and intended behaviors that were more consistent with the Russian norm, not judging them as seriously unethical. Figure 2.7 illustrates this finding. With their experience in Russia, they judged the scenarios with a greater understanding of the local demands and context. We could stop here and debate whether keeping two sets of books, for example, should be universally unethical. But let's change the lens a bit. The authors noted that the two sets of accounting books—which is unethical in many contexts—might be reframed

FIGURE 2.7. *Responses to Ethical Dilemmas*

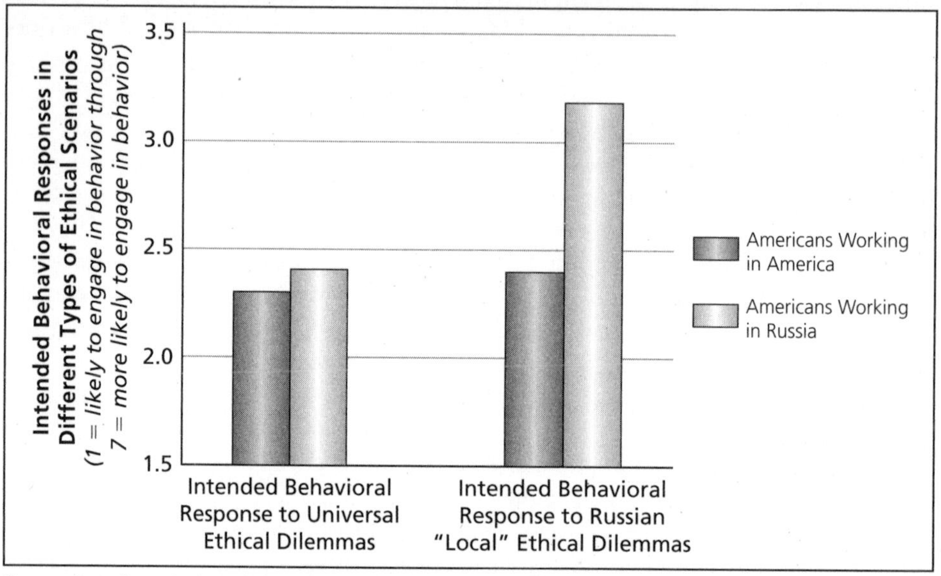

Source: Data from Andrew Spicer, Thomas Dunfee, and Wendy Bailey, "Does National Context Matter in Ethical Decision Making? An Empirical Test of Integrative Social Contracts Theory," *Academy of Management Journal* 47, no. 4 (2004), 610–620.

when the practice is needed in order to keep financial information secret from those involved in organized crime. This is a cultural interpretation that the Americans working in the United States would never have needed to consider—at least, I hope not!

Cultural Minimization

It's probably safe to assume that every organization has certain practices it would like to see maintained consistently around the world. Health and safety standards, codes of conduct, quality standards, fiscal controls, corporate values, and codes of ethics are typical examples of activities that companies typically wish to standardize and control around the world. Global professionals with responsibilities for these areas often are asked to shape and influence the behaviors of colleagues, vendors, suppliers, associates, and subordinates to fit with a corporate or industry norm. In these areas (for example, safety, ethics, and quality assurance), global professionals often need to operate with cultural minimization, working to override any cultural differences and ensure a common standard or outcome. But minimizing differences is often easier said than done. In order to accomplish it, global professionals

Global professionals often need to operate with cultural minimization, working to override any cultural differences and ensure a common standard or outcome.

need to concurrently see (and understand) the cross-cultural differences, and influence others to change or adapt their behaviors. That last sentence has two important moving pieces: (1) an understanding of cultural differences in the desired behavior, and (2) an understanding of how to successfully influence behavior. Cultural minimization is not as easy as it seems—not by a long shot.

Cultural Minimization in Health and Safety Practices   To understand the way culturally agile professionals minimize cultural differences, let's consider safety policies and practices. In this realm, the desired behaviors are relatively clear and objective. You can probably envision the posters in the lunch room: "Are you wearing your safety goggles?" "Is your mobile phone turned off when operating machinery?"

Maddy Janssens, Jeanne Brett, and Frank Smith conducted a study of the adoption of corporation-wide safety practices among production workers in three comparable subsidiary manufacturing plants, one each in the United States, France, and Argentina.[12] Although the policy was the same for the subsidiaries, the production workers from the three countries perceived the same U.S.-based safety policy very differently. For the Argentinian workers, their perception of the importance of the safety policies was deeply connected with their perception of their managers' concern for their safety (as opposed to a concern for production). The French workers, in contrast, made little connection between their managers' concern for their safety and whether safety was a priority in the organization. Now imagine that a well-intentioned senior leader from the U.S. headquarters is visiting each subsidiary to give an impassioned speech outlining the company's safety practices and emphasizing *how much he cares about everyone's safety, over production*. The same speech would be likely to motivate the Argentinian workers to follow safety procedures—while producing bored eye-rolls among the French workers.

Let's stay with safety speeches for a moment. Shell is the world's leading oil and gas company, describing itself on its Web site as a company with health and safety as its "top priority." Shell's safety practices are tightly controlled and allow for no variation, irrespective of culture. In 2007, Shell appointed Darwin Silalahi as country chairman and CEO of Shell Indonesia.[13] With educational experiences including a degree in physics from the University of Indonesia; an MBA from the University of Houston; an executive education program at Harvard; and years of work experiences at BP, the Indonesian Office of the State, and as the Indonesia Country CEO for Booz Allen Hamilton, Silalahi was the first Indonesian to hold this senior-most position at Shell Indonesia.

In a speech to his Indonesian subsidiary encouraging adherence to Shell's strict safety practices in Indonesia, Silalahi emphasized the policy but added a collectivist spin, one he knew would resonate among his group-oriented Indonesian workers: "At Shell, we believe we are all safety leaders. What each of us does individually results in our collective culture. We must each take personal responsibility for creating a culture of compliance and intervention." Silalahi was operating with cultural agility as he leveraged knowledge of the Indonesian culture—appealing to the group orientation to influence behavior—and underscored the importance of Shell's safety practices.

Cultural Minimization: Cultural Messages to Influence Standardization   Successfully maintaining standards takes more than speeches; it requires culturally agile professionals who can be influential across cultures. It's challenging enough to influence colleagues, subordinates, supply chain partners, vendors, and the like in one's own culture, but influencing them in a cross-cultural or multicultural context is fraught with potential misunderstandings, conflict, and feelings of being manipulated. Appropriate influence methods are, in part, culture bound and can be leveraged to achieve successful acceptance of practices and policies that need to be implemented.

Ping Ping Fu and fourteen of her colleagues from around the world conducted an extensive study on cross-national differences in the effectiveness of influence strategies.[14] They found that individuals' social beliefs affect how various influence tactics are perceived. For example, those who believe that life's events are predetermined by fate and destiny perceived being assertive and coercive (as opposed to, say, building a positive social relationship) as an effective influence strategy. In collectivist or group-oriented cultures, building a positive social relationship (as opposed to, say, being assertive and coercive) was considered the more effective influence strategy.

Theo van der Smeede, a culturally agile Dutch professional, knows that being influential is critical to maintaining consistency around the world. When Theo was working as a quality and safety manager and adviser for Exxon Mobil, he was responsible for developing, assessing, and helping implement standard safety management practices and common processes around the world. He worked regularly in refineries, chemical plants, and laboratory sites in Europe, the United States, Saudi Arabia, Singapore, and Chile. Reflecting on the cross-cultural challenges in standardizing practices, he noted that the greatest difficulty in maintaining consistency and standards across cultures was "trying to understand and adjust my approach to influence others from different cultures according to the situation, rather than pursuing my own headstrong approach." Theo stresses that "even with the most straightforward practices, it is wrong to assume that cultural differences don't exist. They do—differing by country, organization, and team." Theo acknowledges that some ways to influence behaviors are shared universally, such as "the need to create ownership for new initiatives rather than pushing these down people's throats." Other methods, he quickly added, are more culturally dependent.

Theo's cultural agility is best seen when he describes the many concurrent factors—organizational, individual, and cultural—that he needs to consider before successfully implementing any standard practice. Theo has seen differences between industries—for example, between oil refineries and chemical manufacturing plants. The refineries themselves are more similar, and those working in them tend to be more willing to adopt common practices, whereas chemical plants are highly diverse, and the professionals who work in them are apt to question a new safety practice. He also notes the differences among individuals and how those differences can affect the implementation. Some people are more interested in adapting the practices put forth, tailoring them a bit for use within their respective units; others are more interested in innovating or being the ones to develop the practice they will eventually follow.

Although he is sensitive to these individual and organizational differences, Theo has also observed many cultural differences affecting the implementation of safety management practices. With an example of how to introduce a new standard safety practice globally, Theo illustrates how he has navigated around the differences. He describes colleagues from his own culture, the Dutch, as being direct, logical, and questioning; they will vigorously debate the points of the new safety practice. With them, he allows the debate to ensue because, ultimately, once they are satisfied with the reasons offered in debate, "they are very committed" to its full implementation. Theo notes that his Belgian colleagues, though more reserved than the Dutch, will also debate prior to buying into the new practice. With them, however, he needs to invite greater debate at the onset, an invitation not needed when working with his Dutch colleagues. Among his British colleagues, the debate cannot be disregarded even though (to his Dutch ear) it sounds less direct, more polite, and more focused on ways to improve the safety practice. His American and German colleagues will buy into the practices they have engineered themselves. Theo has found that bringing them in from the beginning, rather than convincing them of the need for the practice after the fact, allows for greater buy-in. Theo's Saudi, French, and Italian colleagues will debate and discuss the practice, the alternatives, and possible improvements, but will more readily acquiesce to a "this is how it will be" directive from the appropriate leaders within the hierarchy.

With all of these moving parts, Theo revisits an approach, honed over many years in collaboration with safety management colleagues and under the advice of a psychology professor in Germany, to influence safety behaviors across cultures. At the core of this approach, Theo knows that he needs to understand individual, organizational, and cultural differences in several areas, including

- Beliefs or attitudes toward the new practice

- Willingness to change behaviors

- Routines, norms, or habits affecting the desired behaviors

- The consequences of behaving—or not behaving—in a certain way

To the latter point, in particular, he encourages those who are trying to create a common standard to identify positive and negative consequences most appropriate for influencing behaviors in any given cultural context.

As Theo's case illustrates, influencing others to act in a manner that is possibly outside their cultural norm requires culturally agile professionals to thread the proverbial needle—to accurately read and understand the cultural elements embedded in the situation and, at the same time, use the most appropriate influence strategy to change behavior so as to override or minimize those differences. Because cultural minimization requires such advanced skills, I strongly encourage organizations to select their most culturally agile professionals, like Theo, to staff positions that require significant cultural minimization.

Cultural Integration

The previous two sections have presented either end of a continuum. At one end, professionals are placed in situations where their decisions and behaviors (for example, sales and operations management) might require adaptation to the other culture's way of doing things. In these cases, the other culture *controls* the situation either because of the power differential in the relationship (for example, the buyer, the regulatory body or government) or because forcing others to adapt their behaviors to the professional's culture does not make sense. Asking production workers to change behaviors just for the sake of changing behaviors (and not for a strategic need) is often a wasted effort that can backfire. At the other end of the continuum, some professionals' decisions and behaviors (for example, those related to safety and quality) might require that their cultural norms (or their company's norms) be maintained even when they are contrary to those of the host culture. In these cases, the professional is charged with the role of upholding a standard because it is in the best interest of the company (for example, quality standards, accounting rules, codes of ethics) or in the best interest of the colleagues with whom the professional is working (for example, maintaining strict health and safety practices). At both ends of this continuum, the contextual demand of the role, activity, or job is determining the best way to manage the differences in cross-cultural behaviors and norms.

In many professional situations, however, the best approach will not be at either end of the continuum; instead an integrated (or compromised) approach, not fully reflecting either (or any) of the cultures involved, is the most effective. In these cases, global professionals need to understand when—and how—to create an approach that works across cultures. The most common of these situations is the geographically distributed team—that is, one comprising members who belong to different cultures and are located in multiple countries.

Global professionals need to understand when—and how—to create an approach that works across cultures.

Cultural Integration: Creating a Hybrid Team Culture In a series of studies to better understand cross-cultural team functioning, P. Christopher Earley and Elaine Mosakowski found that heterogeneous (that is, diverse) teams functioned better, over time, when they had created a hybrid team culture—their own norms for interactions, communications, goal setting, and the like.[15] These researchers advise that teams work on the "establishment of rules for interpersonal and task-related interactions, creation of high team performance expectations, effective communication and conflict management styles, and the development of a common identity."

Jason Newman, an American culturally agile bioscience researcher who has worked as a global project leader in Germany for CSL Limited (a biopharmaceutical company headquartered in Melbourne, Australia), could provide many examples of the validity of these research findings. Through his experience in leading teams of scientists from diverse cultures, Jason understands firsthand the importance of team-level cultural integration to achieve the team's goals, noting that "team leaders need to recognize the culture lenses of the members and remove the hurdles for a team's unique culture to emerge."

Recognizing cultural differences and becoming culturally agile started in an unlikely way for Jason. He was born and raised in a culturally diverse suburb of New York City. He fondly recalls traveling to Quebec City, Canada, as the first spark to kindle his interest in a global career. He learned something about himself during that trip: that he sensed and deeply appreciated cultural differences, including those related to language, food, and interactions. Jason's cultural interests reemerged a few years later when he was in college, working as a lab technician with scientists from a number of countries. Jason recalls many interesting conversations with colleagues and classmates from Asia, talking about cultural differences while sharing their common interests and academic pursuits in biochemistry and molecular biology in the Microbial Pathogen Department. Later in his professional career, Jason was able to draw on many of the lessons learned during those conversations, recalling that "in college, I learned not to assume similarities; even though we all spoke the same scientific language, the messages were internalized and acted upon in different ways. In retrospect, I was learning to collaborate outside of my own cultural norms."

In 2004, Jason began to hone his global team skills in international roles. Working in a technical sales role for JRH Biosciences, a subsidiary of CSL, Jason now had responsibilities spanning the globe—in the United States, Europe, and Asia. His cross-cultural competencies were used daily and began to grow exponentially. Jason's successful sales campaigns required careful consideration of regional business norms, of differences among his internal and external staff members, and of the importance of cultural differences in developing interpersonal relationships and team cohesion. Jason underscored that "when unaware, even seemingly minor faux pas could have negative consequences on client relations and team success."

CSL noticed Jason's cross-cultural competencies. In 2007, he accepted a position with CSL as a global project leader in the project management department based in Marburg, Germany. In this role, he managed a global development project team with R&D activities in the United States, Europe, and Australia. The diverse cultural backgrounds of his team provided a fascinating work environment—and also some challenges for team leadership. His R&D teams differed in their risk tolerance: some were more conservative, whereas others took greater risks. The teams also differed in their methodological focus—the same tasks that a given team found essential, another team brushed off as trivial.

Jason knew that when he accepted the team leadership role, he also accepted the challenge of building collaborative trust and respect and establishing a team process that would work for everyone, irrespective of culture. He shared that "the lack of personal relationships was undermining the team, and the cultural differences, had they remained unchecked, would have had a powerful negative influence on our team's success." Jason's first course of action was to develop a foundation of cross-cultural understanding.

Recalling the powerful lessons he learned from conversations he had had in college, and calling on the successful methods employed in his professional experience, Jason started with relationship building as the most direct route toward increasing the team members' cultural understanding. He carefully selected team members from each development site to work collaboratively, offering them coaching opportunities for awareness building and reinforcing mutual respect and cohesion. Over time, Jason and his team created a hybrid and high-functioning team culture among his global team members, who were also culturally agile. Jason commented, "When I started working in my current role, I was concerned with the cultural differences and focused immediately on the collaboration aspect to bring together the people, processes, and methodologies. My past experiences had highlighted that without a functional understanding of cultural differences, significant effort is required to build trust and collaboration as a result of cultural misunderstandings. When I see collaboration across sites and cultures and the application of best practices, I am proud of the time spent establishing links and building relationships that will continue to pay dividends." As Jason's example illustrates, the creation of a global team's hybrid culture is critical for a team's success.

Cultural Integration: Does "No Blame" Mean "No Accountability"? Let's consider another example of a hybrid team culture. In preparation for the 2000 Summer Olympics, held in Sydney, Australia, a priority was set to clean up Sydney Harbour—a massive undertaking that would involve a global budget, TV coverage, and a twenty-kilometer tunnel under an affluent neighborhood north of the harbor.[16] Consultants were brought in to work with this extensive alliance of professionals to help create their project team culture. They ultimately helped the team compile a list of value statements, which included two core values—striving to produce solutions that were "best for project" and creating a "no-blame" culture—along with a list of ten principles to guide behavior:[17]

1. *Build and maintain a champion team, with champion leadership which is integrated across all disciplines and organizations;*

2. *Commit corporately and individually to openness, integrity, trust, cooperation, mutual support and respect, flexibility, honesty, and loyalty to the project;*

3. *Honour our commitments to one another;*

4. *Commit to a no-blame culture;*

5. *Use breakthroughs and the free flow of ideas to achieve exceptional results in all project objectives;*

6. *Outstanding results provide outstanding rewards;*

7. *Deal with and resolve all issues from within the alliance;*

8. *Act in a way that is "best for project";*

9. *Encourage challenging BAU (business as usual) behaviours;*

10. *Spread the alliance culture to all stakeholders.*

Although obviously the project was located in Sydney, the guiding principles did not fit any culture completely. For example, one of the Australian project leaders in this alliance expressed concern that the "no-blame" aspect of the team culture was counter-cultural for the Australians. Describing the example of a colleague being late for a meeting, he noted how difficult it was when "you couldn't call anybody up on what they hadn't done. That it meant no one could go up to someone and say 'tighten your schedule, you said you would be here at two o'clock. I've structured my day around you being here at 2 PM and you arrived at 3 PM. I'm losing confidence that you are going to do what you say you're going to do!' . . . I think that [no-blame culture] is something Australians find really difficult to deal with. In Australia it's more like 'Hey, you get lost or something?'"[18] In his view, "no blame" would translate to a lack of accountability.

In spite of the principles' not being fully culturally comfortable for every team member, these professionals adhered to their integrated team culture and worked together exceptionally well. Not only was Sydney Harbour cleaned on time for the Olympics, but all the stakeholders were abundantly satisfied—including three eighty-ton whales who returned to the (now cleaner) waters of the harbor.[19]

Cultural Integration in Mergers and Acquisitions   As with work on cross-cultural teams, other professional situations require an integrated approach to cross-cultural differences. Integrating cultures is also critical when two companies come together through a merger or acquisition. In this context, one of the best examples is Lenovo's acquisition of IBM's PC division. Prior to the acquisition, certain ground rules were set by Lenovo's chairman and CEO, Yang Yuanqing and Steve Ward.[20] These ground rules were characterized as three guiding principles of cooperation for the entire company to follow:

- Candor

- Respect

- Compromise

Yang and Ward also did one more thing: they chose their cultural "battles" carefully. In other words, the Lenovo leaders did not try to impose a consistent approach unless one was needed. Nor did they try to culturally integrate practices if they anticipated that doing so would be overly time consuming and not practically or strategically necessary. In a keynote address to the Academy of International Business, Liu Chuan Zhi, CEO and president of Legend Holdings Ltd. (the parent company that acquired Lenovo), described a salient example of this type of cultural agility and the foundation on which Yang and Ward built their approach to the acquisition. In speaking about cultural compromises between Lenovo and IBM, Liu sagely offered this approach:

In order to promote common interests, we divided issues into significant and inconsequential ones. For the latter, we felt that there was no point in wasting time and energy on them, so that we could focus our attention on the significant issues that need to be addressed. We realized that, if we did not compromise, there would be conflicts where no progress could be made. And it might even lead to destructive factions of two different nationalities within the company. We have yet more work to do in the area of cultural integration. I am happy to say, though, that thus far we are progressing satisfactorily along this front.[21]

It is a reflection on Liu's culturally agile leadership that he was selected as the recipient of the 2006 Distinguished Executive of the Year Award by the Academy of International Business Fellows.

TAKE ACTION

Based on the information presented in Chapter Two, the following is a list of specific actions you can take to begin implementing the first three competencies in the Cultural Agility Competency Framework within the context of your organization:

- Review the competency models currently being used in your organization (for example, the leadership competency model). Are any of the competencies in the Cultural Agility Competency Framework already embedded into competency models that your organization uses? Can you align them to make sense with your existing framework? Which of the competencies are missing from the existing framework? Can some or all of the missing competencies be added?

- Think about the ten most critical positions in your organization. When considering each of these positions in a global context, is there a behavioral response (cultural adaptation, cultural minimization, or cultural integration) that would be most critical for success in the given role (for example, cultural minimization for quality control managers)?

- In considering those critical global roles, is there agreement on the best possible behavioral response—or is the full repertoire of all three behavioral responses needed?

CHAPTER

3

NINE CROSS-CULTURAL COMPETENCIES AFFECTING SUCCESS OF CULTURALLY AGILE PROFESSIONALS

As you've just seen in Chapter Two, the first three cross-cultural competencies in the Cultural Agility Competency Framework (cultural minimization, cultural adaptation, and cultural integration) are distinct because they enhance success only when they are activated at the right time and in the right way. The remaining nine competencies operate in a more intuitive, "more is better" fashion. They enable professionals to be effective in intercultural situations by helping them manage their own response set so as to quickly, comfortably, and effectively work in different cultures and with people from different cultures. These competencies also facilitate culturally agile professionals' abilities to connect with others from different cultures, communicate appropriately, effectively build trust, and gain credibility. These competencies also enable professionals to make appropriate decisions by accurately reading the cultural context—the interconnected system of the countries or cultures in which they are operating—and responding appropriately to it while accounting for the business strategy at hand. Let's delve deeper into these nine remaining competencies.

THREE COMPETENCIES AFFECTING PSYCHOLOGICAL EASE IN CROSS-CULTURAL SITUATIONS

The next time you are in an international airport, spend a few minutes observing people who are entering the country as visitors. For example, if you watch foreigners asking directions to the taxi stand or baggage claim, you can see that some are tense and anxious, and others are at ease. This same tension-ease contrast can be observed among professionals working in cross-cultural contexts long after they've left the airport. Some will feel confident and relaxed from the start. Some will feel like fish out of water at first, but adjust to the host country and feel more comfortable over time. Others will not really feel comfortable again until the moment they return home. All three responses are possible, but only the first two are acceptable for culturally agile professionals.

The Italian executive Rachele Focardi-Ferri remembers being overwhelmed by this fish-out-of-water feeling the day she landed in Mumbai, India, in 2007. Universum Communications, a Swedish-headquartered consulting company specializing in employer branding, had appointed her as its country manager for India, despite the fact that she had never been there. As Rachele recalls, "alone and exhausted . . . I looked around the airport and asked myself how a young woman from Italy would really be able to successfully communicate and do business with the Indian heads of the world's leading organizations."

Rachele's pause at the airport was perfectly understandable. Not only was her mind having a moment of self-doubt; her body was also responding to the experience with feelings of nervous anticipation. Research has found that compared to professionals working in their home countries, many professionals working in foreign countries experience physiological changes in their stress hormones, including increases in prolactin level and decreases in testosterone level.[1] These physiological responses can last for several years in the foreign environment. Global professionals who are equipped with the cross-cultural competencies and individual characteristics that help reduce the psychological discomfort of living in the cross-cultural context tend to do better physiologically as well as psychologically.

Research has found that compared to professionals working in their home countries, many professionals working in foreign countries experience physiological changes in their stress hormones.

The good news is that Rachele packed her cultural agility along with her suitcase. Culturally agile professionals have the cross-cultural competencies necessary to combat their bodies' and minds' reactions to the stress of the cross-cultural context. The ways that Rachele adjusted to living and working in India illustrate these important competencies. First, she had a *high tolerance of ambiguity*, indicated by the fact that she had accepted the role in a country she had never before visited and felt comfortable in the cross-cultural context without the structure of her familiar corporate environment. Second, she had an *appropriate level of self-efficacy*: the humility to realize that she had a lot to learn about India and, at the same time, confidence in her ability to learn to be successful there. Third, she also had a natural *curiosity* about people and cultures and was sincere in her interest to learn about both. Rachele describes how she approached the new experience in India:

> I put on my young traveler's hat—the one I used when I traveled the world as a student with a backpack—and experienced India like a local. I gave up the car service and showed up to meetings on a rickshaw, ate local food at local restaurants, developed friendships with Indian colleagues, and showed a sincere interest and excitement toward the Indian culture—the religion, traditions and all that India had to offer. I asked questions, lots of questions, and learned all I could. The people I met appreciated my enthusiasm and even gave me an Indian nickname, "Rakhi," which is the name of a special bracelet that sisters and brothers in India give to each other to symbolize their bond. To this day, this is still the name many of my Indian clients call me.

Rachele was very successful in India, describing her two years managing the business there as one of the best personal and professional "stretch" experiences of her life. Having honed an even higher level of cultural agility, she now lives and works in Singapore, overseeing Universum's entire Asia-Pacific business.

For the past twenty years, I as well as many others have been conducting research on the competencies that predict success among international assignees, like Rachele, who are living and working outside their home countries, and global business professionals who are working on international activities. Starting with the competencies affecting individuals' psychological ease cross-culturally, as defined in Figure 3.1, we

FIGURE 3.1. *Cross-Cultural Competencies Affecting Psychological Ease*

Competency	Definition
Tolerance of Ambiguity	The internal meter people have that suppresses anxiety or stress in the face of perceived uncertainty (for example, when instructions are not well defined or situations are not clear). People who are tolerant of ambiguity are comfortable in settings where full clarity is not present or possible. For them, ambiguous situations do not produce anxiety or stress.
Appropriate Self-Efficacy	The appropriate confidence individuals have in their skills and their ability to be successful in international or multicultural situations. Humility in regard to one's skills and abilities is related to appropriate self-efficacy; those highest in cultural agility do not overestimate their skills or their ability to be effective cross-culturally.
Cultural Curiosity and Desire to Learn	The interest in learning about other cultures and the tendency to pursue or investigate to form a greater understanding. Those higher in intellectual or cultural curiosity are more likely to ask questions, independently search for information, and read deeply on topics of interest.

can examine the validity evidence—the proof that certain cross-cultural competencies are present in more effective culturally agile professionals.

Tolerance of Ambiguity

Cross-cultural situations are often filled with ambiguities that can potentially be anxiety producing for some individuals. These ambiguities can be major (for example, not being able to accurately interpret behaviors during a high-stakes business negotiation) or minor (for example, being unsure why colleagues from a given culture do not speak up during staff meetings). When a situation is difficult to interpret, the outcome cannot be predicted, producing anxiety for many. People with a higher tolerance for ambiguity, like Rachele, are able to accept the fact that cross-cultural situations often hold some "unknowns." They can remain relaxed and patient until, over time, they understand more about the country, the culture, and the context.

In a study of global business professionals, Ibraiz Tarique and I looked at the relationship between cross-cultural competencies and supervisors' ratings of global business professionals' success on a variety of activities with global scope (for example, managing subordinates from different cultures, managing a budget globally).[2] We found that business professionals who have a greater tolerance of ambiguity are rated by their supervisors as more effective in their global professional tasks. The same result was found in predicting performance among international assignees living and working internationally.[3]

The same result also was found for soldiers who were stationed internationally. Working in conjunction with the U.S. Army Research Institute, researchers Michael McCloskey, Kyle Behymer, Elizabeth Lerner Papautsky, Karol Ross, and Allison Abbe conducted a study to better understand the cross-cultural competencies that differentiate soldiers at a higher level of cross-cultural effectiveness from those at a lower level.[4] Their study identified four levels of cross-cultural effectiveness—pre-competent, beginner, intermediate, and advanced—and evaluated soldiers' responses to assess their cross-cultural competencies. With respect to the characteristics affecting individuals' psychological ease, tolerance of ambiguity and curiosity (or sensemaking, as it was called in their study) are higher among the soldiers at an advanced level of cross-cultural competence. These results are shown graphically in Figure 3.2.

Culturally agile professionals can effectively and *comfortably* work in different cultures and with people from different cultures. If we underscore "comfortably" for a moment, then the need for tolerance of ambiguity among your pipeline of global professionals becomes even more critical. In a meta-analytic study (combining the results of multiple studies), Michael Frone found that those with a higher tolerance of ambiguity are less vulnerable to the negative effects of job-related stress and strain caused by roles with less clarity and more ambiguity.[5] Professionals with a higher tolerance of ambiguity feel more comfortable in uncertain or stressful environments, and are less likely to use negative stereotypes[6]—another useful attribute among culturally agile professionals. You can get a sense of Rachele's high tolerance for ambiguity when she describes why she believes other foreign professionals struggle to be effective in

FIGURE 3.2. *Soldiers' Competencies Affecting Psychological Ease Cross-Culturally*

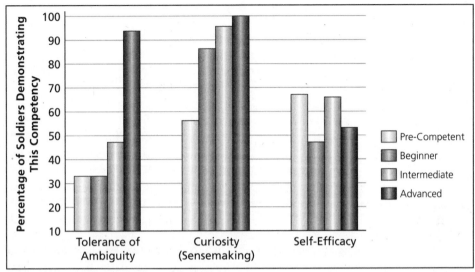

Source: Data from Michael McCloskey, Kyle Behymer, Elizabeth Lerner Papautsky, Karol Ross, and Allison Abbe, *A Developmental Model of Cross-Cultural Competence at the Tactical Level*, Technical Report 1278 (Arlington, VA: U.S. Army Research Institute for the Behavioral and Social Sciences, 2010).

India: "Too many foreign business professionals become very nervous in India when things do not run as smoothly as they do in their home countries. You need to take time to better understand the complexity of how to get things done. It is very different . . . I saw too many foreigners in India openly show their aversion toward the noise, the pollution, the food, and the people. They seemed to be lashing out because of their own insecurities."

Culturally agile professionals can effectively and comfortably work in different cultures and with people from different cultures.

Appropriate Self-Efficacy

Psychologist Albert Bandura coined *self-efficacy* as the term for one's belief in one's ability to succeed in a given situation. As a cross-cultural competence, self-efficacy is the belief in one's ability to perform one's role in a cross-cultural context. Did you notice that of the twelve competencies in the Cultural Agility Competency Framework, self-efficacy is the only one qualified by the word "appropriate"? There is good reason for this. You might recall the study I conducted, described in Chapter One, in which new International MBA graduates *assumed* that they would be successful working internationally on the global rotation of their employers' global leadership development program. Their self-efficacy was high before they actually worked internationally.

The study found that those who were currently on the international rotation of the global leadership development program, or had already been on it, had *lower* self-efficacy in regard to their abilities to be effective internationally. This group had worked abroad and better understood the importance of the cross-national context. Self-efficacy was more *appropriate* among those who understood the context of working internationally.

Professionals who have a high level of confidence in their ability to succeed in a cross-cultural context, but who don't fully understand the powerful influence of the context, generally experience a reappraisal of their self-efficacy and a healthy new appreciation for the effects of the cultural context after they attempt to work in that context. I would have been very concerned for Rachele if she had stepped off the plane in Mumbai believing she had all she needed to be successful. Her initial hesitation and anxiety were important in her adjustment to an appropriate level of self-efficacy. As illustrated earlier in Figure 3.2, appropriate self-efficacy was replicated in a military sample as soldiers gained competence. As with the previous study, those with greater cross-cultural competence had *lower* self-efficacy than those with less cross-cultural competence.

Taken together, these studies offer a clear picture: the more individuals learn about what it takes to be effective in cross-cultural environments, the better they understand the magnitude of the challenges and the more accurately they can appraise their skills and abilities for working in such environments. As professionals become more culturally agile, they learn a more appropriate level of self-efficacy and have greater humility in regard to the skills and abilities they need to be effective internationally. Being aware of how little you know is, in fact, very good when working cross-culturally.

Once professionals gain an appropriate level of self-efficacy, this attribute can help them be successful and further develop their cultural agility. For one thing, self-efficacy is related to professional success.[7] Believing one can succeed produces motivated behavior needed for success. Second, professionals with higher self-efficacy have more contact with colleagues from different cultures and are more willing to seek out new experiences—both of which can increase effectiveness in cross-cultural contexts and further increase cultural agility.[8] Third, self-efficacy is related to international assignees' work-related cross-cultural adjustment.[9]

Cultural Curiosity and Desire to Learn

Rachele Focardi-Ferri described how, when she was in India, she asked questions, lots of questions. Her natural curiosity is an attribute she shares with other culturally agile professionals, those who would also describe themselves as having a relentless desire to learn about cultures and make sense of their new cross-cultural context. Culturally agile professionals are more likely to ask questions about norms, customs, values, behaviors, and other aspects of culture that are unfamiliar. They are more likely to actively search for knowledge about the history, religion, legal system, and other aspects of the cultures of the countries they will visit and the people with whom they will work.

As we can see from the military study illustrated in Figure 3.2, cross-culturally competent soldiers were more likely to engage in these knowledge-seeking or sensemaking behaviors. Curiosity is the grease of the cultural understanding machine, enabling professionals to learn through the contact they have with the people and circumstances of their cross-cultural environment.[10] Combining curiosity with actual opportunities to interact with peers from different cultures—who can, in fact, accurately answer those curious questions and help professionals make sense of the context—will further accelerate the development of cultural agility.

Curiosity is the grease of the cultural understanding machine.

THREE COMPETENCIES AFFECTING CROSS-CULTURAL INTERACTIONS

Have you ever tried a new restaurant and asked the waiter for a meal suggestion? Have you ever been lost while driving and stopped to ask for directions? Have you ever needed to hire a contractor or physician and asked someone you trust for a recommendation? My guess is that you have had each of these experiences at some point in your life. Most of us have. The way we as humans make sense of unfamiliar situations is often through the relationships we forge with others who can guide us. Effective interactions with people from different cultures are not just the *goal* of culturally agile professionals; they are the way in which professionals *become* culturally agile. They are the process, not the outcome. Culturally agile professionals seek to reduce ambiguity and learn to navigate diverse cross-cultural contexts. This is most often achieved through their contact with others, their willingness to develop relationships with people from diverse cultures, and their ability to see things through the lens of those with a different set of values.

In this section, we will examine the three competencies from the Cultural Agility Competency Framework that affect individuals' propensity to engage in these kinds of multicultural interactions. They are listed in Figure 3.3.

Sean Dubberke, a culturally agile professional, has spent the better part of his career helping professionals learn to navigate the cross-cultural contexts in which they are placed. As director of intercultural programs at RW³ CultureWizard, Sean trains corporate professionals on how to develop their relationships and be effective working across cultures. Sean, who is American, also practices what he preaches. Speaking five languages (English, Spanish, German, French, and Japanese) and having lived in Spain, Germany, and the United Kingdom, Sean is aware of how his own cultural agility has grown through the personal and professional relationships he has developed over the years.

The realization that relationships were critical for cultural understanding began early for Sean. When he spent a college year abroad in Spain, he chose to be immersed in the Spanish culture by sharing an apartment with Spaniards rather than living with

FIGURE 3.3. *Competencies Affecting Individuals' Cross-Cultural Interactions*

Competency	Definition
Valuing Diversity	The ease in being with others who do not have a common platform of life experiences. Those more comfortable with diversity tend to associate with colleagues who are from different cultures, generations, and so forth. They are less likely to shy away from cross-cultural settings and interactions with people from diverse cultures. They are at ease with any group of people.
Ability to Form Relationships	An interest in connecting with others on a personal level. Individuals with an ability to form relationships are naturally sociable and seek opportunities to connect with others. They form positive interpersonal relationships and enjoy meeting people.
Perspective-Taking	An ability to see situations from multiple perspectives and reassign meaning to behaviors. Those with this ability tend to suspend judgment while they seek to understand the lens through which a situation can be interpreted.

American students. In addition to his educational pursuit, Sean's goals for living and studying in Spain were to become a part of the fabric of the local community, to improve his Spanish language skills (including colloquialisms), and to understand the nuances of Spanish culture. To help Sean find a flat and roommates in a way Madrileños do, a friend directed him to *Segunda Mano*, a collection of classified ads published only in Spanish. This proved a successful strategy. Sean found a room in a flat with three Spaniards, roommates who later became his close friends. Valuing cross-cultural experiences over the psychological ease of living with fellow Americans, Sean started building his cultural agility.

Although Sean had always been an extrovert, his cultural agility began to snowball after his experience in Spain; his natural curiosity and sociability continue to propel him to seek and form deep relationships with friends and colleagues from diverse cultures and, in turn, to learn about cultures with each cross-cultural experience. A few years after living in Spain, Sean embraced an opportunity to live and work in Leipzig, Germany. Sean credits his success in Germany to his German friends and colleagues, describing how they "helped me learn the German language and guided me as I learned about the culture. They helped me understand the regional mentality toward business and progress—connecting how this was still linked to a rule-oriented, authoritarian past. It would have been difficult to navigate these regional nuances without their guidance."

As a natural extrovert, Sean has an aptitude for using social connectedness in a cross-cultural context to build and practice his cultural agility. In an extensive study examining the successful predictors of globally mobile professionals in many countries, researchers Margaret Shaffer, David Harrison, Hal Gregersen, J. Stewart Black, and Lori Ferzandi found that, among other traits, those who were more extroverted and people oriented were more successful and better adjusted to working internationally.[11]

The results that Margaret and her colleagues found in their research studies were replicated among global professionals; Ibraiz Tarique and I found that global professionals were more successful when they had the natural tendency toward forming relationships and were given the opportunity to do just that.[12] Our study found that global professionals, like Sean, who both are extroverted *and* had high-contact experiences with culturally diverse peers were most successful in their subsequent cross-cultural professional activities.

In the study of soldiers described in the previous section, Michael McCloskey and his colleagues found that soldiers' ability to form relationships differentiates soldiers at a higher level of cross-cultural effectiveness from those at a lower level.[13] As you can see in Figure 3.4, *ability to form relationships* (assessed as both relationship building and rapport building), and *perspective-taking* were higher among the soldiers at an advanced level of cross-cultural competence.

FIGURE 3.4. *Soldiers' Competencies Affecting Cross-Cultural Interactions*

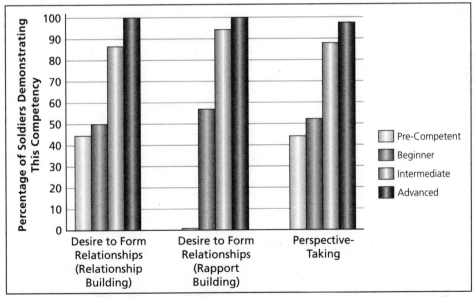

Source: Data from Michael McCloskey, Kyle Behymer, Elizabeth Lerner Papautsky, Karol Ross, and Allison Abbe, *A Developmental Model of Cross-Cultural Competence at the Tactical Level*, Technical Report 1278 (Arlington, VA: U.S. Army Research Institute for the Behavioral and Social Sciences, 2010).

Valuing Diversity

Years before his stay in Madrid as a college student, Sean Dubberke had already been seeking out cross-cultural experiences. He described a time when he was thirteen and petitioned his parents, unsuccessfully, to take him to Japan after experiencing Little Tokyo in downtown Los Angeles. Barely a teenager, and realizing that a trip to Japan wasn't in his immediate future, Sean did the next best thing: he sought out Japanese experiences. Sean dedicated himself to learning the Japanese language, first through self-initiated study at home (memorizing both the Hiragana and Katakana writing systems), then through evening community college courses as a high school student, and, finally, with advanced courses in college and a month-long immersion trip to Japan. Although, as Sean remarked, "the goal was to get to Japan and experience its culture," the steps leading there exposed him to people and places in his own backyard that resulted in an education in Japanese values. "Even without being fluent, I spent time watching Japanese programs on television, attempted to read *manga* that wasn't translated, and surrounded myself with Japanese and Japanophiles alike. Exposure to a diversity of thought was the most influential part of this personal project, which prepared me for life abroad before I knew where I was headed."

Valuing diversity is a critical competence for culturally agile professionals because cultural agility develops over time. The more that professionals seek out and engage in culturally diverse experiences with colleagues and peers from different cultures—as Sean continues to do—the more they will build their repertoire of culturally appropriate skills and continuously increase their cultural agility. Culturally agile professionals value opportunities to be around those who view life through a different lens and are guided by a different set of cultural norms. They don't mind being demographically different from others when they are in other countries or with people from other cultures. On the contrary, they seek and embrace these experiences. Ibraiz Tarique and I found that those global professionals who valued cultural diversity to the point where they sought out opportunities to meet and befriend foreigners—and valued the opportunities to do so—were rated as more effective in their global professional activities.[14]

> *Culturally agile professionals value opportunities to be around those who view life through a different lens and are guided by a different set of cultural norms.*

Ability to Form Relationships

Culturally agile professionals have an advantage when it comes to building a global network of trusted colleagues and business associates. Jon Shapiro, Julie Ozanne, and Bige Saatcioglu conducted a fascinating study of global professionals, North American buyers in the garment industry who spent years working with colleagues in Asia.

The most culturally effective among the professionals in their study were able to accurately scan the environments where they were operating, fully understand the nuances of the host cultures, and respond as needed. These buyers were able to form strong and trusted professional relationships with their Asian counterparts. At this advanced level, the American buyers "personally know their suppliers and business partners' families, socialize with them regularly, and are genuinely committed to working through problems."[15]

This ability to form relationships is also important for those professionals who are living and working internationally. In another study, I found that international assignees from a U.S.-based information technology company with a broader base of host national colleagues and friends were more likely to adjust to living and working in their host countries. As Sean Dubberke's examples illustrate well, his cross-cultural relationships in Spain and Germany facilitated his success in those countries. Culturally agile professionals' ability to successfully form and foster relationships is a critical competence for global professional success.

Perspective-Taking

In the aforementioned research study on American buyers working in Asia, Jon Shapiro, Julie Ozanne, and Bige Saatcioglu found that professionals pass through stages of understanding as they become more accurate in interpreting their cross-cultural environments over time. In the earliest stage, which these researchers call the "romantic sojourner" stage, professionals are still interacting with the foreign culture as a tourist, at a rather superficial level. They are still using their own frame of reference to interpret the different cultural norms around them. Needless to say, an inability to accurately read the cues from the environment results in misunderstandings, problems, mistakes, and failure. They found that those who are at a higher and more skilled level are able to interpret the cues reliably and to "frame-switch" accurately across various cultures.

Perspective-Taking and the Golden Rule Well-meaning professionals, often at the early romantic sojourner phase, often ask me this question: "Wouldn't it make sense to simply treat others the way I'd like to be treated—and not really worry about cultural differences?" This "Golden Rule approach" is a fine way to think about professional intercultural interactions, if (and only if) professionals are willing to adapt the way they "do unto others" to follow the cultural norms of what they wish to be "done unto."

Try taking the Golden Rule quiz (see box) to see whether your behavioral preferences are universally desirable.

Once you have taken this quiz, you will probably be able to guess why the Golden Rule approach is not sufficient without deeper cultural understanding. For example, in some cultures it would be disrespectful to look someone (especially an elder or

Quiz: The Golden Rule

Read each statement and put an X next to those that describe *how you would like to be treated*.

1. I prefer a person with whom I am speaking to look me in the eyes when he or she talks to me.	
2. I would want a friend to accept and open a gift that I give to him or her.	
3. I would not want to be interrupted when I am speaking.	
4. I would want a colleague to actively listen when I am presenting.	
5. I would want to be acknowledged for my professional accomplishments.	
6. I expect my colleagues to respect my time and not be late.	
7. I prefer to be judged at work by my character and knowledge, not by my appearance.	
8. I would want my personal space to be respected.	
9. I would not want to be touched by someone I do not know.	
10. I would want to be honest with a colleague if I thought he or she was wrong about a work-related decision.	

someone more senior on the organizational chart) in the eye when you speak to him or her. In Brazil, it is good manners to open a gift immediately—and to express delight and appreciation. In most Asian and Middle Eastern cultures, it is considered impolite or disrespectful to open a gift in the presence of the person who gave it. In China, refusing a gift as many as three times before accepting it conveys humility and respect. In some cultures, such as Brazil, interruption is a way to show engagement in the conversation. In Japan, being acknowledged for your accomplishment individually would be embarrassing. It is also common in Japan for professionals to close their eyes while someone is presenting to think about what is being said—an act that is almost always interpreted as sleeping by those who are not Japanese. Giving a presentation to people who have their eyes closed is especially difficult for those from interpersonally oriented cultures.

Let's continue down the list. In many of the Southern European countries, time is very fluid and does not have the same sense of value as in Germany and North America. Lateness is accepted and tolerated. In Italy, you will be treated according to your appearance; if you do not care about your own appearance, why should others respect you or trust your opinions?

There is more. You may already know that personal space varies from country to country. What you may not realize is that the violation of the space when communicating—either by being too close or not close enough—causes great anxiety. In certain cultures, a touch on the hand or arm when speaking is merely a sign of conversational connection and should not be construed as flirtation or aggression. Most people think of saving someone from embarrassment in connection with Japanese or other Asian cultures, but it is also critical in Latin American cultures and some European ones, such as France and Italy. For example, a business associate who does not care to have a meeting with someone might repeatedly postpone setting a date or location for the meeting rather than appear rude by stating flatly that there does not seem to be any reason to meet. Professional debate, especially when someone is being challenged, considered healthy in many northern European countries, would be considered rude in many other face-saving cultures.

As this rather superficial test was meant to illustrate, the Golden Rule approach requires some knowledge of cultural differences and the ability to see things from another person's perspective—even if it is not a perspective or value you share. Culturally agile professionals are able to engage in perspective-taking and reassigning meaning to behaviors.

Perspective-Taking and Religion   Sean Dubberke recalls a time when perspective-taking was particularly helpful. He was on his way to a business trip in Oman when a customs official asked Sean about his religion as he crossed the border from the United Arab Emirates. Although that would be an irrelevant and illegal question for government agencies to ask in his home country, Sean sensed that the question was not about judgment but rather that the official was simply curious about the foreigner's religious stance. Having studied Arabic, Sean realized that for many Middle Easterners, it is often hard to understand how someone could not be religious. Sean explains that "atheism and people who don't claim to belong to any religious group aren't visible in the Middle East. It appears vulgar, even selfish, to not believe in any higher power, whatever it may be."

Sean engaged his perspective-taking abilities and responded to the official by saying he "was of an Abrahamic religion." This response was well received. The customs official welcomed Sean with a smile and commented on his belief "that religions are actually not all that different." We can wonder if the official's warm and philosophical response would have been the same if Sean's reply had not demonstrated perspective-taking.

THREE COMPETENCIES AFFECTING GLOBAL BUSINESS DECISIONS

Zsolt Vincze, a culturally agile Hungarian professional, knows that a higher-level understanding of history, culture, economics, and the like will help global professionals make the best possible decisions. Zsolt works for a Dutch firm, BEST Group, that sells products and advises clients in the removal and cleaning of hazardous substances. In Hungary, Zsolt advises clients on asbestos removal—but in doing so must maintain the industry standards and BEST Group's practices, influenced heavily by his company's strict Dutch standards for health and safety. As an Eastern European, Zsolt understands that the similarities in education and job titles belie the ease of instituting appropriate safety practices. He knows that a single approach that does not account for and *integrate knowledge of cultural issues, global standards, and country-level realities* will almost certainly fail. Success requires cognitive complexity, taking multiple factors into account.

When Zsolt works in Eastern and Western Europe, he needs to be *receptive to adopting different ideas* and approaches that will result in the same end—compliance with safety standards. Zsolt understands that in addition to the myriad of cultural challenges, more fundamental challenges related to economics and legal regulations affect whether practices will be followed. For example, in Eastern European countries such as Hungary, there is no regulatory requirement for any type of employee safety training prior to an asbestos removal job—only a voluntary labor safety meeting that might last only a few hours. There is no mechanism in place to regulate compliance with the practices at the organizational level. The opposite is the case in Western European countries. In these countries, associates are required to take an asbestos safety course, which can last between two and five days, with a strict examination and certification. Associates monitor compliance within their work teams and follow the practices with conviction. At the organizational level, there are structured sanctions for not complying with the regulations. Zsolt shares that compliance might not be perfect but that once the safety program is in place, there is widespread adoption in Western European countries.

In Eastern Europe, Zsolt needs to use more of a "macro lens" to be effective in implementing this critical safety compliance. In addition to these regulatory differences between Eastern and Western European countries, there are economic differences. Employees who might otherwise complain about the handling of unsafe materials are fearful of losing their jobs. Zsolt is sensitive to these concerns and takes them into account when developing an approach to safety training. Even with the risk of asbestos as a dangerous carcinogen, it would be inappropriate to recommend an employee-led safety initiative, given that there is great deference to the organization's leaders.

To work around these very practical realities, Zsolt needs to use his skills of *divergent thinking and creativity* to influence at an even higher level. For example, he describes encouraging Eastern European government leaders to consider safe asbestos removal as a government-led *opportunity* for a corporate certification and control system (in other words, one that is revenue generating for the governments) but also a long-term health burden if not addressed. Zsolt forms peer networking groups, mixing leaders from Eastern European firms and multinational companies operating in Eastern Europe. The hope is that when best practices from the multinationals are shared, a more advanced industry norm will be created in Eastern Europe.

Orly Levy, Schon Beechler, Sully Taylor, and Nakiye Boyacigiller would describe Zsolt as having a "global mindset." Their extensive analysis of the human attributes that underlie executives' global mindsets uncovered two factors.[16] First, focusing on the cognitions that make managers successful in global roles, they discovered that managers with a global mindset operate with "cosmopolitanism." They define this as "a state of mind that is manifested as an orientation toward the outside, the Other, and which seeks to reconcile the global with the local and mediate between the familiar and the foreign" and also as "a willingness to explore and learn from alternative systems of meaning held by others." Their examination also found that cognitive complexity was critical given managers' need to understand and integrate broader bases of knowledge and "simultaneously balance the often contradictory demands of global integration with local responsiveness." Zsolt clearly demonstrates both cosmopolitanism and cognitive complexity.

Ultimately, the greatest test of whether your organization's global professionals are successful is related to whether they are able to operate with a global mindset and make the best possible professional decisions in a cross-cultural context. In this section, we will focus on the cross-cultural competencies from the Cultural Agility Competency Framework that contribute to success in this area. They are defined and described in Figure 3.5.

FIGURE 3.5. *Cross-Cultural Competencies Affecting Decisions*

Competency	Definition
Knowledge and Integration of Cross-National/Cultural Issues	The factual knowledge of global issues that individuals possess and the understanding of how the countries of the world are interconnected through political, historical, religious, and economic factors.
Receptivity to Adopting Diverse Ideas	The interest in exploring diverse solutions and willingness to adopt solutions, approaches, or practices that originate from atypical sources. Those who are receptive to diverse ideas tend to cast a wide net for solutions, and ways of doing things. They know that great ideas can come from anywhere in the world. Those who lack cultural humility are more ethnocentric and more likely to be perceived as arrogant by their counterparts from different countries and cultures because they continually assert that the ideas originating from their own country are superior.
Divergent Thinking and Creativity	The ability to generate multiple solutions or approaches to a given situation. Those who can develop multiple ideas have more available solutions to apply to an atypical or novel problem or challenge. Creative individuals can consider complex situations from different perspectives using more outside-the-box thinking. They can also be highly resourceful, inventive, and innovative.

Knowledge and Integration of Cross-National/Cultural Issues

When executives were asked to name the global business capabilities most critical for younger leaders to possess in order to succeed today and in the future, their responses had a clear theme.[17] The most needed areas of knowledge included (but were certainly not limited to) global finance, global strategy, global macroeconomics, and global marketing. They also wanted their leaders of the future to have a worldly awareness and sound judgment, intuition, and decision-making skills. The preceding example of Zsolt Vincze illustrates the need for culturally agile professionals to integrate not only cultural differences but also differences in regulatory, economic, legal, and governmental systems. Zsolt knew that influencing the government and regulatory systems would be more likely to lead to compliance than simply providing safety training to employees in isolation. With a deeper knowledge of global, international, and cultural issues, culturally agile professionals like Zsolt are more likely to understand how the countries are different, interconnected, and aligned. They understand the political, historical, religious, economic, and other factors affecting their organizations' effectiveness. Having a deep understanding of the complexity of these factors enhances professionals' abilities to make more informed decisions in a cross-cultural context.

Do you remember the study described in the previous section by Jon Shapiro and colleagues about highly effective North American buyers working in Asia in the garment industry? They found that the most culturally effective buyers had developed over time the ability to see behavioral patterns within different cultures relative to their own culture, and to use their gained knowledge accurately and effectively.[18] As with buyers in the garment industry, highly effective soldiers operating globally also demonstrate the same cross-cultural competency. Michael McCloskey and his colleagues found that soldiers' *knowledge and integration of global and cultural issues* (assessed as both cultural awareness and integration) was higher among those at an advanced level of cross-cultural competence. Figure 3.6 illustrates this.

Receptivity to Adopting Diverse Ideas

Some of the most stunning, costly, and embarrassing mistakes in international business have been made because business leaders preferred solutions they knew from their home country over solutions that were generated outside their home countries. Consider the case of the world's largest retailer, Walmart. Although Walmart has achieved impressive successes in several countries, its experience in Germany was a dismal failure. In 2006, Walmart sold its eighty-five stores and pulled out of the country, a move that was estimated to cost about $1 billion. During Walmart's eight years in Germany, critics cited a host of cultural mistakes.[19] Some were highly avoidable. For example, Walmart's lack of awareness that German bed pillows differ from American ones in size and shape resulted in an unused inventory of thousands of pillowcases that were impossible to sell.

Other mistakes were more complex. The famously nonunion Walmart seriously underestimated the strength of German labor unions and work councils and its need to

FIGURE 3.6. *Soldiers' Competencies Affecting Decisions Cross-Culturally*

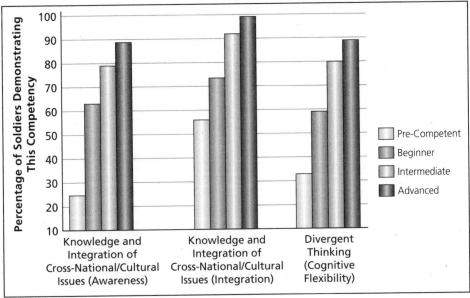

Source: Data from Michael McCloskey, Kyle Behymer, Elizabeth Lerner Papautsky, Karol Ross, and Allison Abbe, *A Developmental Model of Cross-Cultural Competence at the Tactical Level*, Technical Report 1278 (Arlington, VA: U.S. Army Research Institute for the Behavioral and Social Sciences, 2010).

work with them, not against them, as German law guarantees workers the right to organize. Walmart's reputation for offering the lowest price was besmirched when German grocery chains undercut Walmart's food prices. The famous Walmart practice of requiring employees to smile and greet every customer not only was unpopular with employees but also backfired with German customers, who interpreted this behavior as harassment and flirtation.

Being shortsighted about cultural differences in work-life balance preferences ultimately dealt the company the greatest blow in Germany. When Walmart opened its stores, it hired many German executives from the retail chains it acquired, expecting them to relocate. But the U.S.-based firm underestimated the high value Europeans place on remaining rooted in a certain place and connected with extended families. Many German executives quit, leaving Walmart with a dearth of qualified leaders who would have been highly cognizant of these and many other local issues. The Walmart executives' lack of receptivity to a different way of doing business is clearly apparent in their experience in Germany. Since then, Walmart has made tremendous changes to build its pipeline of culturally agile talent and compete more effectively in different countries around the world.

Global professionals who were comfortable and flexible in their willingness to engage in new and different activities were more successful.

Culturally agile professionals are able to adapt to new ways of doing things and do not shun ideas merely because they are different. Ibraiz Tarique and I found that those open-minded global professionals who were comfortable and flexible in their willingness to engage in new and different activities were more successful, rated by their supervisors as more effective in their global professional activities.[20] This competency of being receptive to exploring and accepting diverse solutions enhances cultural agility because having access to a greater number of plausible options relates to the greater likelihood of success in cross-cultural environments.

Divergent Thinking and Creativity

Divergent thinking is the ability to generate multiple solutions or approaches to a given situation, problem, or challenge. You have probably been involved in a brainstorming session at some point in your career. This activity is an example of group-based divergent thinking to generate a wide variety of ideas. Culturally agile professionals are often placed in situations where familiar solutions will not be effective, and alternative, more novel solutions are needed. Zsolt's bringing together leaders in Eastern European countries with leaders from multinational firms operating in Eastern Europe is an example of his use of divergent thinking to come up with a creative solution. Creative people who think "outside the box" are in high demand in almost every industry and professional field today. This is especially true for those who will be working in cross-cultural environments because the decisions to be made, strategies to be developed, and problems to be solved are often new and untested.

American Peace Corps volunteers who have been working globally to help in the HIV/AIDS crisis have been operating almost daily with this cross-cultural competence. Eric Goosby, the U.S. global AIDS coordinator, credits twenty-five hundred Peace Corps volunteers as partners in the implementation of the U.S. President's Emergency Plan for AIDS Relief, the U.S. government's response to the global AIDS pandemic. In forty-six countries, Peace Corps volunteers are involved in HIV education, including initiatives for HIV prevention, care, and support. Eric notes that Peace Corps volunteers demonstrate their divergent thinking to achieve this goal, stating that "Volunteers' 'can do' attitudes mean that they find ways to 'make do.' Where others may see a lack of resources, Peace Corps volunteers see a challenge and they respond with creative solutions . . . I am invariably impressed by the energy, passion and out-of-the-box thinking that volunteers bring to their work in HIV."[21]

TAKE ACTION

Based on the information presented in Chapter Three, the following is a list of specific actions you can take to begin implementing these nine competencies in the Cultural Agility Competency Framework within the context of your organization:

- Review the competencies listed in Figures 3.1, 3.3, and 3.5. How do they fit with your organization's current values or organizational culture? Are they already represented within the organization?

- Identify the critical positions that would most need employees who possess the competencies identified in this chapter—those where success is most critical for the organization's competitive advantage. As a place to start, integrate these competencies into the performance management systems for these positions.

- Collect critical incidents. Identify about ten situations where individual employees either facilitated or impeded an outcome of strategic importance for your organization (from a cross-cultural perspective). For those employees who were successful, identify the cross-cultural competencies they possessed that contributed to their success. For those who were unsuccessful, identify the cross-cultural competencies they lacked—the ones that, if they had had them, would have increased the likelihood of success.

PART

3

ATTRACT AND SELECT THE MOST CULTURALLY AGILE TALENT

People are not born with the twelve cross-cultural competencies in the Cultural Agility Competency Framework. Each competency comprises a mix of knowledge, skills, abilities, and other characteristics that are acquired and shaped over time, often honed by the multicultural situations in which we are placed throughout our personal and professional lives. Individuals will all start from a different place on their road to developing cross-cultural competencies. They start out with different knowledge, skills, abilities, and other personality characteristics. They have different personal and professional life experiences. It is important for you to identify these individual differences as you recruit professionals for your organization, because they affect professionals' ability to develop cultural agility.

At the start of the talent pipeline, your organization will need to attract and select those who are *able to gain these cross-cultural competencies* and, at the same time, to create the training and development opportunities to *build these cross-cultural competencies*. Chapters Four and Five will guide you through the first steps in this process: attracting and selecting candidates who are high in cultural agility or who have the aptitude for attaining it.

CHAPTER

ATTRACTING AND RECRUITING FOR CULTURAL AGILITY

Originally from Argentina, Marcelo Baudino recalls being inexplicably drawn to an international career by the time he was a teenager. His home city of Córdoba is located in the center of Argentina, quite far from the neighboring countries of Chile, Bolivia, Paraguay, Brazil, and Uruguay, countries Marcelo visited briefly as a child on family vacations. His middle-class upbringing was hardly the picture of a cross-culturally rich environment. Marcelo remained in Córdoba for university, attending the Universidad Blas Pascal. Not much changed in Marcelo's transition to university; his friends in college were identical to him on almost every salient demographic dimension. But even with such homogeneity in his life, Marcelo had a deep personal desire to experience the various cultures around the world. He knew he was different from his siblings and some of his friends, who had scant interest in meeting people from different countries or cultures. Whereas they had no interest in careers that would take them out of Argentina, Marcelo could think of no other career that would be satisfying. He wanted an international career and was highly motivated to make this goal a reality.

Marcelo's first exploration was not far—to the corner of a nondescript building within the campus of Universidad Blas Pascal. This small office held a big and life-changing opportunity: it was the International Relations Center, where Marcelo learned about the international programs offered through the university. One of these immediately caught Marcelo's eye: the opportunity to spend a semester studying at the University of Richmond in Virginia. Through dogged persistence and sincere interest, he convinced his parents that this was the developmental opportunity of a lifetime. He was right. During his stay in the United States, Marcelo used every opportunity to learn about Americans, American culture, and the importance of cultural differences. In addition to meeting and befriending Americans, Marcelo connected with other international students from many different countries and enjoyed the rhythm of his new culturally diverse circle. He found their differences and similarities intriguing, and learning about them aroused his curiosity to continue exploring the world.

After returning from his study abroad stint in the United States, Marcelo's psychological pull to see the world was stronger than ever, and he wanted a future career that would provide him with the opportunity to do just that. In Marcelo's mind, this cross-cultural feature of his career was nonnegotiable. Marcelo took every opportunity he could to connect with international professionals. He became very active in the local chapter of the Association Internationale des Étudiants en Sciences Économiques et Commerciales (AIESEC), an organization dedicated to the global leadership development of youth through conferences, international internships, and experiential opportunities in intercultural learning environments.

Making his international career goals known to recruiters and networking relentlessly, Marcelo began working globally upon his graduation from university in 2005. Since starting his career, he has worked in Mexico, Switzerland, and the United States, and his business travels have taken him all over the world, to such countries as Egypt and India and all throughout Europe. In these seven years since graduation, Marcelo has become a well-respected culturally agile professional, speaking three languages and possessing cross-cultural competencies to work effectively in diverse cultures. He is even a sought-after cross-cultural trainer, teaching others how to work effectively with people from diverse cultures.

Marcelo's persistent motivation for an international career accelerated the development of his cross-cultural competencies and cultural agility. Do you know colleagues like Marcelo who seem to have an irresistible attraction to international experiences, an unrelenting desire for cross-cultural professional endeavors?

Finnish researcher Vesa Suutari and his colleagues would describe Marcelo's psychological pull for a global career as his *international career orientation* or *career anchor*.[1] Career anchors and orientations are deep motivating factors propelling people to make career decisions consistent with their self-identities.[2] Like Marcelo, professionals with an international career orientation have personal and professional dedication to international, multicultural, and cross-cultural career activities. The cultural challenges propel them and motivate them. They cannot envision any other type of career. Professionals with this career orientation make career decisions such that their successive career moves are self-reinforcing, and, as a result, they build their cross-cultural competencies and become culturally agile. As professionals who actively build the competencies in the Cultural Agility Competency Framework, they are the exact individuals you will want to attract to your organization.

Through their research interviews, Vesa and his colleagues have captured the attitudes and sentiments of professionals with international career anchors. Here are some examples:[3]

> "I definitely wanted to go abroad—I left for Switzerland immediately after my graduation."

> "After a few years of work I set myself a goal to go abroad, or actually I have had such an intention always."

> "Internationalisation has been an integral part of my career . . . I would have afterwards considered it to be a catastrophe if I had pursued my career just in Finland."

> "Internationalism is of very great importance. It is probably what I would give up last. If I had to consider a job change, an international atmosphere and international connections would be decisive elements."

> "I would not even think about working anywhere else than either in a Finnish international company or in an international company as a Finn, either or. If you work in one country, the job remains very narrow . . . [This kind of job] is more interesting when you can work with all kinds of people."

> "The major issue that interests me [in international tasks] is that things are more complicated . . . [W]hen you talk about accounting as an example, you are not only dealing with numbers but you also work with people from other cultures."

These quotations illustrate how professionals with an international career orientation will seek out and initiate international experiences and thrive on the complexity that cross-cultural activities bring. If you hear any of your colleagues or job candidates sharing sentiments like these, you should look more closely at whether they are being leveraged fully in cross-cultural situations. Once they are equipped with the right set of technical skills, you'll want these individuals in your global talent pipeline.

In most organizations today, the gauge for identifying colleagues with an international career orientation is *broken*. In most firms, accepting or completing an international assignment has been the gauge, erroneously equated with an international career orientation. This gauge is giving organizations far too many false positives. Professionals who have lived and worked internationally do not necessarily have an international career orientation, nor will they necessarily ever gain cultural agility. Vesa Suutari and his colleagues found that only half of the professionals

In most firms, accepting or completing an international assignment has been . . . erroneously equated with an international career orientation.

who had accepted international assignments had international career orientations. The other half accepted their first assignment not because of any desire to work in another country but rather because of job demands, supervisors' requests, a sense of duty to the organization, or the boost in income associated with the international assignment. The old gauge is correct only 50 percent of the time. True international career orientations are deep motivational forces that begin to surface relatively early in individuals' lives, evidenced through successive *self-initiated* career decisions.

The old, faulty gauge for identifying an international career orientation considers only the experiences professionals have had. The new (and highly reliable) gauge considers both the *motivation* for culturally diverse experiences and *self-initiated activities* carried out during these experiences. Udo Fichtner's stellar career as a culturally agile professional illustrates this well. Udo is a German national who has had three significant international experiences. As is the case for most individuals with international career orientations, Udo's interest in cross-cultural experiences began with a trigger event during his teenage years. Unlike most, his trigger event had a tinge of friendly sibling rivalry.

When Udo was thirteen years old, he made his confirmation (a significant milestone in Christian religions). To celebrate, his parents gave him a beautiful piano—a perfect gift considering that Udo was a passionate and accomplished pianist. He was thrilled. Two years later, his younger brother, Wolfgang, made his confirmation and received a comparably valuable gift—one year of high school in Oklahoma in the United States. Wolfgang returned from the United States with his English language skills polished, stories that sounded exotic to teenage ears, and a fully stoked international career orientation. Not to be outdone by his younger brother, Udo was determined to start his international experiences and catch up. Immediately after high school graduation, Udo spent seven months in the United Kingdom as an au pair, living with a British family to hone his English language skills and learn about a different culture.

Udo's second international experience began in 1996 when he was working for Deutsche Bank as a relationship manager for corporate clients and financial institutions. Seeking a deeper international dimension to his career, he actively initiated the opportunity to become the chief representative of Deutsche Bank in Bahrain. This did not materialize as planned; instead he was offered a position in his home country of Germany. But, as is typical of those with an international career orientation, Udo immediately rejected the domestic opportunity and insisted on an international assignment as the next step in his career. Two months later, in early 1997, Deutsche Bank responded by relocating him to Thailand to be a senior relationship manager for corporate clients within the global banking department. Udo's goals for this move were to learn about global business firsthand and, even more important, to gain insights into the way people live and work who are very different from himself. Udo spent two-and-a-half years with his family living and working in Thailand.

While in Thailand, Udo sought out diverse cultural experiences. He learned the basics of the Thai language and connected with his Thai colleagues and friends by cultivating an interest in and appreciation for their religious and social activities. In particular he gained a better understanding of their fascination with the Thai Royal Family. Udo traveled extensively throughout Thailand, not just to enjoy the beautiful beaches as many expatriates do, but also to visit ancient sites and to learn more about the history, culture, and economic development of the country. Breaking away from the traditional German (and Western) expatriate community, Udo fostered relationships with his Thai colleagues, investing time in earning their continued (and unbroken) trust. On the personal side, Udo and his family received invitations to the private homes of his colleagues, a social practice reserved in Thai culture for only one's closest friends. On the professional side, these close relationships enabled Udo to observe and model ways to be an effective professional in Thailand. Udo's cultural agility grew exponentially.

Upon returning to Germany, Udo continued to apply his cross-cultural competencies by taking the lead on a challenging international project, which turned him into a globetrotter. In 2000, now working for the multinational specialty glass manufacturer Schott AG, Udo received an opportunity to design and implement an employee ownership program for the entire corporation *globally*. His integration of the standard Schott AG corporate practice was so well executed that it remains in use today in every subsidiary around the world; to date, every year a new series of Schott Performance Shares are offered in thirty countries. This experience gave Udo a chance to further refine his cultural responses and develop his cultural agility through a significant professional challenge.

In 2004, again propelled by his international career orientation, Udo was looking for a greater cultural challenge and another opportunity to live and work in another country. He was initially offered an opportunity to return to Asia. Although he liked Asia very much, having lived and worked in Thailand, Udo requested a different challenge. Typical of those with a strong international career orientation, Udo wanted to broaden his cross-cultural competencies and gain some exposure to a very different cultural environment. His commitment to his career goals paid off, and he accepted the role of vice president of human resources for the Americas and vice president and general manager of Schott's corporate office in New York. During his three-and-a-half years in the United States, he became deeply embedded in American culture, personally and professionally, just as he had in Thailand. In New York, he learned a different way of making decisions, managing people, and dealing with employee issues—again sharpening his ability to leverage various cultural responses.

Through his experience in New York and his other personal and professional cross-cultural experiences, Udo has been recognized as a true global business leader. In 2008, he accepted a senior executive global leadership role with TRW Automotive in Germany. Three years later, he became vice president of human resources and corporate services at Hirschvogel Automotive Group, a global technology leader and one of the world's largest automotive suppliers in the area of forging and machining. He has a well-worn passport and continues to develop his cross-cultural competencies at the executive level. Udo's career history offers an illustration of how international career orientations unfold for culturally agile professionals through self-initiated activities and motivation for cross-cultural challenges.

In case you were curious, Udo's younger brother, Wolfgang, was also motivated by his international career orientation. His career has included three years in Johannesburg, South Africa; three years in Ohio in the United States; two years in Belgium; and a continued interest in international opportunities.

Finding colleagues like Marcelo and Udo (and Wolfgang), who have demonstrated both motivation for culturally diverse experiences and self-initiated activities during those experiences, is critical for building a pipeline of culturally agile professionals. No business leader should leave this important first step to chance. Today, when more people than ever are traveling, studying abroad, and working internationally, there's a lot of "noise" on the radar screen in the form of professionals who may appear culturally agile on the surface. You will see more people with international experience who might not have commensurate cultural agility. The challenge is to cut through the noise as you search for, attract, and accurately select professionals with an international career orientation—those with the motivation for acquiring cross-cultural experiences and have self-initiated these opportunities in their lives. These individuals are out there. You just need to know where to look for them.

FINDING CULTURALLY AGILE PROFESSIONALS

In your search for talent with international career orientations, you will need targeted recruitment practices, both for new graduates and for midcareer professionals. It is relatively easy to identify an international orientation among new graduates and young professionals because they have made certain decisions while in school that will indicate this orientation. As I've already noted, a reliable gauge for international career orientations accounts for motivation and self-initiation of activities. The gauge is more reliable for this more junior group because, in that phase, almost every extracurricular activity is self-initiated and a function of their individual motivation. Identifying more senior talent is a greater challenge because of the broader influences that can obscure a candidate's real international career orientation. Let's consider both groups—and where you can find those with an international career orientation.

A reliable gauge for international career orientations accounts for motivation and self-initiation of activities.

Finding Culturally Agile New Hires

In the summer of 2010, Goldman Sachs hired thirty-one newly minted graduates from the University of Pennsylvania's Wharton School. This is not surprising; Wharton is one of the world's leading business schools, ranked number one for finance. What might be surprising, however, is that Goldman Sachs hired the same number of graduates from Brigham Young University (BYU), which has a far lower (albeit respectable) ranking of thirty-second.[4] Some have attributed the hiring of these BYU students, many of whom are of the Mormon religion, to preferential treatment whereby senior Mormons hire fellow junior Mormons (the so-called Mormon Mafia). Although that "similar-to-me" bias might be present to a limited degree, this young talent from BYU brings more to the party than Wharton graduates in terms of their cross-cultural competencies and foreign language skills. They have had a significant developmental experience: every male Mormon is required to interrupt his college career (or whatever else he is doing in life) to spend two years in missionary service in another country, after having spent time learning the language and the culture of his assignment.

Jon Huntsman, the former U.S. ambassador to both China (2009–2011) and Singapore (1992–1993), learned how to speak Mandarin Chinese and Taiwanese Hokkien during his Mormon missionary service in Taiwan from 1979 through 1981. Huntsman described his experience in Taiwan as "akin to experience in the Peace Corps, the foreign service or the military. You learn to live a regimented lifestyle, you learn a language fluently and you learn to deal with people at the street level."[5] The obligatory Mormon mission is a profound developmental cross-cultural experience, and a reason why leading global firms such as Goldman Sachs, Google, Apple, Chevron, IBM, Intel, and many others have targeted some of their recruitment efforts at BYU.

International University Programs   Despite its merits, BYU is certainly not the only place to find talented new hires with deep cross-cultural experiences and the propensity to gain cultural agility. Roughly 1 percent of all European college graduates participate in the European Community Action Scheme for the Mobility of University Students (ERASMUS), a program designed to encourage international mobility among (mostly European) university students. ERASMUS is a large and coordinated effort that allows students with the strongest international career orientations to actively pursue an opportunity to study abroad by lifting some of the financial burden of the experience through subsidies. Since its inception, over 2.2 million college students have taken part in exchange programs where they live and study in a different country. Once in their professional roles, these same ERASMUS students are 15 percent more likely to work in a foreign country after graduation,[6] seek employers who will offer international opportunities,[7] and pursue international assignments.[8] Considering that the ERASMUS program comprises roughly four thousand universities in thirty-three countries, it is relatively easy to find new graduates who have participated. For an example of a practice to attract this talent, see "Build Your Employer Brand Among Culturally Agile Young Talent by Hosting Networking Parties" on the next page.

Beyond ERASMUS, there are thousands of other study abroad programs available from almost every university around the world. However, I offer a word of caution on using the study abroad experience as a gauge. You cannot assume that merely engaging in a foreign educational experience as an international or study abroad student is

Build Your Employer Brand Among Culturally Agile Young Talent by Hosting Networking Parties

Your organization could host an ERASMUS program networking party in almost any city to connect with those soon-to-be graduates with international career orientations. More and more students are opting to take a "gap year" to live and work internationally before starting university, or after university before starting their professional lives or entering a graduate program. Similar to ERASMUS program networking parties, gap year parties could help your organization source graduate talent with international career orientations, as well as boost your organization's visibility as an attractive employer for culturally agile new hires. Remember your own college days and how much you appreciated opportunities to learn about potential career paths while having fun and enjoying some free food.

evidence of a new graduate's international career orientation. You will need to consider the nature of the program as an index of the type of experience the student has sought out (see also "The Money Trap" on page 78). Not all study abroad programs are equal in terms of their cultural immersion. In fact, it is not unusual for international students to *seek* culture-free opportunities, either by living and associating with fellow year-abroad students from their home country or by choosing a study abroad location where they can be embedded within a large compatriot immigrant community. For example, parts of New Jersey in the United States have some of the largest concentrations of Indians outside of India. Indian international students who opt to live in those communities could, effectively, have little contact with Americans. (This is akin to the professional expatriate communities in many of the world's major cities, which can also be culture-free zones that serve to buffer any real cross-cultural experience.) I advise you to focus your recruitment efforts on international and study abroad students from university programs where the language of instruction is the host national language, where the students live with host national families or other international students, and where the geographical location does not afford access to a large compatriot community. Students who have selected these highly developmental programs for themselves have actively sought out and completed a cultural immersion experience.

Around the world, we have seen a steady increase in students interested in study abroad programs. Some universities have even changed the design of their programs to encourage more students to study abroad. For example, universities are encouraging students with more technically demanding majors with few available electives, such as engineering and pre-med, to study abroad during their freshman year when they are still taking their general education courses. Other universities are crafting their programs to have richer cultural experiences. *U.S. News & World Report* named the top study abroad programs in the United States based on their academic rigor and their offering of "considerable interaction between the student and the culture."[9] The students who have successfully completed these high-interaction study abroad programs are more likely to have greater cultural agility compared to those students with study abroad experience that limited their interactions with host-country nationals (for example, classes with compatriots, compatriot dormitories).

International Volunteerism Opportunities   Young professionals with international career orientations often engage in international volunteer opportunities as a way to have significant global experiences while concurrently lending their technical abilities to the communities they serve. Thousands of college-educated volunteers return each year, highly motivated to pursue professional careers where they can leverage their newly developed cross-cultural competencies and cultural agility. These returning volunteers are well educated, well trained, multilingual, and highly vetted, making them desirable (and prescreened) candidates for your organization. Although some former volunteers want to continue their work in international aid organizations and nongovernmental organizations (NGOs), many others seek professional careers in private sector organizations—and almost all welcome opportunities to continue enhancing their cross-cultural competencies and foreign language skills.

The largest numbers of volunteers deployed for international service are organized through governments, such as the Peace Corps in the United States and the European Voluntary Service in the European Union. Combined, the Peace Corps and the European Voluntary Service have over ten thousand returning volunteers each year.[10] At the same time, a multitude of volunteers for NGOs also complete their assignments, adding many more to the pool of desirable potential candidates.

You can source these candidates directly through sponsored career fairs, networking events, and Web sites for returning volunteers. For example, the Peace Corps organizes annual career conferences for their thousands of returning volunteers. To date, almost all of the dozens of organizations recruiting at these Peace Corps conferences have been government and aid organizations. With the exception of Disney and Deloitte, private sector employers have missed this opportunity to search for culturally agile talent.

Cross-Cultural Majors, Activities, and Clubs   Christina Biedny is a newly minted MBA in finance with a strong international career orientation. It first became evident when, as a teenager, she was drawn to books and movies set in foreign locations, allowing her to dream of cross-cultural experiences. She jokes that her earliest international trigger was watching the movie *When in Rome* with her younger sister. In the movie, two young girls (played by the twins Mary-Kate and Ashley Olsen) travel to Rome in order to participate in a Model United Nations competition. Inspired by the movie, Christina started a Model United Nations club at her high school and studied French avidly through both high school and college. She also studied Arabic in college and tutored others in French as one of her part-time jobs. As an undergraduate, Christina majored in political science and focused several of her electives on Middle Eastern politics, eventually completing an honors thesis on the Moroccan monarchy.

Christina's international interests also carried over into business school. Under the advisement of an International Business professor, she completed a master's thesis examining the impact of stock market openness in emerging markets. Christina's decisions demonstrate the classic motivation pattern of a new graduate with an international career orientation. Even with a graduate degree in finance, her résumé was filled with self-initiated participation in internationally oriented clubs, organizations, and coursework. Prior to graduation, Christina applied for a position teaching English in Korea. Instead of going to Korea, however, she ended up accepting an excellent offer of a finance position with a top accounting firm. Although the position was located in the United States, one of Christina's first conversations with her supervisor upon accepting the job was about the international opportunities that might exist for her within the firm.

Looking at your candidate pool, consider students with international career orientations, like Christina, who are drawn to internationally oriented fields of study and elective coursework in such areas as international business, affairs, law, development, and politics. New graduates who have combined these or any foreign language concentration with their more technically oriented majors (for example, engineering, accounting) should be considered seriously. Language majors should also be considered closely. In some job families, it will be easier for language majors or internationally oriented social science majors to gain technical skills than it will be for technically competent graduates with no interest in cross-cultural experiences to gain cultural agility. Even if they need some technical training at the onset, internationally oriented students are likely to be valuable in the long run.

The Money Trap

Although culturally rich activities like study abroad programs, international volunteerism experiences, and foreign travel are generally robust indicators of an international career orientation, for some students the ability to engage in these activities is a function of their family's socioeconomic status: can Mom and Dad afford to send their little darlings abroad for a semester or two? Because the indicator should be an international career orientation—and not parents' bank accounts—consider sourcing candidates who have actively sought out low-cost cross-cultural activities, such as internationally oriented majors, foreign language and cultural clubs, and multicultural online networking groups. Also be judicious about evaluating the true interests and aptitudes of candidates who do have international experience. The most effective recruitment efforts will source the best culturally oriented candidates without inappropriately bypassing potentially ideal candidates because of a lack of expensive credentials, or inappropriately selecting candidates whose international sojourn was more fun than substance.

Other places to actively target recruitment efforts are university clubs and organizations designed for students with cross-cultural interests, such as language clubs, Model United Nations, foreign affairs clubs, international business clubs, and the like. Connecting with members of these clubs, organizations, and associations is easier now than ever before given that most of them have an online presence on Facebook, LinkedIn, and other networking sites.

Finding Culturally Agile Midcareer Professionals

When the Peace Corps celebrated its fiftieth anniversary in 2010, I had the privilege of attending a reception at Rutgers University in honor of the first Peace Corps volunteers. Now in their seventies, these men (they were all men) had been in their twenties when they answered President Kennedy's call for young people to serve their country to perpetuate peace through living and working in developing nations. Nicknamed "Colombia 1" for their service destination, the men trained for three months at Rutgers University in the summer of 1961. Thirty-five of the original sixty-two volunteers returned to the place where their life-altering journey started.

At the reception, Kevin Quigley, president of the National Peace Corps Association, described three certainties: "death, taxes, and the fact that the Peace Corps will change your life for the better." The honored guests, those original volunteers, now retired, roared in applause when he spoke those words. It was as though Kevin had shared their treasured secret, a secret they had waited fifty years to pass on. The profound experiences they had in the Peace Corps triggered an international career orientation, launching many successful global careers in business, academe, government, and the military. Periodically breaking into Spanish just for the fun of it, these former American volunteers regaled each other with one story after another recounting fifty years of international assignments, global roles, and travels. Listening, I marveled at their cultural agility.

These original Peace Corps volunteers stood out fifty years ago when relatively few people lived and worked outside their home countries. They self-initiated a profound global experience that, predictably, opened subsequent career doors that may have remained closed to others lacking the cross-cultural competencies they had gained while in Colombia. In past decades, internationally oriented careers were a rarity; even top-level executives lived and worked in their home country with only occasional foreign travel. Those with the interest and aptitude for cross-cultural positions stood out because, typically, they were the only ones with a track record of living and working internationally. Today, with a greater amount of international travel and the ease of technology in connecting people, identifying midcareer professionals with international career orientations is more difficult. There are more false positives when it comes to predicting those who are or will become culturally agile based on having an international experience.

"Oh, God. Here comes the global–village idiot."

Sourcing Culturally Agile Professionals: InterNations

InterNations (www.internations.org) is an example of a networking club for global professionals. Its tag line is "connecting global minds," and it does this successfully. With thousands of members in over 250 cities around the world, InterNations connects international business travelers, those who have international career aspirations, and people who are currently on international assignments. The premise of the club is that those who have true international orientations would like to spend time socially with like-minded individuals, irrespective of country. Populating their social events and networking groups are people who aspire to gain cross-cultural competencies and cultural agility and are highly motivated to do so on their own time. To become better known among this group of motivated internationally oriented professionals, your organization could sponsor a networking event or become one of InterNations' global partners.

In searching for midcareer professionals with international career orientations, consider the pattern of their successive self-initiated career moves, language acquisition, personal development activities, and the like. Professionals who have a strong international career motivation will satisfy their cross-cultural desires through multicultural clubs and associations even when their current roles don't require the use of their cross-cultural competencies. See "Sourcing Culturally Agile Professionals: Inter-Nations" for an example of one of these associations.

Try this exercise: How would you identify adults who are talented and motivated musicians, but are not currently playing professionally? You might look at their previous experiences in music and then consider the types of activities they currently participate in, such as singing in community choral groups, playing in garage bands, taking classes to further their musical talent, attending concerts, and the like. They would be likely to practice their instrument in their spare time, just for fun. The same would hold for midcareer professionals who are motivated to build their cross-cultural competencies. They will independently practice their craft, volunteering their time to engage in cross-cultural activities, learning another language, taking an active interest in the world, and spending free time in multicultural experiences, such as off-the-beaten-path vacations in different countries.

• • •

I cannot emphasize enough that merely having a professional experience in another country is not the same as possessing cultural agility (any more than parents' forcing piano lessons for five years would give a child a love for music). At all stages, *be certain you are recruiting those who are demonstrating their motivation through self-initiated international and cross-cultural experiences*. Your goal in attraction and recruitment should be to meet them where they live—literally or virtually—and showcase to them the international and cross-cultural opportunities available in your organization. The goal is to create buzz for your organization among those with an international career orientation. See the box for an at-a-glance summary of ways to find culturally agile talent.

Where to Find Culturally Agile Talent

- Universities with culturally rich study abroad programs
- University programs with well-regarded foreign language and internationally themed majors
- International volunteerism programs' conferences and alumni clubs
- International and cross-cultural clubs, associations, and organizations
- Social media networking groups with an international, multicultural, or cross-cultural focus

To build a pipeline of globally talented professionals, your organization will need to find the right talent *and* craft your employee value proposition such that these individuals will apply for the jobs and accept the offers if they are extended. Finding culturally agile professionals is only half the challenge. There is not much sense in developing recruitment methods to source culturally agile talent if your offers are not accepted. Once you have found these desirable candidates, you will need to deliver a recruitment message highlighting the cross-culturally oriented benefits, offerings, and developmental opportunities your organization offers that they will find attractive. In doing so, your organization will become an employer of choice for those with an international career orientation. In the next section, I'll discuss a variety of methods to become an attractive employer for culturally agile talent.

Deliver a recruitment message highlighting the cross-culturally oriented benefits, offerings, and developmental opportunities your organization offers.

ATTRACTING CULTURALLY AGILE PROFESSIONALS

In every industry, an organization's ability to successfully recruit the best people for key roles is widely recognized as a source of competitive advantage. The challenge is that the most desired candidates—those individuals your organization most needs in order for it to win the future—will often have plenty of employment options. Why should skilled culturally agile talent select your organization? Leading organizations have effectively developed methods to improve their employer brand and increase their attractiveness as employers. You can apply these same practices to attract culturally agile talent to your organization.

Before we discuss ways for your organization to become an attractive employer, however, it is important to realize that the attraction initiative needs to be part of a targeted and strategic approach geared to maximizing your organization's long-term success. Whatever your organization's key talent needs are—scientists, engineers, culturally agile professionals—becoming an attractive employer for key categories is a *strategic* talent management practice and not a blunt instrument. A scattershot approach to becoming an employer of choice will only result in a larger workload for hiring managers and recruiters, who will then need to sift through an increasing number of subpar applications. Enhancing your employer image generally will only create more work for recruiters, whereas targeting your efforts to burnish your organization's image among the talent you most wish to choose is a valuable talent management strategy.

A scattershot approach to becoming an employer of choice will only result in a larger workload for hiring managers and recruiters.

Tailor your recruitment practices with precision to find and attract the talent your organization needs most—in this case, culturally agile professionals.

Global Image and Attracting Culturally Agile Talent

The attractiveness of your organization's employer brand for culturally agile talent begins with a factor that is likely to be beyond your control—your organization's global image. Organizations with a global consumer brand, cosmopolitan image, or worldwide organizational presence are naturally more attractive employers for culturally agile talent. These organizations are all around us. You know them when you see them—they're the ones whose brands transcend national boundaries in the eyes of their clients, customers, and future employees. These companies, such as Apple, Mercedes-Benz, and McKinsey & Company, are respected worldwide, and their products and services are relevant across cultures. If you work for an organization with a strong and positive global image, it will be easier to recruit culturally agile talent. If you work for an organization with a weaker global image, you will need to be more strategic (and perhaps a bit creative) to implement recruitment practices to attract culturally agile talent.

In speaking about the relationship between consumer brands and employer brands, Danny Kalman, global talent director at Panasonic, notes, "My overriding impression has always been that most employees feel a real sense of pride in being associated with a strong brand, and want to work for one."[11] Candidates are also attracted to organizations that align their consumer brand with their values and self-image. For example, individuals with a cool, fun, and hip self-image are attracted to working for organizations like Facebook, Diesel, Zappos, and MTV because of their cool, fun, and hip consumer brands. Organizations like Siemens, 3M, Intel, and Apple, with innovative, cutting-edge, high-tech consumer brands, tend to attract individuals who want to work with cutting-edge technologies. It is easier for firms with a strong consumer brand to recruit talent, especially among the individuals with values that align with the consumer brand.

The same holds true for those with cultural agility. Culturally agile individuals with an international career orientation will be most attracted to companies known for their global product brands (for example, Coca-Cola, Disney, Starbucks), cosmopolitan image (Gucci, BMW, Cartier), or global organizational presence (Nestlé, Google, Procter & Gamble). These organizations have a global reach that translates to perceptions of their employer brand.

You can see this phenomenon yourself by reading the following lists of "top 10" companies. You will find the complete lists (100 Most Recognizable Global Brands, 100 Most Reputable Organizations, 50 Most Attractive Employers for Those in Business, and 50 Most Attractive Employers for Those in Engineering) in the Appendix.

Attractive Global Employers: The Top Ten Lists

Interbrand's 2011 Ranking of the 100 Most Recognizable Global Brands—the Top 10

1. Coca-Cola (The Coca-Cola Company, USA)
2. IBM (IBM, USA)
3. Microsoft (Microsoft, USA)
4. Google (Google, USA)
5. GE (General Electric Company, USA)
6. McDonald's (McDonald's, USA)
7. Intel (Intel, USA)
8. Apple (Apple, USA)
9. Disney (Walt Disney, USA)
10. Hewlett-Packard (Hewlett-Packard, USA)

Source: Interbrand, *Best Global Brands 2011: The Definitive Guide to the Most Valuable Brands* (London and New York: Interbrand, 2011), http://www.interbrand.com/en/best-global-brands/Best-Global-Brands-2011.aspx. Reprinted by permission of Interbrand.

The Reputation Institute's 100 Most Reputable Organizations—the Top 10

1. Google (USA)
2. Apple (USA)
3. The Walt Disney Company (USA)
4. BMW (Germany)
5. LEGO (Denmark)
6. Sony (Japan)
7. Daimler (Germany)
8. Canon (Japan)
9. Intel (USA)
10. Volkswagen (Germany)

Source: Reputation Institute, "The Global RepTrak™ 100: The World's Most Reputable Companies," 2011, http://www.reputationinstitute.com/events/2011_Global_RepTrak_ 100_Release_08june2011 .pdf. © Copyright 2011. Reputation Institute. All Rights Reserved.

Universum's 2011 World's Top 50 Most Attractive Employers for Those in Business—the Top 10

1. Google (USA)
2. KPMG (USA)
3. PricewaterhouseCoopers (USA)
4. Ernst & Young (USA)
5. Deloitte (USA)
6. Microsoft (USA)
7. Procter & Gamble (USA)
8. J.P. Morgan (USA)
9. Apple (USA)
10. Goldman Sachs (USA)

Source: Universum, "The World's Most Attractive Employers 2011," http://www.universumglobal .com/IDEAL-Employer-Rankings/Global-Top-50. Reprinted with permission from Universum.

Universum's 2011 World's Top 50 Most Attractive Employers for Those in Engineering— the Top 10

1. Google (USA)
2. IBM (USA)
3. Microsoft (USA)
4. BMW (Germany)
5. Intel (USA)
6. Sony (Japan)
7. Apple (USA)
8. General Electric (USA)
9. Siemens (Germany)
10. Procter & Gamble (USA)

Source: Universum, "The World's Most Attractive Employers 2011," http://www.universumglobal .com/IDEAL-Employer-Rankings/Global-Top-50. Reprinted with permission from Universum.

Read the full lists in the Appendix. Do you see the pattern? Roughly half of the companies that appear on the first two lists, those with the best reputations and the most recognizable brands, are also considered attractive employers by job candidates globally. An organization's positive reputation and recognizable consumer brand translate into its becoming a more attractive *global* employer. These organizations have an easier time attracting candidates with an international orientation compared to lesser-known organizations.

Looking at the Universum lists of most attractive employers for both engineers and business professionals, you may have made another observation: almost all of the top ten in each category are headquartered in the United States. This can be explained, in part, by their transnational reach, with subsidiaries and employees all around the world. But there is also another possibility. Reflecting on the high number of U.S. companies appearing on the 2010 list of most attractive employers, the CEO of Universum noted that "American corporations are increasingly the preferred destination for global top talent. They are often perceived as the true international organisations, where nationality will not stand in your way to the top."[12]

The equal opportunity laws, practices, and values that are prevalent in the United States are being perceptually extended to help form the impressions of U.S. organizations as global employers. As the beneficiaries of this positive association, U.S. organizations are being credited with certain values: that they will recognize employees' merit as the basis for promotion (irrespective of nationality) and that they will embrace the diversity of cultures in the workforce. This perception gives U.S. firms an advantage in attracting culturally agile talent globally. However, there are other countries (notably Canada, Australia, Sweden, Denmark, Norway, and Finland) that share these egalitarian values and, therefore, should—with some coordinated communication—share this perceptual advantage when recruiting globally oriented candidates. And, in fact, the *Global Talent Index Report* lists these same seven countries among the top ten with the best capacity to produce and attract talent; the others are Singapore, Switzerland, and Hong Kong.[13] To assess your own organization's attractiveness as a global employer, take the Your Organization's Global Image quiz (see box).

Quiz: Your Organization's Global Image

Read each statement and put an X next to those that apply to your organization.

1. My organization has subsidiaries or locations in more than ten countries.	
2. My organization owns one of the 100 most recognizable global brands listed in the Appendix.	
3. My organization is one of the world's 100 most reputable companies listed in the Appendix.	
4. My organization is headquartered in the United States, Denmark, Finland, Sweden, Norway, Australia, Singapore, Canada, Switzerland, or Hong Kong.	

At this point you may be thinking, "This is very interesting, but what if my company is not located in one of these top ten countries?" The good news is that organizations headquartered in any country can control and leverage the values that are most attractive to internationally oriented candidates. If providing equal opportunity (irrespective of nationality) is a true value of your organization, then this value should be conveyed clearly in your organization's recruitment materials. You can craft your recruitment messages to communicate that the organization embraces diversity of national cultures. With this suggestion on necessary recruitment messages, we turn to the next section, which describes practices you can implement to become an attractive organization for culturally agile talent.

Recruitment Messages to Attract Culturally Agile Talent

As an organization, Nestlé traditionally tops the United Nations Conference on Trade and Development (UNCTAD) list of the most transnational companies in the world.[14] With roughly 280,000 employees and 443 factories in eight-one countries, Nestlé deserves its position at the top of this list of global corporate giants.[15] To compete effectively in almost every country in the world, Nestlé relies on culturally agile professionals in key positions—individuals who can, for example, adapt food and beverage products to local preferences while maintaining Nestlé's standards for operational excellence, product innovation, and ethics.

The message to any job candidate who would like a professional career with Nestlé is unambiguous: to be successful at Nestlé, your career will be global, and you will need to be successful across cultures. These messages start at the top. The last time I visited the home page of the Nestlé careers Web site, the page focused on the Nestlé CEO, Paul Bulcke.[16] Roughly half of that home page contained Bulcke's picture and brief biography listing the many countries where he has worked, including the United States, Germany, Czech Republic, Slovak Republic, Portugal, Peru, Ecuador, Chile, Switzerland, Spain, and Belgium. The other half was a message from Bulcke to anyone interested enough in working for Nestlé to land on this careers page. His message reinforces the global nature of having a career at Nestlé and is designed to attract culturally agile talent (and, in so doing, to deter those with a more local lens). His short message includes the following:

> Nestlé is the world's foremost Nutrition, Health and Wellness Company, committed to serving consumers all over the world . . . We have operations in almost every country in the world, and strive to help our employees to achieve their full potential wherever they are. At Nestlé our commitment to your development can lead to an exciting career that takes you all over the world, as it did for me . . . If you're excited by the prospect of outstanding career opportunities in a global company with ambitious goals, in a truly international culture, Nestlé provides just that.

What message do your organization's careers Web site and other recruitment materials convey to those candidates with (and without) an international career orientation?

Is the message being clearly communicated to attract the culturally agile professionals you desire and need? Your careers home page is important because this is the first impression many will have as the result of actively seeking information about your organization. Step back from your organization's recruitment materials and media for a moment and put yourself in the place of a brand-new candidate. What would a newcomer who knew little about your organization's reputation glean in regard to what the organization values in its employees? Do "cross-cultural competence" and "international experience" spring to mind? If these values are not conveyed clearly, consider adapting the implicit and explicit messages in your recruitment materials.

Does your careers home page force a candidate to immediately "select a country" before being able to navigate further on the site? Dividing position searches by geography makes a certain amount of sense, given practical mobility issues and limits related to visas and immigration. In practical terms, not every job globally is open to every person at every point in his or her career. However, forcing job candidates to immediately select a country sends the message that the organization limits its associates to careers in their home country, which is not the message you want to be sending to those with an international career orientation. Make the "select a country" feature part of the application process or a second level of navigation. Be sure to keep the cross-cultural aspect of careers prominently featured on the careers home page.

Does your careers Web site contain testimonials of your associates? If it doesn't, it should. When candidates perceive that their future colleagues are similar to them on important dimensions related to their self-image, they become more attracted to working for that employer.[17] If your associates are perceived as worldly, cosmopolitan, globally aware, and valuing of diversity, then your organization will be more apt to attract culturally agile talent. If individual associates are profiled in your recruitment materials, is it clear that international experience is valued? Examine the global diversity of associates profiled on your careers home page, throughout your careers Web site, and in your other recruitment materials. Do most of these profiles reflect careers limited to the country of your organization's headquarters? Profiling only those from one country sends the wrong message about the value your organization places on the careers of associates from different countries. Choose the associates represented to reflect the global diversity in your organization. Likewise, focus on their successful global careers and multicultural projects.

The careers Web site is important, but it is not the only opportunity to focus your organization's image to attract and recruit culturally agile talent. Let's consider some other recommendations.

Recruiters Reflect on the first level of face-to-face recruitment in your organization. Are these recruiting professionals able to credibly discuss international career opportunities? Have they themselves worked on multicultural teams or internationally? Do they fully understand the cross-cultural opportunities available within the company? Make certain that your organization's recruiters and search firms can accurately present the variety of cross-cultural opportunities available within the firm. Ideally, they should be able to describe associates' careers specifically, even using their own careers as examples if they can be viewed as typical for the candidate's future career within the organization.

Social Media   What is the social media buzz about your organization's global image? Monitor your image within social media—what are individual employees saying about your organization as an employer?[18] Testimonials from employees are very persuasive, especially when they appear on open Web sites that rate employers, such as Glassdoor, or are more informally discovered on Facebook, Twitter, and the like.

Job Postings   Examine how your job postings are written. Do they convey excitement for the global challenges your associates are able to address? Here are two examples of job postings for a senior finance manager position. The first is from Apple and the second is from HP, two organizations appearing on lists of most attractive global employers.[19]

> *Apple: There's the typical job. Punch in, push paper, punch out, repeat. Then there's a career at Apple—where you're encouraged to defy routine, to explore the far reaches of the possible, to travel uncharted paths, and to be part of something bigger than yourself. Because around here, changing the world just comes with the job description.*

> *HP: From your very first day at HP, you'll notice it—we do things differently around here. You'll be challenged to lead from day one, and rewarded when you do. Because we're in over 170 countries around the world, your work will have a real impact in the lives of people everywhere. So bring your passion to HP; together there's no telling what we can achieve.*

These job postings help candidates visualize a broader career—one that will allow them to expand their mental and physical boundaries. Those who embrace the hope of a globally oriented career with worldwide challenges would find these job postings compelling.

Thus far in this chapter, we have discussed ways to find and attract culturally agile talent. But finding and attracting are only the beginning; you need to be certain that when you extend a job offer, it will be accepted. If desirable candidates turn down your offers, then your targeted recruitment practices become nothing more than an academic exercise. In the next section, I discuss ways to create a compelling value proposition to maximize the likelihood that your offers will be accepted.

CREATING THE EMPLOYEE VALUE PROPOSITION FOR CULTURALLY AGILE PROFESSIONALS

When I was on the academic job market in the early 1990s, I was considering two competing offers. The first university offered 20 percent higher pay, greater prestige, and a highly desirable location. The second university offered like-minded (and fun) colleagues and an opportunity to teach in Singapore each year. To the surprise of many, I accepted the latter university's offer.

The department chair and the search committee of the second university were savvy enough to surmise my career values from my dissertation research (on international careers) and from the fact that I was in India at the time when I was called for an interview. They correctly assumed that I would be most attracted to the international teaching opportunities available in their department. The other university might have had similar international opportunities (as was typical of many business schools starting in the 1990s); if it did, however, the recruiters didn't think to tell me about or "sell me" on them. The value proposition my chosen employer offered—great colleagues and international opportunities—aligned closely with my values and my international career orientation.

Creating an *employee value proposition* for employees means that your organization's jobs have attributes and benefits that, ideally, align with the attributes and benefits your top recruits most desire from their future jobs. In the case of culturally agile professionals, this employee value proposition would include the opportunity to work with people from different cultures, to travel internationally, to work on global projects, or to grow one's career on a global level.

Jyoti Yagnik, a culturally agile professional from India, worked in the banking, hospitality, and education fields after completing her MBA from the University of Pune in India. Although she enjoyed the professional roles she held in India, she wanted to change her career in two important ways: first, she wanted to work in human resources; second, she wanted to have a truly global career. To achieve these two goals, Jyoti decided to return to school and pursue a master's of human resource management (MHRM) degree at a university in the United States. She applied to the top five U.S. MHRM programs and was accepted into each. Ultimately, Jyoti chose Rutgers University in New Jersey, even turning down a scholarship at another top university. She selected Rutgers because of the program's leading record in strategic and international HR management and an opportunity to serve in internships with top global organizations. The Rutgers program satisfied her *student* value proposition, if you will.

Jyoti's decision proved an excellent one. As she neared graduation, she was extended job offers from several leading global organizations. Among the many top companies recruiting her, she was most attracted to IBM, as she had previously interned at the IBM corporate headquarters in Armonk, New York. Recalling her internship experience, Jyoti said how exciting it was "to interact with some of the world's most intelligent people from different cultures, with different languages, professions and perspectives, all working for one globally integrated enterprise called IBM." IBM's world-class talent, global business strategy, rapid foreign market growth, and international opportunities were all a magnetic pull, aligning with the core of her career values.

Upon graduation, she joined IBM's world-renowned and highly prestigious Human Resource Leadership Development Program. For Jyoti, this opportunity at IBM meant she would be able to build her international career, work in different roles in different countries, and work for a company that had strongly held values that had been defined by IBMers themselves. She was attracted to being a part of IBM for its core shared global values that shape the way all IBMers decide, act, and lead. Jyoti said she felt empowered when she joined IBM, a company "where employees are inspired to create innovative solutions to bring about world-changing progress, with dedication, trust, and personal responsibility. I wanted to be a part of it." Jyoti is currently on a rotational assignment, in a leadership role in IBM's HR Center of Excellence in Malaysia.

Jim Kupczyk, an American culturally agile professional, was also looking for an international dimension in his employee value proposition, but in his case it was to work with colleagues from different cultures rather than relocate to different countries. Jim is a senior international supply chain analyst for Rich Products, headquartered out of Buffalo, New York. Originally from Buffalo, Jim wanted a career in which relocation would not be necessary. Part of Jim's employee value proposition was to remain in Buffalo in order to stay close to his family; but, at the same time, his interest in culture made opportunities to work with colleagues from different cultures also highly desirable.

Jim chose Rich Products, a privately held $3 billion organization (specializing in nondairy food products) for its global reach and the opportunity to work with international suppliers and develop deep professional relationships with colleagues from around the world. Jim shares that "this role has reignited my passion for international affairs and how the world is interconnected. Something happening within any country's political system can affect sales . . . Volcanoes or earthquakes in another country affect my decisions on a daily basis—just as much as currency fluctuations or commodity prices. My world is much bigger and far more exciting in this role." For Jim, the international business challenges are an enjoyable aspect of his career.

At the same time, he also appreciates the many opportunities to form relationships with colleagues, customers, and supply chain partners when they visit Buffalo for conferences or meetings. True to Jim's ever-increasing cultural agility, he notes, "I enjoy finding the common ground I have with my colleagues from around the world. Equally, I am fascinated to learn about different cultures—their tastes, preferences, values, worldviews, priorities, family values, and just about any other topic they want to discuss." He credits Rich Products with giving him the opportunity to develop a deeper connection with his colleagues around the world and is happy that he "now has friends on almost every continent."

I share Jim's and Jyoti's stories, along with my own, because they illustrate different ways in which organizations can satisfy the employee value proposition from the perspective of cultural agility. Creating a winning employee value proposition is about aligning your organization's offerings with the values of those you are trying to recruit. In Jyoti's case, it was an opportunity to be on a global rotational program. In Jim's case, it was to work with international

Creating a winning employee value proposition is about aligning your organization's offerings with the values of those you are trying to recruit.

colleagues on international projects. In my case, it was about opportunities to teach internationally. In many organizations, the opportunities and benefits already exist; they just require some repackaging to showcase how they align with what your job candidates are looking for in an employer.

Following is a list of offerings that might already exist within your organization and would be attractive to culturally agile professionals. When targeting these candidates, consider highlighting the following company offerings during networking meetings, in recruitment materials, on social media, and on your organization's careers Web site.

- Your organization's global reach, scope, and orientation for growth in the future

- Career paths that generally include opportunities for international assignments

- International volunteerism opportunities, such as corporate service-learning programs and supported international volunteerism programs

- Language and cross-cultural training offered through the company

- Career paths that include working on teams with diverse colleagues from different subsidiaries around the world

- Global leadership development programs that include an international rotation

- Total rewards that take international careers into account (for example, retirement solutions for employees on international assignments)

This chapter described an important first step for building a pipeline of culturally agile professionals: you will need not only to find but also to attract and recruit those with an international career orientation. You want to implement the practices to acquire the talent among those who have (or have the capacity to gain) cross-cultural competencies, those who have had (or are interested in engaging in) developmental cross-cultural experiences, and those who speak (or are enthusiastic to learn to speak) another language.

TAKE ACTION

Based on the information presented in Chapter Four, the following is a list of specific actions you can take to begin implementing strategies to attract and recruit candidates with the attributes needed to build your pipeline of culturally agile professionals:

- (Re)train recruiters. The ideas in this chapter can be integrated into a training session for recruiters who will be critical in finding and recruiting culturally agile talent.

- Select recruiters for cultural agility. Identify recruiters who will be particularly effective in attracting culturally agile talent because they themselves are culturally agile.

- Revise your careers Web site and other recruitment materials. Select some of the most culturally agile employees in your organization and ask them how they would improve these materials to be more attractive to those who are internationally oriented. Use their feedback as a basis on which to brainstorm possible changes. Implement the best ideas.

- Create a winning employee value proposition. Start by brainstorming the features of your organization and key positions that would be particularly attractive to culturally agile professionals (for example, its global reach, rapid global growth, cross-cultural training offered, international volunteerism opportunities, international assignments, global projects, globally oriented career advancement opportunities). Now refer to the suggestions in this chapter and decide how best to embed these features into your recruitment messages.

- Evaluate recruitment methods. Try a few of the methods for sourcing culturally agile talent suggested in this chapter. Collect yield ratio data (in other words, data on how many applied, how many were selected, how many agreed to join) for each of the talent sourcing methods used. For those who join the organization, also collect performance data and cross-cultural competencies. Over time, you will be able to develop a "source of choice" for recruiting the highest-performing, most culturally agile talent.

CHAPTER

5

ASSESSING AND SELECTING FOR CULTURAL AGILITY

Sudhey Taveras recalls being culturally agile as a young child, long before she could have even uttered the phrase. Sudhey, an American, was born and raised in the Lower East Side of New York City. Her parents, who are from the Canete Tenares region in the Dominican Republic, encouraged Sudhey and her siblings to become bilingual, functionally bicultural, and comfortable in multicultural environments—a lifestyle that was reinforced the moment Sudhey stepped out of her Spanish-speaking home in New York. Describing her earliest indicators of cultural agility, Sudhey recalls that "everyone I knew was from somewhere—Puerto Rico, Italy, China, Bangladesh, and everywhere in between. Among my friends, it was not only OK to be bicultural, it was celebrated. I attended the local public school which celebrated everyone's heritage and culture. I grew up celebrating the Jewish, Chinese, and the calendar New Years. I celebrated Hanukkah, Christmas, and the Dominican Independence Day. As children, we learned to respect each other's differences, and my school made it easy to do just that, fostering an environment which was colorful and inclusive."

Like many of the friends from her childhood, Sudhey looked forward to spending summers with relatives in the Dominican Republic, reconnecting with family and nature. Experiencing cultures and travel became part of her life, and, as she matured, she started traveling farther afield. By the time Sudhey was in college, she had traveled all over the United States, the Caribbean, and throughout Western Europe. She would often travel alone, embracing the opportunity to meet people in different countries. Sudhey enjoys opportunities to leverage her cross-cultural competencies at work; she is comfortable in new environments, naturally finds commonalities and connects easily with others, enjoys diverse teams, and communicates well with people from different backgrounds. She is drawn to the excitement of going to new places and working with people from different cultures. I would describe Sudhey as having a high tolerance of ambiguity. She describes herself as being "sensibly fearless" of the unknown. (Well said.)

Now a successful global professional, Sudhey credits early life experiences with setting the strong foundation for her cultural agility, sharing that "from a young age I knew that I thrived in diverse and inclusive environments." After completing her master's degree, Sudhey was attracted to working for her employer because the organization offered her an opportunity to be on the global leadership development track, enabling her to live and work abroad. In various assignments, she has been able to travel, utilize her Spanish-language skills, and work in diverse environments.

Sudhey would describe her cultural agility as being in her blood, and credits her Dominican *cadena* heritage, which encourages both immigration and a communal desire to work for the betterment of the extended family, for ultimately making her the culturally agile professional she is today. Although it is true that Sudhey had significant international and multicultural experiences as a function of her heritage, her cultural agility is a combination of the many cross-cultural experiences she has had *and* who she is as a person. Sudhey's motivation to succeed, her international career orientation, her language skills, and her dispositional characteristics—such as her openness, extroversion, and emotional strength—are fundamental to the person she is. For those who are truly predisposed to be culturally agile, like Sudhey, their cross-cultural experiences accelerate development.

In Sudhey's case, the organization where she works benefited from her cultural agility from the moment she started. They selected her *for* her cultural agility. For organizations building a pipeline of global professionals, this is the more desirable option: to select culturally agile professionals who can be successful in cross-cultural contexts from the moment they start. The other option is to select individuals with the predisposition to develop from the cross-cultural experiences the organization offers. In other words, you have two options for developing a pipeline of culturally agile professionals: the classic "buy" or "make" approaches to acquiring human talent. A third (and rarely successful) option is to select talent without considering cultural agility and just "hope for the best" in developing the pipeline. This "hope for the best" approach is, thankfully, being employed less often as hiring managers become savvier at assessing individuals for the presence of cultural agility.

Most organizations have two talent needs when it comes to building their pipelines of culturally agile professionals. First, they need culturally agile individuals like Sudhey, who will be effective *immediately* in critical cross-cultural roles. These professionals have already demonstrated their cross-cultural competencies, language skills, and the like, and have shown that they are able to work comfortably and effectively with people from different cultures and in multicultural settings. They not only have experience living internationally or working cross-culturally but also have demonstrated a record of success and progressive development from their rich cultural experiences. These individuals are in high demand and, unfortunately, in short supply.

If your organization needs an immediate infusion of culturally agile professionals, I recommend redoubling your recruitment efforts as suggested in the previous chapter and raising the bar on the selection tools suggested in this chapter. The second talent need of organizations follows from the first. Your organization would be well served to select employees with the propensity to readily gain cultural agility through targeted developmental opportunities.

Select employees with the propensity to readily gain cultural agility through targeted developmental opportunities.

What if you are not sure which jobs in your organization will require cultural agility? It might be the case that certain positions require a high level of cultural agility, whereas others do not. The difference is important. To identify the jobs most needing cultural agility— and even the specific cross-cultural competencies needed—you can apply a *job analysis* method. Job analysis is a systematic way to identify the knowledge, skills, abilities, personality characteristics, education, experience, and competencies needed to perform a given job. See the box "How to Conduct a Cultural Agility Job Analysis" for more information on how job analysis can be used to tailor a selection system for cultural agility. Knowing the level of cultural agility needed for a given job, job family, functional area, or business unit will help you tailor your selection system with the assessment tools suggested in this chapter.

How to Conduct a Cultural Agility Job Analysis

You can use job analysis to systematically analyze the positions that will most need cultural agility. You are advised to apply this approach under the guidance of HR professionals or industrial and organizational psychologists who are trained in the technical aspects of conducting job analysis. The following are the general steps:

1. Identify subject matter experts from across your organization who are successful in their globally oriented roles.

2. Have the subject matter experts identify the *critical activities* (functions, duties, tasks) of their jobs.

3. Ask your subject matter experts to review the Cultural Agility Competency Framework. For each of the critical activities of their jobs, have them identify the level of cultural agility needed.

4. You can take this analysis one step further and ask your subject matter experts to identify, for each of the critical activities of their jobs, the necessary level of each of the cross-cultural competencies.

5. Assess whether a pattern emerges regarding the cross-cultural competencies.

6. Apply this same process to jobs, job families, functional areas, or business units where cultural agility is a critical requirement.

The remainder of this chapter describes the components of the *Cultural Agility Selection System*, including a multimethod approach for assessing the cross-cultural competencies in the Cultural Agility Competency Framework (presented in Chapters Two and Three). Given that each cross-cultural competency has its own configuration of knowledge, skills, abilities, motivations, and dispositional underpinnings, each will require a somewhat different approach to assessment. Figure 5.1 provides a matrix for the tools included in the Cultural Agility Selection System. It also summarizes the selection methods your organization should consider using to build its pipeline of culturally agile professionals.

RÉSUMÉ SCREENING

You should sensitize your recruiters, hiring managers, retained search firm partners, and even your applicant tracking systems to ways to screen résumés for evidence of the competencies related to cultural agility. Both humans and machines will likely need to work together to identify résumés of the culturally agile talent or those who have the propensity to gain cultural agility. If résumés will be "read" first by computer software, you will need to make sure that your system can detect those applicants who might have cultural agility. More than 60 percent of employers, both small and large, are using applicant tracking systems to scan résumés.[1] If your organization has one of these systems, your candidates' résumés will be read by a recruiter, hiring manager, or professional from your retained search firm only *after* they pass the system's filter. The filters are keyword scans designed to detect the technical experience (usually nouns, mostly technical jargon) on the résumés. If the goal is to find those who might also be culturally agile or have the propensity to gain cultural agility, you will need to broaden the keyword filters appropriate for the position you are trying to fill. Consider some of the following categories and some sample keywords:

Languages: French, Mandarin, Spanish, Hindi, and so on

Subjects: International Relations, International Affairs, International Business, International Law, and so on

Terms: Foreign, International, Global, Globally, Abroad, Overseas, Cross-Cultural

Following the computer scan, it will be time for human eyes. At first pass, most hiring managers will spend only between five and twenty seconds reading a résumé. Much like the applicant tracking system, they are scanning, looking for keywords, accomplishments, experiences, and skills. If you will be the one reading the résumés, look for patterns of engagement in progressively challenging cross-cultural activities. Spend more time on the résumés of candidates who have lived abroad for a significant period of time, even if the experience was not work related (for example, study abroad, volunteerism), and then sought out opportunities to work in international or multicultural situations. These activities will likely indicate, at minimum, a greater comfort

FIGURE 5.1. *The Cultural Agility Selection System*

	Résumé Screening	Foreign Language Assessment	Knowledge Assessment	Personality Assessment	Situational Interview	Self-Assessment
Competencies Affecting Behavioral Responses						
Cultural Minimization			X		X	X
Cultural Adaptation			X		X	X
Cultural Integration			X		X	X
Competencies Affecting Psychological Ease Cross-Culturally						
Tolerance of Ambiguity	X			X	X	X
Appropriate Self-Efficacy					X	X
Cultural Curiosity	X			X	X	X
Competencies Affecting Cross-Cultural Interactions						
Valuing Diversity				X	X	X
Ability to Form Relationships		X		X	X	X
Perspective-Taking		X		X	X	X
Competencies Affecting Decisions in a Cross-Cultural Context						
Knowledge and Integration of Cross-National/Cultural Issues	X		X		X	X
Receptivity to Adopting Diverse Ideas				X	X	X
Divergent Thinking and Creativity		X		X	X	X

cross-culturally (in other words, a greater tolerance of ambiguity and more cultural curiosity), given that humans rarely seek out perpetually uncomfortable situations.

Scan résumés for a self-reported indication that your candidates have fluency in foreign languages. Then look more closely for any opportunities the candidates may have had to actually *use* those foreign language skills. For example, a candidate who is not from Germany who lists on her résumé fluency in German and *also* lists that she lived in Germany as a student and works for a German company should be considered more closely than someone who merely lists fluency in German. A diversity of experiences where the candidates' language skills were used suggests that they would likely possess a greater level of, at the very least, some country-specific knowledge beyond their home countries.

FOREIGN LANGUAGE ASSESSMENT

Being able to converse with people in their own language improves one's chances of forming relationships and working effectively in a country where that language is spoken. (I realize that this sounds like it might best belong in the *Journal of Obvious Conclusions*, but it is often an overlooked issue when companies send professionals to different countries for work.) If the goal is to form relationships with peers, subordinates, partners, or clients whose first language is not English, having proficiency in their language does, in fact, help. It allows others to clearly convey their thoughts in their first language, even if they are reasonably proficient in English.

Beyond this somewhat obvious benefit of improved communication, there are additional benefits of selecting bilingual individuals into your organization. Fluently bilingual individuals have a variety of cognitive advantages over their monolingual counterparts. Numerous research studies have demonstrated the link between bilingualism and enhanced problem-solving skills, cognitive flexibility, learning strategies, abstract reasoning skills, and working memory.[2] The research on bilingual cognitive complexity is fascinating, especially if you are trying to improve your memory or become better at solving problems. However, most relevant for cultural agility is the research that has linked bilingual fluency to divergent thinking and perspective-taking.

Let's test this out. First, take a moment and stare at the images in Figure 5.2. What do you see? Hint: each image contains two objects. To see both objects, you will need

FIGURE 5.2. *Do You See Two Objects in Each of These Ambiguous Images?*

to shift focus and reassign a different meaning to the same feature of the image. For example, to see the face-vase image, you will need to visually allow the chins in the profiled faces to also be the base of a curvy white vase in the center of the image. (If you are stumped, please visit www.culturalagility.com for the answers to the other three.) Ellen Bialystok and Dana Shapero found that bilingual children were better able to reassign interpretations to figures in the ambiguous images.[3] In a professional context, those who can interpret the same scenario in multiple ways should have a higher capacity to suppress their original interpretations, allowing for a different interpretation to emerge (perspective-taking), and to see things in ways they had not previously considered (divergent thinking or creativity).

There are a variety of ways to assess foreign language proficiency (see box below). As an assessment of the ability to form relationships, foreign language tests should assess listening and speaking, ideally in the target language of the location where your colleagues will be working. The assessment of foreign language skills for the purpose of assessing divergent thinking and perspective-taking does not need a destination country. The desired candidate would be bilingual or multilingual, irrespective of the languages needed for professional communication. For this assessment, you should consider assessing both active language skills (reading and speaking) along with passive language skills (writing and listening).

Bio-data items can also be used to assess foreign language skills or the use of those language skills in various circumstances. Bio-data items are verifiable behaviors that indicate the presence of a certain attitude or trait. The premise of bio-data is that our past behavior is likely to be the best predictor of our future behavior. For example, those who

Assessments for Foreign Language Proficiency

- Language Testing International is a licensee of the American Council on the Teaching of Foreign Languages (ACTFL) and assesses language proficiency in over sixty languages. The ACTFL standards offer a structured rating based on the internationally recognized test of language proficiency. Visit www.LanguageTesting.com.

- The Center for Applied Linguistics also uses the ACTFL structured ratings in its Simulated Oral Proficiency Interviews to assess language skills. Visit www.cal.org.

- The United Nations (UN) has language proficiency examinations to test written and verbal skills in each of its six official languages: Arabic, Chinese, English, French, Russian, and Spanish. These are only available to organizations related to the UN and within the UN family. Visit http://www.un.org/exam/lpe.

- Transparent Language offers free written language proficiency tests online for thirteen different languages. These are self-scoring and assess standard grammar and vocabulary. Visit http://www.transparent.com/language-resources/tests.html.

Bio-Data Assessment for Foreign Language Usage

Using a scale, such as 1 = Never; 2 = Rarely (a few times in my career); 3 = Sometimes (on average, about once per year); 4 = Often (on average, monthly); 5 = Frequently (on average, weekly), you can ask candidates to rate the frequency with which they have used their foreign language skills, depending on their level or position. Items are

1. I speak in a language other than my native tongue (or first language) when I interact with colleagues at work.
2. I participate in meetings where my native tongue (or first language) is not spoken and I am expected to speak in the language used at the meeting.
3. I have given a presentation for work in a language other than my native tongue (or first language).
4. I write professional correspondence using a second language.
5. I read professional correspondence that has been written in a second language.

Those with a score close to 25 would be more actively using their foreign language skills.

---

have a history of trying different ethnic recipes, using unfamiliar ingredients in cooking, and so on will have bio-data evidence of a positive attitude toward ethnic cuisine. Asking these questions should be a more reliable indicator of an individual's attitude toward ethnic food than asking directly the question "Are you open to trying new foods?" See the box "Bio-Data Assessment for Foreign Language Usage" as an example.

KNOWLEDGE ASSESSMENT

Think about the past five countries you have visited, either for vacation or a professional activity. For each, are you able to name the country's capital, head of state, type of government, most salient cultural norms, and national bird? Unless you happen to be an ornithologist, the national bird might not be a critical piece of knowledge; knowing the basics about a country's dominant institutions and cultural norms is, however, helpful. In many, especially more senior positions, a deep knowledge base regarding countries and cultures is needed to make well-informed decisions and to respond effectively in cross-cultural contexts.

We all might agree that it would be unrealistic to expect culturally agile professionals to know every sociopolitical issue, religious or cultural norm, legal and regulatory statute that exists in this world. After all, there are nearly two hundred countries on the planet. At the same time, there are some jobs and professions where knowledge about countries and cultures is so critical for success in their jobs that testing candidates and employees on their level of knowledge on these topics is warranted. Diplomats, for example, should be highly knowledgeable in international affairs and how countries and cultures are interconnected. The selection system for U.S. diplomats, not surprisingly, includes a written exam, the Foreign Service Officer Test. This exam assesses, in part, knowledge of global current affairs, regional issues, world history, and geography. Not all global professionals need the same level of knowledge of countries and cultures as diplomats. For some jobs this knowledge might be "nice to have," but for others, it will be critical.

If you have some critical roles where country and cultural knowledge is essential for success, then knowledge tests can be used to assess candidates and employees. This would be especially important for professionals, like diplomats, whose knowledge would be applied from the first day on the job and cannot be gained over time. This time distinction is relevant for gaining knowledge, given that of all the competencies in the Cultural Agility Competency Framework, knowledge and integration of cross-national and cross-cultural issues will be the easiest for your organization to increase through training. Methods for increasing knowledge in this area will be discussed in Chapter Six.

PERSONALITY ASSESSMENT

If you have children, nieces and nephews, or younger siblings, you have probably directly observed the stability of natural personality traits. Perhaps you observed your child as a toddler having such an extreme natural curiosity and sense of fearlessness that you ended up installing industrial-strength baby gates. You might have observed your young nephew's ease around strangers, melting hearts with his toothless smile, or how content your little sister was to be left alone playing with her toys. Have you noticed how those traits have manifested themselves as your little ones have matured? These stable traits are not unique to the children in your family; all humans have a constellation of stable and relatively immutable personality traits, and they have been found across time, contexts, and cultures.[4] Psychologists have nicknamed the five most robust and stable personality characteristics the "Big Five":

1. Openness

2. Emotional stability

3. Extroversion

4. Agreeableness

5. Conscientiousness

The degree of expression of these five basic personality traits varies from person to person, but the extent to which an individual displays these traits will be relatively constant throughout his or her life.

Personality assessment is important for building a pipeline of cultural agile talent, for three reasons. First, these basic personality traits underlie many of the competencies

Your employees have certain personality traits when they are hired that are unlikely to change once they are in your organization.

in the Cultural Agility Competency Framework. Second, these traits have been found to be accelerators for the developmental opportunities your organization offers, such as international assignments. Third, the traits are relatively stable. This means that your employees have certain personality traits when they are hired that are unlikely to change once they are in your organization. In the case of personality traits, selection is critical because the traits directly affect your professionals' cross-cultural competencies and their abilities to gain them in the future.

Personality Traits Affecting Psychological Ease Cross-Culturally

Two personality characteristics, *openness* and *emotional stability*, will predispose your professionals to be more comfortable and well adjusted and to derive greater satisfaction from working in different cultures. Let's first consider the most intuitively important trait—openness. Individuals with greater openness engage in international experiences and multicultural opportunities because of their natural curiosity. Those higher in openness are receptive to experiencing new and different ways of doing things. When your global professionals are more open, they will generally feel more comfortable with the ambiguity of the cross-cultural context.

Do you recall the days before cars came with satellite navigation systems, when we used an old-fashioned device called a map? If you remember those days, you can probably remember missing an exit or two when driving to unfamiliar destinations. What was your reaction to the missed exit—were you calm and resigned, or nervous and frustrated? The response to this scenario is one sample indicator of your personality (in this case the characteristic of emotional stability). *Emotional stability* is a basic personality trait that enables individuals to cope with stressors and ambiguities. There is ambiguity associated with working in a cross-cultural context, especially in situations where professionals will be traveling or living internationally. My research, along with the research of my colleagues, has found that emotional stability is particularly important for global professionals' performance and their psychological comfort working internationally.[5]

Personality Traits Affecting Cross-Cultural Interactions

When building your pipeline of future global professionals, consider focusing on the personality characteristics that underlie the competencies associated with cross-cultural interactions. Two of the basic personality characteristics, *extroversion* and *agreeableness*, predispose people to form relationships, and are especially valuable for global professionals in their relationships with colleagues from different cultures. As we discussed in the previous chapter, relationships enhance professionals' ability to be more effective cross-culturally.

Let's first consider extroversion. Many people think of extroverts as the life-of-the-party types, when in fact it is more appropriate to think of extroverts as those who enjoy attending the parties and speaking to people while they are there. Extroversion is the tendency to prefer to be with others, as opposed to a tendency to prefer solitude.

Although there are many globally effective introverts, my research has found that professionals who have a higher level of extroversion are comfortable asserting themselves in social settings to form interpersonal relationships with colleagues from different cultures and, as a result, tend to be more likely to effectively learn the social culture when operating in a different cultural context.[6] Introverts need to push themselves beyond their natural comfort levels when working cross-culturally. Learning about cultures from peers and colleagues from different cultures is core to the development of cultural agility—making extroversion more important for global professionals.

The same is true when professionals are more affable and collaborative—or agreeable, as it is called in the Big Five list. Don't we all prefer to spend time with those who are nice, rather than with those who are surly and demanding? Of course we do. Being agreeable should not, however, be thought of as being a pushover. We don't want global doormats in the organization's talent pipeline; we want those who are strong professionals and, at the same time, reasonable people who others enjoy being around. My research found that international assignees who are higher in agreeableness report greater cross-cultural adjustment and better performance on the assignment in their host countries. Possessing the combination of extroversion and agreeableness will help your professionals form relationships—a competency that helps them succeed in diverse cultures.

Personality Traits Affecting Decisions in a Cross-Cultural Context

Making effective business decisions in a cross-cultural context requires more effort—they entail greater investigation of a broader range of options, more potential risks, and a higher number of unknowns that need to be understood fully. Cutting corners when working globally usually results in costly mistakes. Your global professionals should have a high level of *conscientiousness*, which includes perseverance, self-discipline, maturity, and resourcefulness. Wouldn't you prefer that the global professionals in your organization have the natural tendency to stay committed to their work long enough to explore their options and make the best possible decisions? Immature and less conscientious individuals tend to lack perceptual skills and the cultural sensitivity needed to consider their options. Those who are higher in conscientiousness also tend to be more resourceful. This feature is especially important when your professionals will be working in another country, because often the resources available are quite different from those at home. Not surprisingly, my research found that conscientious global professionals are more likely to be rated as higher performers.[7]

Testing for Personality Characteristics

Building a pipeline of culturally agile professionals should start with an assessment of the Big Five personality characteristics. These characteristics will accelerate professionals' development of cross-cultural competencies and help them be effective in a cross-cultural context. Personality assessment will help you assess what your organizations' professionals "will do" rather than what they "can do" (for example, technical skills and cognitive abilities).[8] The Big Five personality traits have also been found to be linked with leader effectiveness, making them important for selecting global professionals in your talent pipeline who will also assume leadership roles.[9] The box offers a list of some excellent commercially available personality tests that have shown validity evidence in predicting success among professionals.

Personality Tests

Caliper Profile: http://calipercorp.com/

Hogan Personality Inventory (HPI): http://www.hoganassessments.com

NEO Five Factor Inventory: www.parinc.com

Occupational Personality Questionnaire (OPQ): www.shl.com

Example of a Bio-Data Assessment of Openness

With my colleagues Rick Jacobs and Jim Farr, I developed the Attitudinal and Behavioral Openness Scale (ABOS), which assesses *openness to experience* and *openness to people*. The items in this scale assess actual activities and experiences in which individuals have engaged. In both cases, a higher score (40 is the maximum for *open to people*, and 16 is the maximum for *open to experience*) indicates a higher level of openness. Our research found that individuals' scores on these openness dimensions related to other cross-cultural competencies, namely tolerance of ambiguity and receptivity to diverse ideas (that is, novelty).

Bio-Data Assessment for *Openness to Experience*

Using the scale provided, rate the frequency with which you have done the following things.

1 = Never; 2 = Rarely; 3 = Sometimes; 4 = Often; 5 = Very Frequently

1. When I am in my home country, I eat at a variety of ethnic restaurants.
2. When I am in my home country, I attend foreign films.
3. When I am in my home country, I read magazines that address world events and other countries.
4. When I am in my home country, I watch world news programs on television.
5. When I am in my home country, I attend ethnic festivals.
6. When I am in my home country, I visit art galleries and museums.

7. When I am in my home country, I attend the theater, concerts, and other performing arts productions.

8. When I am in my home country, I travel within my home country—visiting different states, national parks, historic sites, and so on.

Bio-Data Assessment for *Openness to People*

Using the scale provided, rate the extent to which the following statements describe your friends.

> 1 = The same (100% identical on this dimension)
>
> 2 = Almost all the same (80–99% identical on this dimension)
>
> 3 = Somewhat diverse (50–79% identical on this dimension)
>
> 4 = Very diverse (less than 50% identical on this dimension)

1. My friends' first languages are . . .

2. In general, my friends' careers are . . .

3. My friends' ethnic backgrounds are . . .

4. My friends' religious affiliations are . . .

Source: Paula M. Caligiuri, Rick R. Jacobs, and James L. Farr, "The Attitudinal and Behavioral Openness Scale: Scale Development and Construct Validation," *International Journal of Intercultural Relations* 24, no. 1 (2000): 27–46.

Food Attitude Behavior Openness Scale (FABOS)

For fun, you might also like to try the bio-data and attitudinal assessment on the topic of openness to foods. Lakshman Rajagopal and Fayrene Hamouz developed this assessment and found that individuals' openness to food was related to individuals' tolerance of ambiguity. As bio-data items should be verifiable, think of all the interesting restaurants where you can host interview lunches to verify your candidates' tolerance of ambiguity.

Following are two of the four dimensions from the FABOS. A higher score indicates a higher level of food openness.

> 1 = Completely Disagree; 2 = Slightly Disagree; 3 = Neither
> Agree nor Disagree; 4 = Slightly Agree; 5 = Completely Agree

Seeking Novelty Items *(behavioral example)*:

1. I am constantly looking for new cuisines to try.

2. My family and I frequently try new cuisines.

(Continued)

3. I eat ethnic cuisines whenever possible.

4. It is very likely I would eat at a new ethnic restaurant when one opens in town.

5. I make an effort to attend ethnic festivals to eat the different foods they serve.

6. I frequently eat at ethnic restaurants.

Enjoying Novelty Items *(attitudinal example):*

1. I enjoy trying new cuisines and recipes.

2. I am always excited to eat new kinds of foods.

3. When presented with a new cuisine, I am very excited.

4. I think it is enjoyable to eat at restaurants serving different cuisines.

Source: Lakshman Rajagopal and Fayrene L. Hamouz, "Use of Food Attitudes and Behaviors in Determination of the Personality Characteristic of Openness: A Pilot Study," *International Journal of Intercultural Relations* 33, no. 3 (2009): 254–258.

INTERVIEW

A world-class executive who displays an enviable level of cultural agility is Andrea Jung, who served as CEO of Avon Products from 1999 to 2012, when she stepped down but remained with the company as chairman of the executive board. She is a first-generation Chinese American who grew up balancing Chinese and North American cultures. "My parents kept the best aspects of the Asian culture, and they Americanized the family," Andrea said in an interview for the online newspaper *GoldSea*. By the time she finished high school, Andrea had studied Mandarin, Cantonese, and French. She was accepted at Princeton and graduated magna cum laude with a degree in English literature, planning to become a lawyer. At this point, however, she ran into a cultural barrier of a different sort. Before applying to law school, she accepted a position with the Bloomingdale's department store chain, planning to spend two years gaining a thicker skin and firsthand knowledge of how business is done in the real world.

Her academically inclined parents (her father was an MIT architecture professor and her mother a concert pianist who had previously achieved recognition as a chemical engineer) were aghast. When Andrea decided to pursue a career in retail over the long term, according to a *GoldSea* article, they "complain[ed] bitterly that she was dumping all they had invested in their little girl into the waste heap and lowering herself into the same class as street hawkers and used car salesmen."[10] Working in retail sales was simply not acceptable as an appropriate career option in the culture in which Andrea had been raised. Her goal of becoming less thin-skinned had to be fulfilled in more ways than one: she learned not only to hold her own in the pushy world of retail but also to disagree with her parents without alienating them.

As she worked her way up the corporate ladder, she was challenged by another cultural divide. Although women do most of the shopping in high-end department stores, the executives in these corporations are predominantly male. Being a woman in top management meant working in a male-oriented corporate culture where the one who was louder, stronger, and faster was the winner. It took discernment to seek out successful, supportive female role models and to initiate campaigns to give female customers the products and the store ambience they truly wanted. Tuning in to women's desires became even more critical when Andrea joined Avon in 1993. The century-old cosmetics company badly needed a new, more up-to-date image. To reshape Avon in popular culture and attract younger women, Andrea launched the Just Another Avon Lady and Olympic Woman campaigns, which tied in to the 1996 Olympic Games and featured such athletes as Jackie Joyner-Kersee and Becky Dyroen-Lancer.

Avon's global reach gave Andrea the opportunity to come full circle with her childhood lessons in Mandarin. In her first year as CEO, she traveled to twenty countries, including China, where she addressed Avon employees in their own language. "I know that women today are far more alike than not," she told *Harper's Bazaar*. "Consider the business opportunities that we're giving women in China, and then they see a Chinese American at the top. It's not so much about me; it's more that these women see that it's possible."[11]

Andrea's experiences, both personal and professional, have shaped her cultural agility. Her biography includes many examples of times when she effectively overcame cultural differences, behaved in a countercultural way when the occasion called for it, used her language and cultural skills to adapt, integrated bicultural perspectives— the list continues impressively. If you were interviewing her for a position in your organization, you would quickly see the pattern of evidence of her cross-cultural competencies.

Not all candidates will have such an impressive repertoire of experiences from which to draw, but it is helpful to conduct interviews as part of the talent management approach for developing cultural agility in your organization's workforce. Interviewing candidates is the most comprehensive way to assess their cultural agility—but it is also the most time consuming. In an interview, you can go deeper than surface-level experiences to determine whether the candidate or employee is truly culturally agile. As we have discussed, it is possible for individuals to, for example, live in another country but not have any connection with the culture by staying mostly within their expatriate communities or by befriending compatriots. The interview gives you a chance to assess not just what they've done but also their reactions, preferences, motivations, and results.

I've provided a sample excerpt from my Cultural Agility Interview and scoring guide. (You can contact me at www.culturalagility.com for more information about the full Cultural Agility Interview and scoring guide.) The sample includes the behaviorally anchored rating scales (BARS) associated with one of the twelve cross-cultural competencies, cultural minimization. BARS will enable those who are conducting the interview to standardize their ratings and focus on the interviewee's behaviors rather than on the rater's impressions of the person. When reading through the BARS for this sample dimension, please keep in mind that the points on the BARS are *examples* of

Cultural Agility Interview and Scoring Guide: Sample from Tolerance of Ambiguity

Instructions: This interview protocol directly assesses the twelve competencies in the Cultural Agility Competency Framework. [The sample for one cross-cultural competency, *tolerance of ambiguity*, is provided.] Although there is some conceptual overlap among these competencies, every attempt was made to make each competency distinct. Each cross-cultural competency in the interview protocol has suggested questions. There are more questions than you will be likely to use in a typical interview. Select or draft questions most appropriate for the level and target position of your candidate or interviewee. It is most important to standardize the questions within a target group (for example, new hires, high-potential leaders) at various stages in your talent pipeline. This standardization of interview questions will enable you to compare your candidates "apples to apples," so to speak, and make the interview assessment more reliable. Each competency has a behaviorally anchored rating scale (BARS) listing behaviors as examples that would justify a high score (5), a low score (1), and so on. *The listed behaviors are only examples.* You may find that no one example perfectly fits the individual you are assessing. It is up to you to judge where the individual falls on the scale after listening to his or her responses too all questions for each competency. *The examples are only there to help you make that judgment.*

Tolerance of Ambiguity

Definition: Individuals who are tolerant of ambiguity are able to suppress anxiety in the face of perceived uncertainty (for example, when instructions are not well defined, the environment is complex, or the situation is novel). Those who are tolerant of ambiguity are comfortable in work settings in which full clarity is neither present nor possible. For them, ambiguous situations are not stress-producing and might even be their preferred work situations—the ones in which they thrive and are most successful.

Sample Interview Questions to Assess Tolerance of Ambiguity

1. Under what conditions do feel as though you are able to work at your best and are most successful? What about the opposite (that is, your least preferred work settings)?

2. There are situations when you might not have the necessary information or instructions to complete a project, task, or job. It might be because the situation is either novel for the organization or possibly that it is more complex than originally expected. Describe your experience in this type of situation. How did you handle it? What was the outcome?

3. Describe the most complex or ambiguous environment in which you've worked. What made the environment complex? How did you manage the ambiguity? What was the outcome?

4. Describe a time when you experienced social or interpersonal ambiguity—when you could not interpret the social cues of others (for example, when working in another culture or with people from another culture). What was the situation? How did you feel during that situation? What did you do?

Sample Behaviorally Anchored Rating Scale for the Tolerance of Ambiguity Dimension of the Cultural Agility Structured Interview

	1 Unacceptable	2 Poor	3 Fair	4 Good	5 Excellent
Behavioral Examples	Dislikes projects with novelty, ambiguity, or complexity. Describes experiencing anxiety when instructions are vague or incomplete. Clearly prefers a predictable, familiar, and structured work environment. Is visibly anxious when describing complex, changing, or ambiguous work situations. Is upset at the thought of work situations with ambiguity. Speaks about cultural differences in a derogatory way.	Generally prefers a predictable work environment over one with ambiguity. Seems to have a limited tolerance for novel or ambiguous work situations and admitted to being hesitant to work in them. Experiences frustration when instructions are vague or incomplete. Has never worked in a situation with any level of ambiguity or uncertainty. States that he or she dislikes change but reluctantly admits that some change is needed.	Generally seems to tolerate ambiguous situations without becoming too anxious but might not have been fully tested yet. Is reasonably comfortable in situations when instructions are vague or incomplete but does not describe a preference for these work situations. Is generally comfortable when instructions are vague or incomplete but clearly prefers (and expects) clarity. Describes some reasonably good strategies for handling uncertainty.	Voices a general preference for professional challenges that are novel, complex, or ambiguous. Is quite comfortable when describing situations involving vague or incomplete instructions. Has been tested in work situations that have a reasonable level of ambiguity. Has employed effective strategies for handling uncertainty and ambiguity. Enjoys working with colleagues who are different from him or her.	He or she doesn't just tolerate ambiguity; he or she thrives in it. Expresses an active desire or passion for work settings with greater complexity, novelty, or ambiguity. Has been tested and has been extremely successful in highly novel, complex, and ambiguous work situations. Remains calm and confident in situations that most people would find unnerving. Is visibly enthusiastic when recalling work situations involving ambiguity.

(Continued)

Sample Behaviorally Anchored Rating Scale for the Tolerance of Ambiguity Dimension of the Cultural Agility Structured Interview

	1 Unacceptable	2 Poor	3 Fair	4 Good	5 Excellent
Behavioral Examples	Has been unsuccessful in situations because of his or her inability to manage ambiguity.	Describes situations as "ambiguous" that really were not ambiguous.	Situations described as ambiguous did not seem contain too much ambiguity.	Has worked in situations with incomplete instructions and has been successful in them.	Describes highly successful strategies for handling very challenging, complex, and ambiguous situations.
	Blames others inappropriately for his or her inability to succeed in ambiguous or novel work situations.	Admits to being uncomfortable or nervous in uncertain, changing, or ambiguous work situations.	Seems open to work challenges which involve ambiguity but he or she does not have enough experience in these situations to fully justify that feeling.	Seems to be ready and willing to take on more complex roles—ones that will have higher levels of uncertainty.	Exudes an appropriate high level of confidence for his or her ability to work effectively in ambiguous situations.
	Describes novel experiences in a negative way.	Does not appreciate novel situations, describing the differences as generally uncomfortable.	States being interested in cultural or novel experiences but has not sought them out.	Has made past career decisions which suggest he or she has some tolerance of ambiguity, taking some risk when the outcome was not fully predictable.	Has been acknowledged for his or her masterful handling of an ambiguous, novel, or complicated project.
	Has actively avoided any type of change in his or her career.	Believes that most organizational changes are inferior to what was already in place.	Talks about novel situations in neutral ways—is neither enthusiastic nor opposed to them.	Has worked with people from different cultures and speaks positively about the experience.	Prefers working with colleagues who are different from him or her, seeking many opportunities to do so.
	Blames managers inappropriately for work situations that had ambiguity.	Is visibly frustrated when describing work situations with ambiguity or uncertainty.	Appreciates novel situations as an observer but does not believe he or she can learn much from them.	Articulates and supports the positive role change has in the organization.	Equates ambiguous situations with an opportunity to be creative.
	Dislikes being around colleagues who he or she is unable to understand fully.				

the responses you might hear in interviewees' responses. They are not a checklist for what you should hear or a comprehensive guide to what you will hear.

When training your hiring managers in the use of the Cultural Agility Interview, you should mention two rating errors assessors frequently make that are unique to cultural agility. One error is to assume that someone who appears to come from a multicultural background is, necessarily, culturally agile. The opposite assumption is likely to be equally erroneous: that someone from a majority group would necessarily be devoid of cultural agility. Do not prejudge or assume cross-cultural competence (or the lack of it) from overt appearances or accents. Assess it. Another error is to be self-referential when judging others' interview responses. Hiring managers must try not to hold up their own life experiences as the standard against which to judge others. There are many ways these cross-cultural competencies might manifest themselves. Managers need to allow the candidate to share her own story, and judge her level of cross-cultural competency on her response, not on the manager's impression of the candidate's experiences themselves. For example, some people who have traveled very little in their lives can exhibit tremendous cultural agility.

SELF-ASSESSMENT

We believe it was Socrates who gave us the sage advice approximately twenty-five hundred years ago to "know thyself." This is especially great advice for your organization's associates who think they might be interested in careers requiring cultural agility. Self-assessment is different from all the other assessments discussed in this chapter. Self-assessment is self-discovery, not evaluation. It gives candidates or employees an opportunity to consider their strengths and weaknesses relative to what it will take to live comfortably and work successfully in another country or with people from diverse cultures. As will be discussed more in Chapter Eight, self-assessment is often used by companies to help professionals make a decision regarding whether an international assignment is really right for them.

You don't need to be sending people on international assignments to use a self-assessment tool. Including self-assessment for cultural agility at the start of your selection system is a relatively low-risk, low-cost, and high-return tool. These assessments are private and confidential. The scores and interpretations found in the tool are for self-awareness and allow for a self-nomination to the next step of your selection system. In truth, these self-assessment tools weed out very few people (only about 2 percent), but they have some added benefits:

- They build self-awareness and appropriate self-efficacy when your candidates and employees discover that they have what it takes to potentially be successful as a global professional.

- They point out developmental opportunities without risk, given that they are private and confidential.

Self-assessment tools are not foolproof. If you've ever listened to karaoke, you have probably heard people who have an overly inflated perception of their strengths. It is human nature to overestimate one's strengths, and as a result, not everyone will internalize self-awareness data accurately. At the opposite extreme, however, some people underestimate their strengths, refusing to believe that they possess the raw talent that others see in them. Given that global success often requires a fair dose of humility, the underestimation end of this continuum concerns me less. Low self-efficacy for international work can often be enhanced appropriately when presenting clear evaluations of what it takes to be successful, a feature of most self-assessment tools. In any case, though, internalized accuracy in regard to personal strengths is needed.

Those who take self-assessments will often want to know how to improve their competencies. This piece is very important, as self-awareness should be followed by self-development for those who want to build a global career. As we will discuss in the next few chapters, some cross-cultural competencies are easier to change than others. (For example, gaining knowledge about another country's legal system is easier than building a tolerance for ambiguity.) Your self-assessment tools should consider the level of mutability of cross-cultural competencies when offering feedback on developmental opportunities. I encourage you to explore the Cultural Agility Self-Assessment (CASA) as one option for self-assessment. (Chapter Nine includes more information and provides access to a single-use trial of the CASA.)

There are clear indicators to help identify culturally agile professionals who will be, from day one, effective in cross-cultural or international settings. Although many more individuals might be able to gain cultural agility over time, your organization no doubt has some critical roles for which there will be no time to ramp up, no time to develop talent into culturally agile professionals. Consider using the Cultural Agility Selection System to identify those who possess cultural agility and those who will continue to develop their cultural agility.

It is important to remember that in assessing for cultural agility, you are identifying those professionals who will succeed in the cross-cultural job context. This means that you are predicting success in the *context* of the job, not the *content* of the job. However, I'm not suggesting that you ignore the content for the sake of the context; technical skills are also necessary for success. Sending a culturally agile professional to do a job that requires engineering skills will not result in success unless the professional does, in fact, possess the necessary engineering skills. It helps to think of the Cultural Agility Selection System as a piece in a sequential process; this selection system helps build a pipeline of professionals who can be effective in cross-cultural contexts. From that full pipeline, your organization should be able to effectively assign professionals to roles on the basis of their technical skills.

What's Next?

To this point in the book we have discussed ways to attract and select those with the greatest likelihood of having cultural agility or the ability to gain cultural agility once they are in your organization. The goal in building a pipeline of globally successful professionals now shifts from talent acquisition to talent development. In Part Four, I will outline the learning system that enables talent to continuously increase their cross-cultural competence and enhance their cultural agility.

TAKE ACTION

Based on the information presented in Chapter Five, the following is a list of specific actions you can take to begin implementing strategies to assess and select for cultural agility in your organization.

- Tailor your approach for résumé screening. Using the tips offered in this chapter, your applicant tracking system and recruiters can more effectively screen for candidates who will likely possess or be able to gain cultural agility.

- Test for foreign languages, knowledge, and personality traits. If you plan to use the tests recommended in this chapter, base your test selections on the cultural agility job analysis. You can conduct a validity study under the guidance of HR professionals or industrial and organizational psychologists who are specifically trained in the technical aspects of test validation. As with all employment testing, it is important to ensure that the tests you are using meet accepted standards of reliability and validity. Your selection system should be adapted for your organizational context and for key jobs, job families, functional areas, and business units.

- Use a structured interview. A sample of the Cultural Agility Interview protocol is offered in this chapter. For more information about the entire Cultural Agility Interview protocol, please visit www.culturalagility.com.

- Offer a self-assessment tool, such as the Cultural Agility Self-Assessment (CASA), to anyone who might enter your talent pipeline of global professionals. The CASA can also give job candidates a way to structure and think about their cross-cultural competencies and understand the importance of cultural agility in your organization.

PART

TRAIN AND DEVELOP CULTURALLY AGILE TALENT

I've emphasized throughout this book that developing cultural agility is a continuous process, not an achievement. Professionals gain cultural agility through an ongoing learning system, not a single event, such as a one-time training course or single experience abroad. As professionals move from being novices to culturally agile experts, they internalize the pieces of knowledge they gain, developing an unconscious, internal "grammar" of cultural differences. And the more they use this grammar in their professional interactions, the more "fluent," or culturally agile, they become.

This is where you come in. You will need to design your organization's learning system for developing cultural agility to expand along with professionals' increasing fluency. To help you achieve this, the next three chapters will provide the foundational components for your organization's learning system. The learning system includes two parts: *cross-cultural training* (Chapter Six) and *experiential developmental opportunities* (Chapters Seven and Eight).

CHAPTER

6

BUILDING THE FOUNDATION FOR CULTURAL AGILITY WITH CROSS-CULTURAL TRAINING

Asif Zulfiqar is a culturally agile professional from Pakistan who has lived and worked in the United States, Finland, and the United Kingdom. Asif understands the subtle power of country-specific differences, noting that "even basic behaviors, such as saying 'hello,' can be culturally bound and can be misinterpreted if not done correctly. For example, American colleagues don't shake hands every day—only after not seeing each other for a long time; a subtle nod or simple 'hello' would suffice." He adds that this same behavior would be rude in his home country of Pakistan, where "it is polite to acknowledge another person with a handshake and a verbal 'Assalam-o-alaikum' every time you see him throughout the day—even if it's the tenth time you've seen him." When his American colleagues pointed out the difference, it was easy for Asif to adapt his behavior. However, Asif added that "it took a few months before my mind allowed me to feel comfortable with the behavior. It was still signaling that I was being rude when I was acting appropriately."

In preparation for relocating from the United States to Finland to work for Nokia, Asif received a one-on-one orientation session with a cross-cultural trainer. In this training, Asif learned that Finns are highly egalitarian, honest, direct, reserved, and soft-spoken, and that they prefer not to engage in small talk, even in social settings. There is one exception: saunas, a staple of Finnish personal and, in some situations, professional life. The cross-cultural trainer had shared with Asif that he should expect different—more expressive—conversations in the sauna. Just as the Finnish social norm is to be physically naked in the sauna, conversations and emotions are also "naked" in that setting. As an expressive and talkative person, Asif thought this would be an easy adjustment to make.

A few weeks after starting to work in Finland, Asif recalls, "At the end of a long day of meetings, some colleagues—men, thankfully, for the sake of my modesty—decided to go to the gym downstairs and finish up our business conversation. While I had been a regular at the Nokia gym, I never used the sauna because I was a little shy about the 'dress code.'" The cross-cultural trainer was correct. Asif observed that his Finnish colleagues were more relaxed, humorous, and very talkative when in the sauna; he shared that "once I adjusted to the 'dress code'—which took a few minutes of self-consciousness—I came to appreciate this and all of our animated sauna conversations. We always had great conversations about work—and usually laughed a lot in the process." Asif deeply appreciates the Finnish culture, their reserved, honest, and direct communication style—and now appreciates the health benefits of going to the sauna from time to time.

Asif's cultural agility is evidenced by the fact that he can now easily overcome the feelings of psychological discomfort with culturally appropriate behaviors—whether greetings or the sauna dress code. He now makes psychological adjustments quickly and comfortably. His brain is trained, if you will, to ascribe multiple meanings to the same behaviors. Although cross-cultural training programs cannot retrain one's emotional responses, they can explain the process of cross-cultural adjustment. This type of cross-cultural training offers the "fair warning" that there will be some disconnect between physical behaviors and psychological responses for some period of time. Knowing is different from experiencing. Even so, it helps to know that the feelings are normal and that becoming culturally agile requires some mental conditioning.

As Asif's example illustrates, cross-cultural training can be a very valuable first step in developing cultural agility—provided that the training covers the right content, is delivered in the right way, and is offered at the best possible time. Even if one possesses the best set of predisposing personality traits, as Asif can attest, knowledge about how cultures differ is important. Cross-cultural training is any instructional method—such as instructor-led courses, one-on-one orientations, videos, cultural coaching, online tools, or older siblings with content knowledge—designed to impart knowledge about the ways in which cultures differ (generally) and the differences one might experience when working in a given country or culture (specifically). Cross-cultural training can help build a pipeline of successful global professionals by helping them learn to interpret behaviors and respond appropriately in a cross-cultural context. It can also help professionals form realistic expectations with respect to working in a different country or with people from different cultures.

Cross-cultural training is a very common practice, but one that is still largely available only to professionals who are living and working internationally. Brookfield's 2011 *Global Relocation Trends* reported that 74 percent of organizations offer cross-cultural training for their international assignees, with 25 percent of the companies making it mandatory.[1] At a minimum, your company should be offering cross-cultural training to international assignees who will be spending an extended period of time in another country. Duration, however, should not be the only factor determining who will receive training. Although often offered to international assignees, cross-cultural training is even more important for professionals who are taking important business trips or working on short-term projects with those from different countries. They need to arrive with the knowledge already in their toolbox; unlike international assignees, they will not have the luxury of taking time to learn through observation. I strongly recommend that you offer cross-cultural training to the widest possible swath of professionals engaged in cross-cultural interactions.

> *Although often offered to international assignees, cross-cultural training is even more important for professionals who are taking important business trips or working on short-term projects with those from different countries.*

WHAT TO INCLUDE IN A CROSS-CULTURAL TRAINING PROGRAM

When offering cross-cultural training, it is important that the training begin with the *general cultural differences*—a cultural framework. This cultural framework provides the professionals in your organization with a mental filing cabinet, if you will, a method to sort and store the future information they acquire about cultures. Another learning goal for cross-cultural training should focus on *culture-specific knowledge*: the behaviors, norms, attitudes, and values that can potentially influence professionals' success in a given context. The third learning goal is *methods for discovery*, or ways in which professionals can build their knowledge store by interacting with people from different cultures and in different cultural contexts. In a sense, the goal for this aspect of cross-cultural training is to help professionals "learn how to learn" from their experiences. The fourth common learning goal of cross-cultural training is an *understanding of the adjustment process* to help professionals prepare for what they might experience as they interact in an unfamiliar culture.

Learning Goal 1: Build a Framework for How Cultures Differ

Regardless of the delivery method and whether the provider is internal to your organization or an external vendor or consultant, the cross-cultural training offered should begin with a solid cross-cultural framework, a basis for understanding the ways in which cultures differ. Ask to see the provider's cultural framework and evaluate it: Is it comprehensive (but not too academic or theoretical)? Is it logical and useful?

An effective cultural framework will serve as the platform for discussing the cross-cultural differences affecting how global professionals gain credibility, communicate

FIGURE 6.1. *A Sample Cross-Cultural Framework*

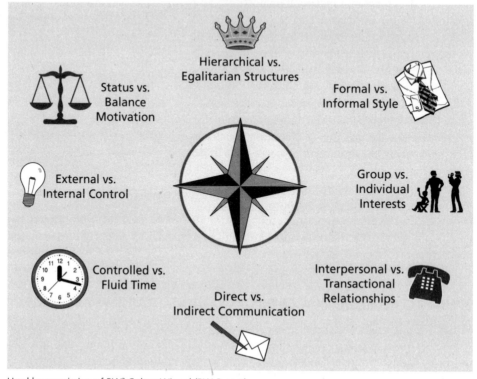

Used by permission of RW³ CultureWizard (RW-3.com)

effectively, and collaborate. Figure 6.1 offers a cultural framework from RW³ Culture-Wizard, one of the popular providers of cross-cultural training.

All cross-cultural frameworks have their roots in anthropology and sociology. Those written for professional audiences will emphasize the dimensions most relevant in professional and business contexts.

Learning Goal 2: Gain Culture-Specific Knowledge

An effective cross-cultural training program will equip the professionals in your organization to understand specifically how cultural dimensions in a given context could affect the outcome of their work. Training on culture-specific knowledge before international business trips, negotiations, global team meetings, and other cross-cultural endeavors will lay a foundation for your colleagues to be more successful in a specific cultural context. Over time, when this training is successfully put to use, a repertoire of behavioral responses are built that can, in turn, be leveraged in subsequent professional cross-cultural situations.

Read More about Culture: Suggested Books for Understanding Cultural Differences

Geert Hofstede, *Culture's Consequences: International Differences in Work-Related Values*, 2nd ed. (Thousand Oaks, CA: Sage, 2001).

Geert Hofstede, Gert Jan Hofstede, and Michael Minkov, *Cultures and Organizations: Software of the Mind*, 3rd ed. (New York: McGraw-Hill, 2010).

Charlene M. Solomon and Michael S. Schell, *Managing Across Cultures: The Seven Keys to Doing Business with a Global Mindset* (New York: McGraw-Hill, 2009).

Fons Trompenaars and Charles Hampden-Turner, *Riding the Waves of Culture: Understanding Diversity in Global Business*, 3rd ed. (New York: McGraw-Hill, 2012).

To illustrate culture-specific knowledge, let's take the example of "establishing credibility" as a critical starting point for many intercultural interactions (and one that is laden with potential cultural nuances). I often joke to my students that I lose credibility in some parts of the world by merely "showing up" as a woman and appearing younger than expected (although the latter problem has resolved itself over the years). I also lose credibility in certain countries by sharing that I was born into a blue-collar family in which my parents worked hard to send their five kids to school, each of us achieving advanced degrees and professional occupations. Although that personal fact is admired by some, a portion of the world would downgrade my credibility for my not being "born well"; in their eyes I am a person who inappropriately tried to overcome her lower-class destiny.

I've worked all over the world—even in some countries where I have had to overcome a sex-age-birthright "triple whammy." How have I managed to work effectively? Not by changing the "skin suit" I wear in different countries. Rather, through training, coaching, and experience, I have learned the culture-specific ways to negotiate around these cultural differences in expectations of how experts should look, to mitigate the effect of first impressions associated with age and sex, and to highlight different aspects of my biography as the cultural context demands. These are tangible skills that can be learned the hard way through reflection on one's mistakes. But, having tried this, I would not recommend it as a human talent development strategy. Instead, it is much more effective and efficient for these skills to be taught via culture-specific cross-cultural training. To work with this example for your own personal case, review the questions in the box "Cultural Factors in Building Credibility" to determine the factors that might affect how your professional credibility is established in a given culture.

Establishing credibility is merely one example of a situation where country-specific knowledge is relatively easy to impart via cross-cultural training, and where a lack of knowledge can be professionally devastating. Another example is the difference in

Cultural Factors in Building Credibility

1. How important is my educational attainment and the name of the university from which I graduated? How will my educational background be perceived?

2. How important is my family background or birthright? How will my life story be perceived? Do I know what pieces of it I should disclose openly?

3. Do leaders in this country tend to be older, male, or both? How will I be perceived given my age and gender?

4. How important are personal contacts and formal introductions in this culture? How will I be introduced—and by whom?

5. How important is it to build relationships before business is transacted? What will I do to build these relationships?

6. How important is organizational rank? How will my own rank be perceived?

7. How important are visible signs of status, such as dress and appearance? How will my appearance be perceived?

communication styles across cultures. Cultures vary on what their words connote (as opposed to what is literally said) and how speech is interpreted. In cultures with more indirect or high-context communication, many things are left unsaid, as people expect the context to fill in the true meaning of what was intended. Communication in high-context cultures is subtle and nuanced; an outsider who doesn't know how to read the cues can find it difficult to interpret.

This challenge works in the other direction, too: people from high-context cultures may find the communication of those from low-context cultures inappropriately direct and abrupt. In a training class for English-speaking computer help desk employees in India, the global IT services company Wipro Technologies observed that "as a high-context culture where what is communicated is more internalized (say, in a family), Indians can seem to be beating around the bush to Americans, who are part of a low-context culture in which communications need to be more explicit. 'If you like to talk and you're dealing with a low-context person,' explains the instructor, Roger George, 'you might want to keep it simple and get to the point.'"[2]

Languages, like cultures, vary in their formality. Even when professionals are speaking a lingua franca, such as English, the language is used and interpreted in different ways. In cultures that are more formal, people are often called by their title. In these cultures, there is little discussion of personal issues at work, a greater use of formal greetings, and stricter observance of the rules of etiquette. Cultures also vary in the extent to which communication is expressive and emotional or unemotional. Passionate speech denotes enthusiasm in more expressive cultures, but it may be considered bombastic in less expressive ones. Speakers in more emotional cultures will use higher volume, more gestures, and greater vocal modulation compared to those in less expressive cultures.

The list of culture-specific "good to know" factors could continue at some length. It would include how individuals integrate and balance their work with their personal lives—do they "live to work," or do they "work to live"? This dimension will manifest in the amount of effort expended for work-related activities at the expense of a personal life and vacation time, whether work will be brought home or done over the weekend, and the like. The list would also include the extent to which time within a given culture is controlled and treated as a commodity ("time is money") or with a more fluid approach. This will manifest in adherence to deadlines, punctuality, and the extent to which long-range planning is conducted. Your professionals should also know whether their colleagues from a given culture value the group's needs over one's individual needs or vice versa. This difference will manifest in the ways teams work together and are rewarded, the way promotions are awarded, and the way work is prioritized.

Your organization's cross-cultural training programs should enable professionals to learn about culture differences for the contexts in which they will be expected to work. The broader learning goal for culture-specific training is that your professionals are able to correctly read a situation and accurately assess the meaning of another person's behaviors. An accurate understanding of the situation enables professionals to make better and more strategic decisions regarding the most appropriate behavioral response. As discussed in Chapter Two, engaging in the most appropriate cultural response—adaptation, minimization, or integration—will require professionals to first understand the potential cultural influences of a situation and then determine the extent to which culture will affect the best way to respond.

Learning Goal 3: Learn Methods for Cross-Cultural Discovery

Imagine that you are single and on the dating scene. You walk into a bar, and a good-looking person makes eye contact and then looks away. The interpretation of the brief gaze will depend on a myriad of contextual features: Is he or she with a date, alone, or with friends? Did a smile accompany the eye contact? Is the place crowded, or are you the only two in the bar? Did you trip over a chair, creating an attention-grabbing crash? In evaluating this scene, you are reading the contextual cues through your personal lens. The ability to accurately read contextual cues is exactly what culturally agile professionals are able to do. The difference is that they are able to change lenses and continually reframe and reinterpret social cues, depending on the cultural context. Accuracy in any given cultural context should improve over time as the professionals in your organization discover and internalize the new meanings for behaviors across contexts.

Although personality and culture-specific knowledge will accelerate the process, discovering the nuances of an unfamiliar culture comes down to one thing: repeated interaction with (and observation of) people from that culture. Riall Nolan, a cultural anthropologist from Purdue University who has spent much time living and working in Senegal, described to me how this discovery process works:

> *The way in which one uncovers a new culture is similar to the way one would learn about a new neighborhood. You meet people and start asking questions. You put the pieces together. Eventually, you start to see some patterns about what is important in the community, preferences, and values. At that point, you become more discriminating in your observations, and your questions become more precise. The answers are more helpful to you. Many people have engaged in this process of discovery previously in their lives, if they have ever moved, gone away to school, or started a new job. With every new move, you need to discover and learn how to read the unfamiliar culture.*

Truly cultural agile professionals know and use these discovery methods effectively. They are keen observers who can quickly "read" any new cultural context. Cross-cultural training can provide a structured way for the professionals in your organization to use these discovery methods to focus observations, interpret cues, ask the right questions, and, when ready, see the patterns inherent in the culture (without jumping to hasty inaccurate conclusions). This type of cross-cultural training offers the professionals in your organization the methods for *how* to observe to accurately read the situation. The goal of this type of cross-cultural training is twofold: both to structure observations and to give professionals a way to categorize the observations so that they can use them effectively and in a logical manner.

The use of these discovery methods is a skill. As is true of all skills, it requires practice. You will need to give the professionals in your organization an opportunity to learn these discovery techniques and then build their skills by applying them. The learning goal is to enable professionals to continuously build their understanding of cultures and effectively read them more quickly and more accurately with each successive experience. As an example, the box "Do You See What I See?" offers a list of five possible observations (of hundreds) that professionals can make when entering an unfamiliar country or culture for the first time, to help them read a culture more accurately.

Give the professionals in your organization an opportunity to learn these discovery techniques and then build their skills by applying them.

Learning Goal 4: Understand the Cross-Cultural Adjustment Process

At the beginning of this chapter, I described how Asif Zulfiqar adjusted to the casual style of greeting that was the norm among his U.S. coworkers. As you recall, he was able to readily adapt his behavior and abandon the handshake and formal greeting he had been brought up to use in his native Pakistan. Behaviorally, the change was easy,

Do You See What I See? Five Sample Observations to Make When Entering an Unfamiliar Culture

1. Watch local television (even if you cannot understand what is being said) and observe prototypical leaders and experts, such as the local TV news reporters, political leaders, and business leaders. How do they look and act? Are they effusive or stoic? Are they formally attired or casually dressed? Are they more polished in their appearance or more natural? These observations can often provide a good indication of the extent to which expressiveness, elegance, or formality is the cultural norm among professionals.

2. Walk into public establishments and observe the way associates in retail stores or restaurants greet customers. Is everyone greeted in a warm and friendly way, or are those warm greetings reserved for friends who happen to walk in? Is the greeting to clients formal and professional or more informal? If you are staying at a local hotel (as opposed to a large chain catering to business travelers), ask for recommendations of restaurants, shops, and so on. Listen to what is justifying the recommendation (is it the five-star rating or the fact that a cousin owns the restaurant and the recommender knows you will be treated well)? These observations can often provide a good indication of the extent to which a culture is more relationship oriented or task oriented.

3. Observe the amount of personal space people maintain with each other when speaking in casual conversations. Do people stand close together or comparatively far from each other? These observations can often provide a good indication of the distance you should use when speaking with members of the host culture.

4. Observe the name plates on office doors and the extent to which colleagues refer to each other by their titles. Are first names used? Is there a difference in how names are used depending on the level in the organization? Do the placards on office doors reflect both an honorific and a title, or just the person's name? These observations can often provide a good indication of the extent to which hierarchy or egalitarianism is the cultural norm among professionals.

5. Observe the extent to which public transportation is on time. Also observe the accuracy of (and presence of) clocks in public spaces. These observations can often provide a good indication of the extent to which time is either fluid or controlled within the culture.

but at the emotional level he felt uncomfortable with the U.S.-style informality, and his discomfort persisted for months.

What Asif experienced in the subtleties of greetings is an issue whenever your professionals move from learning about behaviors to actually living them. Cognitive understanding—knowing that a handshake is considered overly formal—is only the

Developing Cultural Intelligence

David Thomas and Kerr Inkson have written extensively on how to build one's cultural intelligence. In their book *Cultural Intelligence: People Skills for Global Business* (San Francisco: Berrett-Koehler, 2004), Thomas and Inkson offer a three-stage process for the self-development of cultural intelligence. The first step is to gain the knowledge to understand the principles of cross-cultural interactions, including the ways cultures might differ and how those differences could affect behavior. The second step is to practice mindfulness, really focusing your attention to attend to cues and reflect on what is being observed. The third step is to build a repertoire of behavioral skills and possible ways to adapt in different cultural contexts. For more information about cultural intelligence, I recommend Thomas and Inkson's *Cultural Intelligence: Living and Working Globally*, 2nd ed. (San Francisco: Berrett-Koehler, 2009).

first step. Changing one's behavior to fit the host culture is different from emotional adjustment and feelings of psychological comfort with the new behavior. Christopher Earley and his colleagues would describe Asif's experience as a demonstration of his cultural intelligence (CQ) and note that Asif engaged his mind, body, and heart in the process.[3] Asif's experience illustrates how CQ is a combination of cognitive understanding of the differences (his mind observed the differences between the Pakistani and American greeting styles), the ability to change behaviors (his body used the U.S. greeting style), and feeling comfortable with the differences over time (his heart accepting the U.S. greeting style as an appropriate method for greeting in that context). The box "Developing Cultural Intelligence" offers information about further reading in becoming more culturally intelligent.

If your organization's cross-cultural training program includes building understanding of this aspect of the adjustment process, professionals will realize that a certain amount of psychological discomfort is normal. This realization is an aid to emotional regulation. Instead of being frustrated or perplexed, professionals who understand the process will be more likely to give themselves time to settle into the new behavior and allow their emotional responses to catch up.

DELIVERY METHODS FOR CROSS-CULTURAL TRAINING

As we saw in the preceding section, developing cultural agility in the workforce requires employees to have four kinds of tools in their cross-cultural toolbox:

1. A solid foundation for understanding how cultures can potentially differ

2. Culture-specific knowledge targeted for jobs and roles

3. Methods for cross-cultural discovery (the skill needed to learn how to be effective in a given country)

4. An understanding of the cross-cultural adjustment process to better regulate their emotional responses while working cross-culturally

Some methods for delivering this cross-cultural training are *Web based*; others are *person led*. Many organizations use a *blended* approach, combining the convenience of the Web-based tools with the tailored approach of person-led instruction and coaching.

Web-Based Delivery Methods

With the inception of e-learning in many organizations, cross-cultural training programs are beginning to be delivered via the Internet, mobile device applications, and organizations' intranet systems. According to the Brookfield study, roughly 32 percent of organizations are now offering cross-cultural training for their international assignees through a Web-based program, a number that is steadily increasing each year.[4] The use of Web-based cross-cultural training is scalable, making the training affordable for business travelers and members of global teams, rather than being limited to international assignees, as the more expensive face-to-face training often is.

These Web-based training tools can be a cost-effective way to build cross-cultural training into your organization's learning system. They are rarely homegrown. Rather, organizations offering Web-based training tools generally purchase access to existing tools from providers specializing in cross-cultural training. When evaluating the best possible Web-based cross-cultural training tool for your organization's professionals, remember that not all tools provide the same level of utility. (See the box "Web-Based Cross-Cultural Training Tools" for a list of some popular providers.) Consider the strategic needs of your organization with respect to countries covered and the focus of the employees to be trained (for example, business travelers, members of global teams, international assignees). Web-based cross-cultural training tools should be assessed and compared on the following ten features:

1. Does the tool offer an explanation of what culture is and how cultures form within societies or groups? Assess whether the explanation is clear.

2. Does the tool provide a framework for understanding cultural differences, including clear explanations of the dimensions of culture? Assess whether the framework is comprehensive and the dimensions can be clearly understood.

3. Does the tool cover all the countries of strategic interest to your organization?

4. Does the tool offer a self-assessment of every participant's own cultural values so that culture can be explained from a personal frame of reference? Assess whether the assessment tool and report offer useful and practical feedback to individuals about their cultural values.

5. Does the tool provide a comparison approach to better understand one's personal values compared to a given country's cultural values? Assess whether the information is accurate and current. Keep in mind that there are almost two hundred countries in the world, and some organizations operate in all of them.

6. Does the tool offer a practical focus for a professional audience? Assess how applicable the content is for your organization's business. Be certain the content is practical and not too theoretical.

7. Does the tool offer a comparison of multiple cultures concurrently? More sophisticated Web-based training programs can handle multiple cultures concurrently and offer advice on how to work within a multicultural team whose members represent many cultures.

8. Does the tool accommodate a variety of learning styles? The content of the cross-cultural training should be offered in different ways. Look for interactive modules, visual components (such as videos), and interactive tests for understanding.

9. Is the tool easy to use? Assess whether the tool is self-directed, available 24/7 in real time, available across multiple platforms (for example, intranet, Internet, device applications), easy to navigate, and generally enjoyable to use.

10. Is the tool accessible? Assess whether the tool is available for associates with disabilities who use assistive technologies and those who are using older computer platforms or mobile devices.

Person-Led Delivery Methods

Otis Shepard is an American culturally agile professional who has been on both sides of person-led cross-cultural training when working in Europe and Asia. Before his international assignment in Poland for PepsiCo as division training manager for Eastern Europe, Otis received person-led cross-cultural training. Since he had not yet worked in Poland, he appreciated the culture-specific knowledge he received from

Web-Based Cross-Cultural Training Tools: Some Popular Providers

RW³ LLC's CultureWizard: www.rw-3.com

Living Abroad's Culture Compass: www.livingabroad.com

TMC's Cultural Navigator: www.tmcorp.com

TMA World's Country Navigator: www.tmaworld.com

World Trade Press's Global Road Warriors: www.worldtradepress.com

international colleagues currently on assignment in Poland, and some strategies for communicating effectively with Polish colleagues from his assigned coach, who was based at the Polish head office. The coach advised Otis on business protocol and important country customs, such as the focus on relationships and more formality, especially at first.

This was good advice. Within days of arriving in Poland, Otis recalls that "the advice of the cultural coach took shape when I started working. Exactly as he advised, I adapted to a more formal and more relationship-oriented style—and even tried to use the words of Polish I was learning." Following the norms of the Polish culture to develop collegial relationships helped Otis readily become effective. He credits his Polish colleagues, saying that "since I took the time to build the relationships, my Polish colleagues supported me, enabling me to adjust to business and personal life in Poland."

Otis, in turn, became the in-house cultural trainer for non-Polish colleagues arriving in Poland, whether for international assignments or business trips. He recalls providing colleagues with instrumental support (for example, helping them learn how to get around the city, rent an apartment, find a medical doctor, shop for food and clothing) as well as emotional support (helping them deal with their frustrations with delays and bureaucracy, vestiges of Poland's former Communist years). Otis coached them on how to build relationships, negotiate, communicate, and lead in the Polish context. This in-house coaching paid dividends for PepsiCo; Otis was able to help colleagues quickly and effectively negotiate the Polish business landscape, operate with less stress in the Polish culture, and achieve their business goals.

Although Web-based tools' being real-time and 24/7 makes them particularly convenient for busy professionals, Otis's example illustrates that there are times when a "live person" is the most effective way to help the professionals in your organization navigate through a specific context. Cross-cultural coaches work with professionals directly to build country-specific knowledge, usually in preparation for a specific work-related activity. They guide professionals on how to modify their behaviors to be effective in a specific task, such as delivering an important speech in another country or negotiating an international joint venture.

In addition to role-specific cross-cultural training designed to help employees accomplish a specific task, organizations also offer cross-cultural training to their international assignees to help assignees and their family members live and work in a host country. Over 70 percent of organizations offer person-led cross-cultural training to international assignees and their families prior to their relocation to another country (predeparture cross-cultural training) or upon arrival. This tailored and often family-oriented cross-cultural training is designed to facilitate assignees' success and the entire family's adjustment to life in the host country. However, as anyone who has relocated to another country or around the block can attest, the weeks immediately before, during, and immediately after the relocation are stressful and busy (to say the least). Not surprising, the cross-cultural training offered for international assignees and their families often remains unused, given the many other conflicting demands on the international assignees' and their families' time. For the person-led cross-cultural training to be useful, the international assignees would need to view the training as a tool essential to their effectiveness on the international assignments.

Blended Learning

Both Web-based and person-based cross-cultural training programs have their pros and cons. Web-based programs might not be able to address the specific nuances of a given colleague's situation, and person-led training might not be cost-effective or logistically practical. The best of both worlds is sometimes a blended learning approach that mixes online e-learning tools, simulations, exercises, and modules with personal coaching, instructor-led training, seminars, and action learning projects. This blended approach is gaining favor as the "best practice" across organizations. Brookfield's 2011 *Global Relocation Trends* reported that roughly one-third of companies used a Web-based cross-cultural training platform; among them, nearly 30 percent used the Web-based training in conjunction with person-led training.[5]

Blended learning is typically structured according to the following protocol: the basics of cross-cultural differences are taught online as prework before the more expensive and time-intensive person-led training begins; the face-to-face portion of the instruction is then targeted to the specific situation of the global business professional's need, such as an international assignment in Singapore, a business negotiation in France, or a global team distributed across five countries.

Many organizations use blended approaches to reinforce cross-cultural learning and ensure that employees have the cultural knowledge necessary to achieve their performance goals. For example, a global financial information company, opening offices in Asia, Europe, and Latin America to support a major new global product initiative, engaged in blended cross-cultural training. In this company's case, cross-cultural understanding was of strategic importance because team members from these three regions needed to be able to communicate effectively regarding complex technology issues. The communications were mostly generated through teleconferencing and emails, with the team leaders also having face-to-face meetings. At the onset, these multicultural groups, which were operating virtually, experienced many communication problems leading to frustration, resentment, and some failures. Their solution was to combine the RW[3] CultureWizard Web-based cross-cultural training tools with in-person team training. The participants were able to identify their own cultural values, their colleagues' cultural values, and how these differences affected collaboration. Ultimately, as a great example of cultural integration, the teams developed their own standards for team communication and interactions.[6]

LANGUAGE TRAINING

Whenever professionals will be working in a country where another language is used, language training is an essential complement to cross-cultural training. Professionals can hardly be expected to succeed without the language skills they will need to communicate with colleagues who speak the target language. However, much like cross-cultural training in organizations, language training is usually reserved for professionals on international assignments. Whether Web or classroom based or with a private instructor, instruction in the host-country language is typically provided both before and during the international assignment. Language instruction is also generally extended to the family members of international assignees to help smooth the transition to the host country.

The other pockets of language training activity are the courses offered company-wide to train employees globally in a lingua franca, the common company language. The lingua franca in some cases is not the language of the headquarters country, but rather the language most useful for the business from a strategic perspective. The Japanese retailer Rakuten, for example, decided to adopt an English-only lingua franca policy throughout its organization; signs, meetings, communications, documentation, and even its cafeteria menus in Japan are written in English.[7] Rakuten has over seven thousand (mostly Japanese) employees who are actively learning or improving their English skills, some of whom are enrolled in English language classes. Managers are expected to pass an English proficiency test to be promoted. As a part of the company's globally oriented business strategy, language skills training helps Rakuten improve its cultural agility at the organizational level, facilitating communications among associates and clients outside Japan.

TIMING AND SEQUENCING OF CROSS-CULTURAL TRAINING

Have you ever attended a training session and felt as though you were experiencing "information overload"? This might manifest as the inability to absorb more information, loss of concentration on what is being taught, or lack of connection between the material covered and its practical application to the work setting. Ibraiz Tarique and I conducted research on the issue of overload in the context of cross-cultural training, specifically on the timing and sequencing of training delivery.[8] We found that when cross-cultural training is offered without context, trainees can fail to absorb the training content because it does not build on prior knowledge. Without any prior experience of cultural difference, individuals find the cross-cultural training to be too far removed from their reality. Once employees have had some cross-cultural experience, the content of cross-cultural training has heightened relevance as the individual can "feel" and internalize the differences, rather than merely learn about them intellectually. Learning in this context is more memorable because it is offered in real time. The knowledge gained in cross-cultural training will be "stickier."

Our research found that effective cross-cultural learning systems optimize both elements:

- *Sequencing* cross-cultural training content to ensure that new knowledge builds on existing knowledge

- *Timing* cross-cultural training to ensure that content is matched to the needs and the readiness of the trainees

Brookfield's 2011 *Global Relocation Trends* survey found that almost half of the responding organizations offered cross-cultural training to their international assignees once they were in the host country.[9] For reasons of both timing and sequencing, this type of cross-cultural training is likely to be more efficacious in building assignees' knowledge. Once the assignees begin to experience cultural differences in their host country, the cross-cultural training will be more relevant and useful.

However, I want to emphasize that it is *not* advisable to postpone all cross-cultural training until professionals are in the host country or working with colleagues from a different culture. Throwing your professionals into a new culture without advance preparation could result in some cultural missteps early on that might damage professional relationships, stunt the adjustment process, or, at minimum, bruise an ego or two. When professionals in your organization have make-or-break negotiations or business-critical presentations in a country where they have never previously worked, it is critical to provide cross-cultural training *before* they begin any cultural interaction. This intervention type of cross-cultural training can be timed to occur at the onset of the formation of a global team, giving the team some heightened awareness of their cultural differences and a structured way to create their team's norms. The goal for the cross-cultural training program is to deliver the appropriate information at the right time, neither too early nor too late. Both the *timing* and the *sequencing* of cross-cultural training are important.

READINESS FOR CROSS-CULTURAL TRAINING

Arms crossed. Eyes rolling. "Who cares?" attitude. Anyone who has ever conducted cross-cultural training has had the occasional trainee in the session who, quite frankly, just should not be there and definitely should not be working cross-culturally. These individuals believe that the cross-cultural training is teaching irrelevant soft skills—skills that cannot possibly matter when they are being asked to use their technical skills in a cross-national context.

From my experience offering cross-cultural training, I find that these individuals fall into two categories. The first category is made up of those who have never worked interculturally before and underestimate the power of cultural differences. These cross-cultural newbies often believe that their company's culture will be the same globally, and underestimate the extent to which their technical skills are bound by culture. Generally, they quickly grow to appreciate cross-cultural knowledge, usually seeing the light once they have taken a few cultural missteps. Those who underestimated the role of culture tend to become converts, seeking out cross-cultural training before their subsequent business trips.

Cross-cultural newbies believe that their company's culture will be the same globally, and underestimate the extent to which their technical skills are bound by culture.

The second group comprises the professionals who have traveled extensively for business but engaged in little significant intercultural interaction in the process. They are more intractable. Professionals in this group rarely "come around" to grasp how much *more* effective they could be if they would only take cultural differences into account when working internationally and interculturally—even in professional situations which demand that they override cultural differences via cultural minimization. They are generally not given feedback on their behaviors in different cultures; furthermore, they are almost always working in situations where their seniority, expertise, or position suggest that there are few people around who could even comfortably provide such feedback. In a nutshell, they lack openness even to accept that cultural differences exist, and are much less likely to willingly adapt their behavior when needed. These individuals lacking in openness are the least successful in cross-cultural training.[10] Unfortunately, they are also the ones who would benefit from it the most.

I have also observed that these two groups of employees who lack readiness for cross-cultural training are nonexistent, or nearly so, in organizations fully committed to building a pipeline of culturally agile professionals. When they work in organizations with culturally agile role models and mentors in prominent leadership positions, those without experience cross-culturally want to model their behavior after their culturally astute senior leaders. They seek cross-cultural training because they know it can help them be more effective in their roles, and the importance of the knowledge is reinforced throughout the organization. Those who truly lack openness (a personality trait that is unlikely to change, irrespective of training) generally do not make it far in the talent pipeline of organizations that place a high value on cultural agility.

EVALUATING THE EFFECTIVENESS OF CROSS-CULTURAL TRAINING

Cross-cultural training is an investment of organizational resources. As for all investments in human capital, organizations should look at their dashboard and assess whether their most important strategic needles are moving in the positive direction—and whether there is a return on the knowledge gained as a result of the training provided. Organizations should consider three metrics as they evaluate whether their cross-cultural training programs are helping build a pipeline of culturally agile professionals:

1. Knowledge gained and retained

2. Time-to-effectiveness cross-culturally

3. Professional success

Let's consider each of these in turn.

Knowledge Gained and Retained

If organizations offer foreign language training, assessing whether trainees have increased their proficiency in reading and writing in the target language as a function of having been through the language training course is relatively straightforward. We could assess their language proficiency before and after the language course to measure their knowledge gained. We could assess them again months after the language training course to measure their knowledge retained. The same is true for cross-cultural knowledge. You can assess whether the professionals in your organization who have taken the cross-cultural training course are able to identify the general ways cultures differ, the specific ways a target culture differs from their own culture, the methods for cultural discovery, and the phases of cross-cultural adjustment.

The box "Testing Cross-Cultural Knowledge" offers a sample of items from a test to assess individuals' knowledge of how cultures differ. It should be noted, however, that these knowledge-based cultural tests will reveal only a portion of your professionals' true understanding. The real test when evaluating the effectiveness of cross-cultural training is whether professionals are able to effectively use the knowledge in international or multicultural settings.

Testing Cross-Cultural Knowledge: Five Sample Items from a Knowledge Test to Evaluate Cross-Cultural Training

1. The cultural dimension of "hierarchy" is characterized by which of the following?
   a. The directness or subtleness of the language people use.
   b. The preference for autonomy or collaboration.
   c. The extent to which individual-level or group-level contributions are valued.
   d. The allocation of power and responsibility.

2. Individuals who are egalitarian would tend to believe that . . .
   a. Authority and power should change depending on the situation.
   b. It is good to share personal information with the team.
   c. The leader is the only one who should provide direction.
   d. Work-life balance is important for happiness.

3. In a work setting, group-oriented teammates would likely prefer to . . .
   a. Focus on personal responsibility in the context of the team's goals.
   b. Act with independent initiative to further the team's progress.
   c. Create a team identity and a shared sense of purpose.
   d. Make fast and efficient decisions—and then revise them later if needed.

4. When compared with colleagues who are indirect, colleagues who are direct will be more likely to . . .

   a. Use nonverbal communications.

   b. Show humility and preserve dignity.

   c. Prefer a more egalitarian organizational structure.

   d. Openly discuss differences of opinion as they arise.

5. In a work setting, colleagues with a fluid sense of time will tend to . . .

   a. Constantly bring new ideas and information to the group.

   b. Create short-term goals rather than long-term plans.

   c. Develop and implement timelines for deliverables.

   d. Desire work-life balance.

Answers: 1-d, 2-a, 3-c, 4-d, 5-a

Time-to-Effectiveness

At the start of this book, we defined cultural agility as professionals' ability to quickly, comfortably, and effectively work in different cultures and with people from different cultures. This definition intentionally starts with "quickly"; most firms today have a sense of urgency as they compete in the global economy. Waiting for professionals to become effective cross-culturally—and allowing them to make developmental (and costly) missteps along the way—is a luxury most companies cannot afford. In evaluating the effectiveness of cross-cultural training, organizations should assess whether they are accelerating professionals' time-to-effectiveness cross-culturally as a function of the training offered.

Professional Success

The most relevant test of whether cross-cultural training has been effective is, ultimately, whether professionals are more successful as a function of having been through the cross-cultural training program. It is with this higher-order evaluation that the return on investment can be assessed. It is also the most challenging to isolate, given the many factors beyond cross-cultural training that can potentially affect someone's performance in a cross-cultural context. One recommendation is to measure professionals' level of success in professional tasks requiring cross-cultural competence. With these measurements, the line of sight between cross-cultural competencies (and the cross-cultural training that helped promote them) can be more clearly compared to a financial marker or an overall effectiveness rating. You might want to assess your

Sample Tasks Requiring Cross-Cultural Competencies

- Working with colleagues from other countries
- Working as a member of a geographically distributed team
- Interacting with external clients from other countries
- Interacting with internal clients from other countries
- Supervising people who are from different countries
- Developing the organization's or unit's global strategic plan
- Managing the organization's or unit's budget worldwide
- Negotiating with people from other countries
- Managing foreign suppliers
- Managing risk across countries

business managers who have received training, for example, on the sample tasks requiring cross-cultural competencies (see box).

Methods for Evaluating Effectiveness

In discussing the metrics for cross-cultural training evaluations, we also need to discuss the methods for conducting them. The most conclusive training evaluations are those that can effectively measure change on a dimension of strategic importance. For the sake of illustration, let's say your organization is most interested in cross-cultural knowledge. To conduct this evaluation of whether cross-cultural training affects knowledge, we would need to first randomly assign employees into two groups: one group of employees will receive cross-cultural training, and another group of employees will not receive cross-cultural training. All of those participating in this evaluation would need to be assessed on their knowledge at two points in time: before the training program and after the training program. Before the training program, both groups should be the same in terms of cross-cultural knowledge because we have not yet offered cross-cultural training. This is the baseline. While the one group receives cross-cultural training, the second group does something unrelated (for example, plays Angry Birds). The employees from both groups are then tested again on their cross-cultural knowledge. For the cross-cultural training to have been effective, the group receiving the cross-cultural training should now have higher scores in cross-cultural knowledge compared with the group who played Angry Birds.

Is It Working? Three Methods to Measure Cross-Cultural Training Effectiveness

1. *Knowledge tests*. The content of the cross-cultural training program can be used to create pretraining and posttraining knowledge tests to assess knowledge gained. (An excerpt of a knowledge test used to evaluate cross-cultural training in a large European financial services firm appeared earlier in this chapter.) Ideally, you will want to test the trainees twice; once before the training to assess the baseline of their knowledge and again after the training to see what has been learned. You could also wait three, six, or more months to test one more time to see what knowledge has been retained.

2. *Performance on realistic simulations*. Some work sample or simulation can be created to assess whether trainees are able to use the cross-cultural knowledge gained after training. The U.S. Army, for example, conducts realistic simulations, with full operating villages and realistic role players, at the Joint Readiness Training Center at Fort Polk, Louisiana. In these simulations, the created villages are so believable that "by all appearances . . . [they] could have been in Afghanistan."* The soldiers run through training scenarios in these villages, interacting with role players. The scenarios are debriefed, performance is evaluated, and lessons learned are discussed.

3. *Performance measurement*. Cross-cultural training efficacy can be assessed by comparing two groups, one that has been trained and one that has not. One U.S.-based oil and energy company allowed its international assignee candidates to be randomly assigned to two groups, with one group receiving online instruction to help improve members' efficacy or confidence for an international assignment. The efficacy for the two groups was compared one month later, and the group with access to the knowledge about the assignment reported greater efficacy compared with the group without access.**

*Zach Morgan, "JRTC: Roleplayers Add Authenticity, Culture to Rotations," May 10, 2010, http://www.army.mil/article/38849/.

**Paula M. Caligiuri and Jean M. Phillips, "An Application of Self-Assessment Realistic Job Previews to Expatriate Assignments," *International Journal of Human Resource Management* 14, no. 7 (2003), 1102–1116.

In about twenty years of working in this area, only one client has requested (or allowed me to conduct) an evaluation this rigorous; the resistance is generally related to the fact that this type of assessment requires cross-cultural training to be withheld from a randomly assigned group of employees. Although this method remains the gold standard for evaluating the effectiveness of cross-cultural training, it is rarely carried out. The good news is that there are several acceptable methods for evaluating the effectiveness of cross-cultural training that are slight variations on this design. Most typically, organizations will pilot-test a cross-cultural training method with employees from one representative unit and compare them to the rest of the organization on some strategically relevant dimension (for example, global team effectiveness). Other organizations match two relatively comparable units and offer cross-cultural training to just one, evaluating whether the trained unit is more successful on some strategically relevant dimension (for example, cross-cultural knowledge). Another approach is to phase in cross-cultural training across the organization, assessing whether the level of success across the organization is increasing on some strategically relevant dimension (for example, international assignees' ratings of effectiveness in the host country). See "Is It Working?" for some suggestions of other methods that could be used to evaluate your organization's cross-cultural training programs.

TAKE ACTION

Based on information presented in Chapter Six, the following is a list of specific actions you can take to begin implementing cross-cultural training strategies and placing a direct business value on them in your organization.

- Lead by example. Professionals in your organization will be more receptive to cross-cultural training if the organization's prominent leaders support it and engage in it themselves. Use your organization's communications to encourage prominent leaders to share how cross-cultural training has helped them succeed.

- Offer cross-cultural training to a strategically important group of employees, such as a highly visible global project team or your international assignee population. Regardless of the group with whom you start, be certain that the cross-cultural training is highly effective in making a positive difference. Ideally, this first group's example will establish a track record and illustrate the benefits of cross-cultural training.

- Evaluate the effectiveness of your investment of organizational resources in cross-cultural training. Set up an evaluation with each training program to determine how well you are spending those resources.

- Consider the value per employee; for example, in comparison to a person-led training program for individuals, a Web-based cross-cultural training program with open access on your organization's intranet site will enable you to train more people.

CHAPTER

7

CRAFTING DEVELOPMENTAL CROSS-CULTURAL EXPERIENCES TO INCREASE CULTURAL AGILITY

A learning system to develop cultural agility needs to include two parts, *cross-cultural training* and *experiential developmental opportunities*. Chapter Six focused on cross-cultural training, including methods for laying the foundation of cross-cultural knowledge within the workforce. For cultural agility to be created, however, professionals need to interact in different cultures and with people from different cultures. We cannot learn to swim by taking even the best land-based swimming lesson. At some point, we need to get in the water. Similarly, professionals need to learn to be effective in cross-cultural situations by *experiencing* cross-cultural situations. This chapter focuses on how professionals build cultural agility through developmental cross-cultural experiences.

Chris Steinmetz is a culturally agile professional who recalls many significant developmental cross-cultural experiences throughout his life, several occurring long before the start of his professional career. Chris was born in Quito, Ecuador; his mother was a German-born Ecuadorian employed by the U.S. Embassy in Quito; his father was an American diplomat and Georgetown University graduate. Chris's childhood was one of continuous cultural immersion; his family changed countries every four years for his father's next assignment. Chris recalls his multicultural upbringing fondly, now appreciating having had the opportunity to live in Ecuador, the United Kingdom, the United States, Brazil, and Mexico before he was a teenager. These were especially rich developmental experiences given that Chris's family eschewed expatriate neighborhoods for more typical local ones.

Chris learned to be culturally agile at an early age. When he was five years old and his family lived in Belém, Brazil, a city at the mouth of the Amazon River, Chris remembers being "scared to death" to attend a Portuguese-speaking primary school. His fear quickly subsided; "fortunately, my brother and I adapted quickly—we were young so we made new friends and learned the language easily." Adjusting to a different cultural context is a powerful lesson at any age, but foundational for a five-year-old. From that point forward, Chris met all cross-cultural challenges with excitement rather than trepidation, and that feeling still remains with him today as a successful international business professional.

With an MBA in international business, fluency in three languages, and several well-honed cross-cultural competencies from his years living internationally as a young adult, Chris was a natural fit for internationally oriented professional roles. He began his career with Rich Products (a privately held organization specializing in nondairy food products) in 1988, at a time when the company was beginning a tremendous global expansion. In 1990, at twenty-six years of age, Chris had his "baptism by fire" in international business when he was assigned to open the Mexican market for Rich Products. He relocated to Mexico City and traveled throughout Mexico, ultimately visiting and experiencing thirty of Mexico's thirty-one states over a five-year international assignment. Chris recalled "feeling a bit like MacGyver on a stretch challenge, I was forced to be resourceful and creatively solve business problems every day."

Chris developed his business acumen quickly while working in Mexico, but the experience was not all smooth sailing. In the early 1990s, Mexico was in a precarious position economically, which was challenging for even the most seasoned international business professionals. Chris will never forget one short day in 1994 when the Mexican peso devalued over 100 percent, and interest rates surpassed 100 percent. Like many other American firms operating in Mexico, Rich Products sold goods imported from the United States in U.S. dollars. Unlike other American firms that started closing their Mexican operations to wait out the economic crisis, Chris recommended to Rich Products that the company remain and continue to invest in Mexico. His recommendation was based on his on-the-ground knowledge of the socioeconomic changes happening in Mexico, his understanding of Mexican traditions and culture, and the relationships he had built over the course of the assignment. It was a white-knuckle year that ended well for Chris professionally. He shares that "we lost a lot of money in 1995 while subsidizing the peso devaluation, but, in the end, we solidified our relationships—gaining confidence, earning the trust of our local customers, and leading to an increase of 25 percent in market share in one year." With well-deserved pride, Chris notes that "still today we are the dominant market leader with number-one market share in a field of ten competitors, including some of the biggest food companies in the world."

Chris understood the Mexican culture and how to succeed in it. In a surprising twist, in 1995, Chris agreed to step down from the leadership role of the Mexican business, the very business he had just spent five years (and countless sleepless nights) helping grow. He did this to allow a more senior Mexican manager to lead their newly created joint-venture organization. "While I started the business, I knew it would take someone with better connections in Mexico to take it to the next level," Chris noted. In that simple act of stepping aside, Chris's cultural agility shines; he demonstrated both cultural humility and also a deep understanding of what it takes to be successful within a cultural context.

Now the vice president for Latin America at Rich Products, Chris uses his knowledge to develop his staff, manage his region, and build cross-cultural competence within the organization by "promoting high-potential associates quickly and creating cross-cultural stretch opportunities in an effort to develop them, while fostering effective expansion and growth to meet our company's aggressive global growth goals." True to his cultural agility, Chris knows when to push and when to adapt to cultural differences. For example, staying true to the egalitarian values he shares with his organization, Chris successfully promotes women and junior managers, rare in the male-dominated and hierarchical culture in Latin America. He uses his understanding of the Latin American culture to persuade local (senior, male) leaders in the host national organizations to embrace an "unconventional" approach to staffing the organization. Rather than leading with the importance of diversity (another value he and his company share) to persuade, he leads with the business case for his associates' top-notch skills and fresh perspectives because he knows that "all could agree that ultimately it is the results that count." With respect to his U.S.-based colleagues' interactions with Latin American colleagues, Chris is steadfast in fostering respect and peer-level collaborations. He has zero tolerance for condescension, nipping it in the bud and replacing it quickly with cultural humility, mutual respect, effective communication, and positive relationships. Chris and his team continue to be successful in Latin America.

HOW CROSS-CULTURAL EXPERIENCES BECOME DEVELOPMENTAL

Chris Steinmetz can easily point to many significant developmental cross-cultural experiences he has had throughout his career, almost all of them occurring when he rolled up his sleeves and began working alongside his host national counterparts. "To become effective in international business, you need to experience culture deeply," Chris notes. I agree—and the research supports this conclusion.

A great challenge to the development of cultural agility today is the highly efficient business-class travel (hotels, airport clubs, car services, and so on) that has evolved over the years, now pervasive in almost every big city around the world. Although these resources have made travel infinitely more comfortable and efficient, they have created the cultural equivalent of an around-the-world vacation without ever leaving the culturally homogenized cruise ship. Here is the paradox: international travels are now easier, but using them to develop cultural agility has become harder.

Truly developmental experiences, such as the ones Chris shared, are stretch opportunities for intercultural learning that allow professionals to understand the limits of their cultural assumptions and progressively increase their cultural agility. Cross-cultural developmental experiences have three conditions, or qualities, that make them truly developmental. They enable the professionals in your organization to

1. Engage in meaningful interactions with peer-level colleagues from different cultures

2. Use their knowledge, skills, and abilities in different cultural contexts

3. Receive feedback on their performance in roles requiring cultural agility

Many firms . . . have been surprised to learn that cross-cultural experiences their organization offered actually lacked the qualities to make them developmental.

All three features are important and can be embedded into the learning system for building cultural agility in the workforce.

I encourage you to conduct an evaluation of the cross-cultural experiences in your organization's learning system; many firms I have worked with have been surprised to learn that cross-cultural experiences their organization offered actually lacked the qualities to make them developmental. Let's consider each of these key qualities a bit more closely.

If You Meet Me While Traveling . . .

If you run into me in an airport lounge, a coffee shop with a Wi-Fi hotspot, or the lobby of a big chain hotel, please know that I am not being a hypocrite. Like every other international business traveler on the planet, I appreciate the cosmopolitan standards available around the world—but I also know that what is making me more productive is unlikely to be making me more culturally agile. The latter requires richer experiences.

Engage in Meaningful Peer-Level Interactions

The first important feature of cross-culturally developmental opportunities is meaningful peer-level interactions with people from a different culture or cultures. Meaningful interactions allow peers to work collaboratively toward a common goal in an environment that supports their collaborative success. Peer-level colleagues working together in the same department for a few years have more potential for meaningful interactions, compared to the same two colleagues attending a weeklong off-site meeting together. At the same time, working in adjacent offices for a few years could have little developmental value due to lack of collaborative work, whereas the offsite meeting might be highly developmental if it included an action learning project.

Meaningful experiences are not always the most comfortable ones. Almost everyone who has worked cross-culturally or internationally can point to a cultural faux pas that was costly, either to the organization or the ego. Early in my career, I had a deep developmental lesson, thankfully embarrassing only to me. It happened while I was teaching in Singapore for an executive master's program, a joint program between the Singapore Institute of Management and Rutgers University. On the last day of an executive class titled Managing the Global Workforce, some of my students approached me during break and invited me to a restaurant for dessert after class at about 3:00 PM. Honored to be asked, I checked my calendar and said in American English, "Thanks for the invitation—that should work. The dinner I have tonight starts at 6:00 PM." At the end of the class, I noticed that many of the students were leaving. Wondering where everyone was going, I asked the student who had extended the invitation. Looking confused, he said it was their understanding that I had politely declined the invitation. "I did?" I asked. "Yes, when you told us about your dinner this evening," he said. I spent the next fifteen minutes trying to round up people from the parking lot, while apologizing for the misunderstanding. We all laughed at the miscommunication over dessert.

There were a few cultural missteps I made in this example, but for the sake of illustration, I'll focus on one lesson learned: the difference between high-context speech and low-context speech. As described in Chapter Six, in low-context communication cultures (including my culture, U.S. American), speech is interpreted directly. In high-context communication cultures, such as Singaporean, meaning is interpreted from words in the context of the situational cues surrounding them. I know the difference between high- and low-context speech. I even taught the difference between high- and low-context speech in my Managing the Global Workforce class (oh, the irony!). At the time, however, I was not experienced enough to apply it to this situation. I failed to realize that opening my calendar and explaining the potential conflict would be interpreted as a polite way of declining the invitation. This was a meaningful interaction that taught me to double-check for intended meaning in high-context cultures. Lesson learned!

If professionals receive enough knowledge, coaching, and feedback, these meaningful developmental experiences need not be professionally or emotionally risky.

Chris Steinmetz, for example, actively encourages interactions between his U.S. and Latin American team members. Given his functional biculturalism and depth of experience, he is able to "run interference" between cultures when needed. In addition, he is able to be proactive in fostering respectful collaboration in a way that is comfortable enough for most, and that makes the interactions truly developmental.

Use (New) Knowledge, Skills, and Abilities in Different Cultural Contexts

In developing cultural agility as in developing many other skills, practice makes perfect. Chris Steinmetz describes his approach in Mexico as, initially, "more of a trial and error—the more knowledge and experience I gained, the more successful I became." Over time, he gained knowledge and a better understanding of how culture affects customer tastes and client preferences, and had the ability to build trusting relationships with clients and suppliers, negotiate effectively, and motivate team members. The knowledge, skills, and abilities Chris gained in Mexico helped Rich Products create a template for global growth, an approach for how to expand through South America and other countries. With this template, Chris and his internationally oriented colleagues were able to use their knowledge to point out the aspects of the company's approach that should be synchronized and the other aspects that should be adapted to the cultural context. "Trial and error was no longer needed once enough of us had knowledge about how to open a new country." The knowledge accumulated through these cross-cultural experiences was critical. Chris noted, "When you are selling cakes, as we do, it is important to know that Mexicans prefer sweeter-tasting cakes compared to the Brazilians." Chris continued, "Not knowing the details of differences, at first, is not the real problem. You can do your homework and learn. The real problem is not even realizing there might be differences in the first place."

Greater participation in cross-cultural experiences will enable the professionals in your organization to gain culturally appropriate behaviors and foreign language skills—and also to understand the role of the cultural context. Using new skills and abilities in a cultural "stretch" situation affords opportunities to practice different cultural norms for working on a team, leading, presenting, negotiating, and the like. Over time, these experiences build higher levels of cross-cultural competencies by increasing knowledge, building skills, and improving their ability to reproduce culturally appropriate behaviors when appropriate.[1]

Receive Feedback on Performance in Cross-Cultural Roles

Judging our own abilities and performance is not easy for us as humans. We tend not to see ourselves as others see us; instead, we often either make excuses for our shortcomings or criticize ourselves more harshly than is warranted. This human tendency is what makes feedback from others so valuable. And it is why cross-cultural experiences, in order to be truly developmental, should include opportunities for receiving feedback on culturally appropriate behaviors and language skills. Seeking and receiving feedback from colleagues and managers is one way this occurs. As we all know from our own professional experiences, certain contexts are easier than others for feedback to be sought out, perceived as appropriate, and even welcomed. If the professionals in your organization are in senior leadership roles, they might not feel comfortable trying new knowledge, skills, and abilities at the risk of making credibility-depleting cultural or linguistic mistakes. Similarly, subordinates may not feel comfortable giving feedback to a senior leader.

Ideally, cross-cultural developmental experiences should include situations where making cultural or linguistic mistakes would not be embarrassing or socially risky, either professionally or personally, and where feedback is offered to employees by those who accurately understand how their behaviors are being perceived in the cultural context. This feedback should be provided in a respectful fashion, in a setting that is comfortable, supportive, and welcomed. A cultural coach or a bicultural manager is often the best person to offer such feedback. Chris Steinmetz, for example, will debrief with and coach his junior associates when they start working in the Latin American region. He knows this is a developmental process and wants to foster cross-cultural competence among his associates, adding that "I know I made some mistakes, at first, when I was in Mexico, so I try to provide the coaching I wish I had had back then."

It is no surprise that people who have grown up in multicultural households, as Chris did, are often very culturally agile. The family setting in the home is typically a comfortable, supportive place to learn about two cultures and practice two languages, and feedback is frequent and readily available. These home situations often provide multiple supportive "coaches" in the form of parents, grandparents, and other relatives. Compared to one's family life, the professional setting—where one is charged with leading a subsidiary, managing a team, and working with colleagues from different cultures—tends to be comparatively less comfortable. The stakes are higher: a promotion, or even one's job, can hinge on how well one does in the cross-cultural professional situation. Professionals who grew up being accustomed to receiving feedback from family members often find it easier to give and receive feedback in these more risky professional settings.

• • •

Now that we have examined the three qualities that I consider key for making cross-cultural experiences truly developmental, I encourage you to turn to the assessment of developmental potential (see box). If you employ it to evaluate the experiences in your organization, it will help you step back and analyze, in the aggregate, whether the learning system in your organization is actually designed to do what is intended: build cultural agility in the workforce.

Developmental Potential: Assessment of the Developmental Properties of a Cross-Cultural Experience

You can use the following six questions to assess an individual cross-cultural experience for its developmental properties. A higher overall score suggests that the given developmental experience had greater potential for developing cultural agility. This assessment can be used to measure the developmental nature of a type or group of experiences (for example, global rotational program, international assignments). The assessment here is written such that you can reflect back on a given cross-cultural experience. The same assessment can be reworded to assess future experiences.

1. When you were in this experience, recall the number of significant peer-level interactions you had with a person (or people) from a different culture (or cultures). Examples of significant peer-level interactions would include a friendship with a person from a different culture or working closely with someone from another culture.

    This experience gave me . . .

    3: many opportunities for significant peer-level interactions

    2: some opportunities for significant peer-level interactions

    1: few opportunities for significant peer-level interactions

    0: no opportunities for significant peer-level interactions

2. When you were in this experience, recall the extent to which you worked collaboratively toward a common goal with a person (or people) from a different culture (or cultures). Collaborative interactions might be, for example, working on a project together for work or school, or being teammates on a sports team.

    This experience gave me . . .

    3: many opportunities for collaboration

    2: some opportunities for collaboration

    1: few opportunities for collaboration

    0: no opportunities for collaboration

3. When you were in this experience, think about how much the environment of the situation supported and encouraged your interactions with a person (or people) from a different culture (or cultures). Examples of supportive environments might be support from your supervisor encouraging you to succeed on a global project team, or support from your university encouraging you to work with classmates from different cultures. Examples of unsupportive environments might be growing up in a diverse neighborhood where people from different cultures did not mingle much, or studying abroad in a program where you stayed with students from your own country.

This experience gave me a . . .

3: very supportive environment

2: somewhat supportive environment

1: not very supportive environment

0: not at all supportive environment

4. When you were in this experience, think about how many opportunities you had to practice culturally appropriate behaviors and foreign language skills. A robust example is actively using a language you are learning while working or studying abroad. A more subtle example is learning how to be a student, teammate, or colleague in a situation with different cultural norms for how to behave.

This experience gave me . . .

3: many opportunities to practice cultural and/or language skills

2: some opportunities to practice cultural and/or language skills

1: few opportunities to practice cultural and/or language skills

0: no opportunities to practice cultural and/or language skills

5. When you were in this experience, think about how many opportunities you had to receive feedback on your culturally appropriate behaviors and/or language skills. An example might be growing up in a home where two languages were spoken and receiving parental feedback on both behavior and language. Another example might be receiving feedback on your working style from colleagues from different cultures.

This experience gave me . . .

3: many opportunities to receive feedback on culture and/or language skills

2: some opportunities to receive feedback on culture and/or language skills

1: few opportunities to receive feedback on culture and/or language skills

0: no opportunities to receive feedback on culture and/or language skills

6. When you were in this experience, how comfortable did you feel making cultural or linguistic mistakes, such that making a cultural or linguistic mistake was not embarrassing, not professionally or personally risky, and so on. For example, growing up in a multicultural household is generally considered a very comfortable place to learn about two cultures and practice two languages, whereas speaking to subordinates and leading a subsidiary are generally considered less comfortable places to make mistakes.

During this experience, I generally felt . . .

3: very comfortable making cultural or linguistic mistakes

2: somewhat comfortable making cultural or linguistic mistakes

1: rarely comfortable making cultural or linguistic mistakes

0: never comfortable making cultural or linguistic mistakes

SUGGESTIONS FOR DEVELOPMENTAL CROSS-CULTURAL EXPERIENCES

As I've just discussed, cross-cultural experiences are developmental when they provide opportunities to practice newly learned behaviors in a meaningful and collaborative context that includes receiving feedback on their effectiveness, and when they do so in an environment that is professionally safe for learning. Within your organization there are likely to be several opportunities for these developmental experiences that are consistent with your organization's business goals and strategic needs. They include, but are not limited to,

- Mentoring programs

- Buddy programs

- Global project teams

- International volunteerism programs

- Global rotational programs

Let's examine each of these in turn.

Mentoring Programs

Mentoring or coaching programs are generally associated with the formal or informal matching of a successful senior manager with an associate who is more junior or less experienced. Through work-related advice-giving interactions, the knowledge of the more senior person can be transferred to the more junior person. This is particularly powerful for developing organization-level cultural agility when the mentor–mentee dyad does not share the same nationality. Having a mentor of a different nationality allows the mentee's behaviors to be interpreted through at least two different cultural lenses.

In their research, Shawn Carraher, Sherry Sullivan, and Madeline Crocitto found that among international assignees, those who had host national mentors enjoyed a variety of career-enhancing benefits from the relationship, including organizational knowledge, improved performance, and promotability.[2] Especially for international assignees, I encourage your organization to establish formal mentoring programs that promote the high value of mentoring relationships and that reward host national mentors not only for participating but also for the success of their mentees. These programs should also be fostered more informally; international assignees should be encouraged to actively seek out professional relationships with more senior host national managers while on assignment.

Buddy Programs

Unlike mentoring programs, which are characterized by a hierarchical difference between the mentor and mentee, buddy programs involve the pairing of peers from different countries for the purpose of knowledge sharing. An example is IBM's global mentoring program, which is consistent with the company's goal of creating a globally integrated enterprise. This program connects IBM employees from emerging markets with comparably placed IBM employees from more mature markets. These pairs build relationships and share information via phone and email, in addition to connecting face-to-face when business travels enable them to do so. One example is described as follows:

> *Taiwanese software programmer David Lin paired with Danny Chen, an engineer who was born in Taiwan but works in Austin. Chen taught Lin how to develop ideas that were patentable, and Lin set up an invention team in his office and began publishing a newsletter full of tips for new inventors. Last year the Taipei lab got five patents, up from one in 2005. For his part, Chen got valuable advice from Lin on how to do business in China.[3]*

Global Project Teams

There has been an increase in the number of organizations using cross-border, virtual, and global teams composed of members from geographically dispersed units. Participation in cross-border teams allows for the development of cross-cultural competencies, including in-depth knowledge about different cultures, ability to form relationships, cross-cultural communication skills, and perspective-taking. Given their collaborative and peer-level team interaction, they can provide rich cross-cultural development opportunities.

In addition to being developmental, cross-national project teams are also strategic. For example, as a part of its leadership development program, Unilever creates teams of high-potential employees from around the world who collectively investigate trends in emerging markets and develop ways in which Unilever can respond to these trends. Working over a few months in a variety of modalities including face-to-face workshops, site visits, and distance components, these project teams collaborate on developing proposals and presenting their ideas to Unilever's senior executives. The most viable proposals are then implemented.[4]

All cross-cultural encounters carry a significant potential for misunderstandings. To address this potential concern, many leading organizations are now using online tools specifically designed to foster cross-cultural understanding and ease cultural challenges that might arise in the course of collaborations. These tools help make peer-level interactions both effective and developmental by addressing communication challenges and opening the dialogue to create the best working relationship among colleagues from different cultures. Read about RW[3]'s Global Teams Tool (see box) for more information about online cross-cultural training tools to facilitate the effectiveness of multicultural teams.

International Volunteerism Programs

In a survey of more than three hundred organizations, the Deloitte Volunteer Impact Survey found that although cash donations have declined during the recent recessionary years, the number of firms adopting corporate volunteerism programs is rising steadily.[5] International volunteerism programs are formal programs in which companies sponsor release time, ranging from a few weeks to several months and supported by regular compensation, for their interested highly skilled employees to volunteer with targeted

Global Teams Tool: Learning to Collaborate Cross-Culturally

The Global Teams Tool from RW³ CultureWizard allows online learners—the culturally diverse team members—to quickly see where they might encounter challenges when working in multicultural teams. The tool visually represents readily recognizable behaviors that differ among members' national cultures to identify potential differences. The Global Teams Tool is a platform for dialogue and enables teams to comfortably discuss team-level ground rules.

Sample Screenshot from the Global Teams Tool Illustrating the Cultural Differences Among Team Members in a Cross-National Team

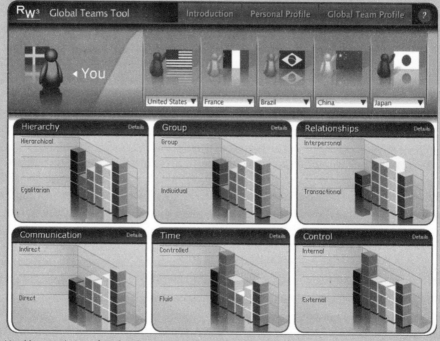

Used by permission of RW³ CultureWizard (RW-3.com)

nongovernmental organizations (NGOs) in developing countries. In the years from 2007 to 2010, we have seen a plethora of leading organizations, such as GlaxoSmith-Kline, Dow Corning, PepsiCo, FedEx, and IBM, benefiting from their international volunteerism programs. These programs serve a variety of strategic business needs, including an increase in the corporate social responsibility reputation of the firm, improved retention among socially responsible high-potential employees, higher employee engagement, and improved employer attractiveness among the millennial generation, whose members are more dedicated to service.

When designed well, these international volunteerism programs can build cross-cultural competencies and create new knowledge about developing markets. I worked with Ahsiya Mencin, the director of GlaxoSmithKline's PULSE Volunteer Partnership (see box for more information), and my colleague Kaifeng Jiang to conduct a broad stakeholder analysis identifying the characteristics conducive to a high-quality volunteerism assignment.[6] We gathered stakeholder data from business unit leaders, NGO leaders, and the employees, assessing the employees at three times:

1. At the start of the volunteer assignment

2. At the end of the volunteer assignment (which lasted, on average, more than five months full-time)

3. Six months after the completion of the assignment

Our study found that corporate-sponsored volunteerism created sustainable value across multiple stakeholders under the following conditions:

- Volunteerism assignments should be selected carefully such that employees are assigned to truly meaningful projects. The employees want to make a difference in the lives of those they are serving through the work of the NGO. Although stuffing envelopes and taking inventory of supplies may be necessary tasks for the NGO, highly skilled corporate professionals are unlikely to perceive this routine office work as meaningful.

- Volunteers should be placed in assignments where the NGO staff members and managers support the volunteers. In the most rewarding and satisfying assignments, the volunteers felt comfortable interacting openly and sharing feelings of mutual acceptance and respect with NGO leaders and staff members.

- Volunteers should be placed in assignments where they are able to offer significant value to the NGO through the use of their highly relevant professional skills. The volunteer experience should be designed as a stretch assignment that fully utilizes—and pushes—the volunteers' professional skills in the NGO environment.

- The organization should recognize and leverage the knowledge and skills that the volunteers gain during the volunteer experience. Employee engagement was highest when the volunteers sensed that as a result of the volunteerism program, their newly honed skills were highly valuable in the eyes of the organization.

- NGOs should have the resources available (for example, time, money, talent) to sustain the volunteers' projects after the volunteers leave.

The PULSE Volunteer Partnership at GlaxoSmithKline

As noted on GlaxoSmithKline's PULSE Volunteer Partnership's Web site (www.gsk.com/community/employee_involvement.htm), PULSE is a skills-based volunteering initiative within GlaxoSmithKline that empowers employees to make a sustainable difference for communities and patients in need. Through the PULSE program, employees are given an opportunity to use their professional skills and knowledge during a three- or six-month immersion experience within a nonprofit or nongovernmental organization (a "Partner"). During the assignment, the volunteers address a Partner need and, at the same time, develop their own leadership skills. According to the Web site, PULSE has a threefold mission: "PULSE aims to create a positive, sustainable difference for non-profit organisations and communities; support the leadership growth and development of [GSK] employees; and foster a culture of simplification, creativity, ingenuity, proactivity and teamwork in the Partner organisation, and ultimately back at GSK."

In the past three years, PULSE has sent nearly two hundred volunteers from 26 countries working with fifty-eight Partners in 39 countries. These volunteers worked full-time for an average of 5.4 months. PULSE partnered with thirty-one different organizations focused on health, education, and the environment. The following (quoted from the Web site) are examples of just some of the projects from the PULSE Volunteer Partnership:

PULSE Volunteer Julie L. worked with the Clinton Health Access Initiative (CHAI) in Togo, Africa—Julie improved the drug supply chain in order to facilitate the access of care for patients with HIV/AIDS in Togo, in accordance with WHO recommendations. Specifically, she created a functional coordination unit to enable better information gathering and sharing, support various antiretroviral (ARV) distribution activities, and enable management tool capability transfer in order to improve Togo's response to the [population's] health needs.

PULSE Volunteer Kerry M. worked with Pro Mujer, Bolivia (PMB)—Kerry changed the way PMB purchased and distributed medications in sixty-five health clinics throughout the country. Because of Kerry's work, the women and children of PMB now have access to more affordable medications from their medical home, a place that they trust and place confidence in. With medications in place, clients will recover more quickly from illness, therefore allowing them more time to focus on their work and take care of their families and communities.

PULSE Volunteer Michelle W. worked with the Millennium Cities Initiative in Kumasi, Ghana—Michelle supported the educational development of Ghanaian junior high school students by training their teachers to use the Internet to find relevant, interesting math and science lesson materials and to build partnerships with teachers in the United States.

PULSE Volunteer Hilary B. worked with Direct Relief International (DRI) and AMREF in Uganda—Hilary supported the Lake Victoria Basin Integrated Health Initiative. She drafted the first Kalangala District report, which was adopted as official policy by AMREF and was shared with the Ugandan Ministry of Health as a strategic plan for the next five years.

- Employees should be selected carefully for volunteerism assignments, given that not everyone will benefit from these developmental opportunities. To reap the maximum developmental benefits from these volunteerism experiences, employees should be selected who are open, flexible, and emotionally strong.

Global Rotational Programs

International assignments offer rich opportunities for employees to gain cultural agility through immersion in host countries. Generally lasting over one year, international assignments enable employees to live and work in host countries, potentially providing an opportunity for significant and meaningful collaboration with host nationals. Without question, this has been the single most developmental method organizations use to build cultural agility. Although Chapter Eight is fully dedicated to international assignments, this section of Chapter Seven covers a specific type of international assignment: the global rotational program.

Many leading organizations, such as IBM, Johnson & Johnson, Dow, Nokia, and GE, have created global rotational programs to build cross-cultural and functional competence within their firms' most critical functional areas. These global rotational programs offer high-potential employees exposure to working in one or more host countries, spending between six months and two years in a given context before moving to the next location. Global rotational programs are generally offered early in employees' careers, usually to new graduates from targeted master's degree programs, with the hope that the participants will gain critical cross-cultural competencies to successfully manage and lead anywhere in the world.

The experiences of assignees in global rotational programs are designed to increase peer-level interactions with host national colleagues. After the experiences, these assignees report that they have developed an appreciation for new or previously unfamiliar things, gained cultural sensitivity, and learned to respect values and customs different from their own.[7] Professionals' increased understanding of the extent to which their skills and abilities are culturally bound is one of the most powerful lessons learned from these rotational assignments.[8] For you to maximize the developmental components of the global rotational program and ultimately see a return on investment from the perspective of cultural agility, I recommend that you assess whether the international portion of your organization's global rotation program contains the requisite qualities of a developmental experience (discussed earlier in this chapter). In addition, your organization should initiate the following three talent management practices:

1. *Careful selection of participants.* Selection for key personality traits is critical: global rotational programs will be more effective when participants are predisposed to gaining cross-cultural competencies. As most of these participants will be newly hired university graduates, your organization is encouraged to use both personality tests and a structured interview to assess for the most critical attributes. (See Chapter Five for selection and assessment tools that can be used for this purpose.)

2. *Performance management of participants.* Throughout the rotational assignment, assess whether the participants are gaining cross-cultural competencies. Host-country leaders and peers would be best able to provide these assessments. Intervention strategies can be developed to address any developmental needs the participants might have (for example, coaching, mentoring, and cross-cultural training).

3. *Use of competencies gained.* A global rotational program, at its core, is a strategic investment in the future leadership talent of the organization. Be sure your organization has a way to measure—and then effectively integrate—the cross-cultural competencies acquired by participants. Leveraging their competencies will reduce the risk of participants' choosing to leave your organization for opportunities elsewhere where their competencies can be used.

TAKE ACTION

Based on information presented in Chapter Seven, the following is a list of specific actions you can take to begin crafting cross-cultural experiences that will be truly developmental for professionals in your organization.

- Offer cross-cultural experiences. Implement experiential opportunities, such as those described in the chapter, that will promote meaningful interactions among peer-level colleagues from different cultures. Structure opportunities for your employees to use and stretch their knowledge, skills, and abilities in different cultural contexts.

- Evaluate cross-cultural experiences. Brainstorm with organizational leaders the possible experiences that would serve a functional need while also offering a developmental benefit for the employee. Evaluate the experiences on two dimensions: Are they filling a business need? Do they have the potential to develop cultural agility?

- Create opportunities where it is professionally safe to make mistakes. In order to learn, employees need to receive feedback on their cross-cultural competencies. Arrange for employees to receive feedback on their performance in roles requiring cultural agility. Ideally this feedback will come from functionally bicultural professionals, those who understand the nature of the mistakes employees make.

CHAPTER

8

DEVELOPING CULTURAL AGILITY THROUGH INTERNATIONAL ASSIGNMENTS

Among the experiential opportunities companies can offer, the most often used—and potentially the most developmental—is the international assignment or expatriate experience. To round out the learning system, this chapter focuses on how international assignments can be best structured to build cultural agility in the workforce.

Jake Shannon, an American culturally agile professional, recalls many significant developmental cross-cultural experiences throughout his life, some occurring long before the start of his professional career. Jake was born in Japan and lived in five states in the United States as well as Germany on two separate occasions. These eight moves, three internationally, all occurred before Jake turned twenty years old.

As a child, Jake recalls several experiences where he learned, firsthand, the importance of being culturally agile. "I remember when I was eleven years old being invited by a German family to spend a weekend with them and their son at their small vacation home in southern Germany. Everything about that weekend was different from what I had grown up with—the style of their home, the food that they ate, and the Sunday morning worship service that I experienced." Even with all of Jake's time spent in different countries and states as a child, that weekend was salient because it gave Jake his first real experience of full cultural immersion with host nationals, one of the most developmental cross-cultural experiences one can have. Reflecting on that weekend, Jake says, "At first, I found the experience a bit odd and kind of awkward—but by the end of the weekend I was thrilled by it. It felt like an adventure, like I was discovering the culture and enjoying it."

When Jake was in his thirties, he returned to Germany, only this time as an international assignee for the global health care company Merck and Co. (Merck). Jake's wife, RuthAnn, and their four children, whose ages at the time were 11, 8, 5, and 3, accompanied him. Having lived in Germany as a child, RuthAnn also speaks German fluently. The couple embraced the opportunity to return to Europe. Jake and RuthAnn not only share with each other a strong, supportive, and loving marriage but also a deep interest in immersing themselves in different cultures, a value that they have fostered in their children as well. This shared family value for experiencing different cultures is important; in fact, it is a secret ingredient for international assignee success. My research on the predictors of success among international assignees found that a family's communication, cohesion, adaptability, and interest in living internationally will directly affect the *entire* family's level of adjustment, which, in turn, spills over to the international assignee's work performance.[1] Jake didn't need my research to tell him that RuthAnn and his children were a positive influence on his ability to be effective in the host country. He notes that "RuthAnn's flexibility and adjustment to living in Germany made it easier for me to focus on my work. I knew the home front was OK. She and our children were happy."

The characteristics of Jake's family, already well-adjusted, supportive and cohesive, became even more crucial when tragedy struck about five months into his assignment. Without any precondition or warning, Jake and RuthAnn's youngest daughter was admitted into the intensive care unit of the local hospital with a very rare and life-threatening illness. As Jake says, "Under normal circumstances, this kind of shocking experience would have been devastating for a parent, to say the least, but to experience it three thousand miles away from home and in a completely different hospital setting was unnerving." After one month in the intensive care unit, Jake and RuthAnn's daughter thankfully survived the illness. She was released to go home with her parents to continue home therapy in order to relearn how to walk, talk, and eat.

The worst of the ordeal was over, but was Jake's international assignment also over? Jake shared that "even though my daughter was receiving world-class medical care, we seriously contemplated returning to the United States. The location was just one more stressor we just didn't need." When the cloud of the most imminent threat to their daughter's health was lifted, the need to return to the United States also faded. Jake notes, "We realized that we could provide the best possible care for her and still remain in Germany." Jake and RuthAnn's decision to remain in Germany was based not only on the excellent medical care and their daughter's improving health but also on one more factor: the emotional support his family was receiving from their host national colleagues and friends. Jake says, "Even though we had just moved into the area, we felt that everyone from the local community—including new friends from church, school, and work—were rallying behind us during this difficult time."

My research has found that even in the best of circumstances for international assignments, emotional support is critical for international assignees' adjustment to living in a host country.[2] Again, Jake did not need my research to tell him that. After this initial setback, which appropriately changed his priorities to focus entirely on his family, Jake returned to the work he was sent to do and continued with his international assignment.

Even though Germany was a country Jake already knew well, he still views the Merck experience in Germany as highly developmental for his cultural agility. The core of what made it so developmental was the fact that it was a *full immersion*. Jake worked directly with his German colleagues, often conversing only in German. Jake recalls, "Even though I thought I knew what I was getting into from a cultural perspective, I still found certain elements of the experience to be completely new. Even something as subtle as the best way to give presentations was different. I needed to adapt to the German way of working to be successful." Jake went deeper into the German culture, sharing that he "also learned that there were differences between regions within Germany. The professional behaviors that were appropriate for success in one area would not work in another. I found that even with what I thought was a deep understanding of the culture, there were still many things I had to learn." Jake's comments reflect his true cultural agility—the deep desire to learn more about the cultural contexts in which he finds himself.

A professional milestone for Jake came after he had been on his international assignment for one full year. He and his German colleagues worked tirelessly as they collaborated on an important presentation to be delivered to approximately 120 of Merck's most senior leaders in Germany. They presented as a team, and when it came to Jake's section, he delivered it in German. Jake recalls that "both during and after the presentation I sensed that my German colleagues were impressed not only with the content of the presentation but in my ability to truly 'speak their language.' After that, I felt like I was accepted—not as an expatriate—but more like a local." Jake noted that the experience at the presentation was a turning point for his international assignment and deepened his professional relationships with his German colleagues.

Reflecting on his international assignment and professional development, Jake notes that "it was in those interactions while on the international assignment that I realized how important it is to truly be able to see things from another person's perspective—really walk in someone else's shoes." He underscored the value of language skills, sharing that "it is so important to speak the host-country language—even if not completely fluently." Today, Jake appreciates the cross-cultural competencies he had gained in Germany, saying that "my experience in Germany has definitely given me credibility when working with professionals from all over the world. The experience also taught me how to really listen, not just to the spoken words, but to cultural cues and the subtleties of the context." His roles have expanded over the years, and he now works with more global client groups within Merck. Jake credits his assignment in Germany for being developmental, personally and professionally, sharing that it "has definitely helped me not only be a better person but a better employee—and a better agent for change."

International assignments like Jake's remain the most popular method by which cultural agility is developed in organizations.[3] However, merely labeling Jake's international assignment "developmental" did not make it so. As you'll recall from Chapter Seven, for international assignments to be truly developmental from the perspective of building cross-cultural competencies, they need to satisfy three conditions:

1. International assignees engage in meaningful interactions with peer-level host nationals.

2. They use culturally appropriate knowledge, skills, and abilities in the host country.

3. They receive feedback on their performance as international assignees.

Jake's international assignments included all these features—and he was supported by a cohesive and well-adjusted family, also critical for assignment success.

The right type of assignment and his supportive family were helpful indeed for Jake. However, Jake also possessed some personal attributes that helped in his development. Jake has an open personality, which facilitated learning in the host country. He had language skills that enabled him to collaborate with his host national colleagues. And he had successive cross-cultural experiences throughout his career, which helped accelerate his development of cross-cultural competencies in the host country. If you were reverse-engineering the development of Jake's cultural agility, you would carefully select the professional for the assignment, support the family in the host country, identify how this experience fits into his or her broader career plan, and craft the type of cultural experience that would foster the desired development. In other words, you would *strategically* manage international assignments.

This is not as difficult as it might sound. Managing assignments strategically requires your organization to align the performance goals of its international assignments with its international business strategy and, in turn, the talent management practices that support that strategy. That was a mouthful. Let's start with the most basic of strategic questions that you should be able to answer:

• Among your international assignee population, do you know who you have where—and why?

• What is each international assignee being asked to do? What is he or she being asked to develop, if anything?

Were you able to answer these questions? The most globally competitive organizations can. These organizations use different type of assignees for different strategic purposes. Through our research, Saba Colakoglu and I found that the most globally integrated organizations align the use of international assignments with the way in which they compete around the world. The firms with global integration business strategies made greater use of developmental international assignments, had a higher number of senior managers with international assignment experience, and had a stronger focus on leadership development through international assignments.[4]

The most globally competitive organizations align their talent management practices with the strategic decisions regarding where and when to send employees as international assignees. These organizations know who they have on international assignments and why they are there from the perspective of the assignments' strategic goals. In turn, these organizations are able to leverage the competencies gained from the international assignees' experiences upon their return. For example, in a survey of their corporate clients in Europe and the United States, TraQs Consulting found that organizations with a greater integration of international assignments into talent management systems reported greater success in the use of international assignments as developmental experiences.[5] We need to keep in mind that from the perspective of strategic alignment, all international assignments are not intended to be developmental. Let's go deeper into this.

INTERNATIONAL ASSIGNMENT GOALS AND CULTURAL AGILITY

Many organizations categorize international assignments based on the assignees' hierarchical level in the organization, or on practical factors, such as tax equalization needs and visa requirements. These practical categories, which are useful for the administration of international assignment programs, do not differentiate assignments on the basis of their strategic importance to the organization. They should. International assignments do not all have the same strategic goals: some are designed for developmental purposes; others fill technical needs or skill gaps in the host countries; still others provide technical transfer of information from the assignees to the staff within the host national subsidiaries.[6] An understanding of these differences is critically important for developing cultural agility through international assignments.

International assignments do not all have the same strategic goals. . . . An understanding of these differences is critically important for developing cultural agility.

From the perspective of performance goals, there are two broad categories of international assignments: *demand driven* and *learning driven*.[7] Demand-driven assignments are created for assignees to accomplish tangible goals, most often to fill skill gaps in the host countries and manage functional areas or units to align with the parent company's standard or culture. Within the broad category of demand-driven assignments, there are two types of assignees, *technical assignees* and *functional assignees*. Technical assignees do not have much need to collaborate with host nationals in order to accomplish their goals, whereas functional assignees need to work collaboratively with host nationals to be successful. Even though development is not a strategic goal of these assignments, your functional assignees are more likely than technical assignees to gain cross-cultural competencies, given their higher level of collaboration with host nationals. (This issue becomes particularly important for retention upon repatriation, a topic I will discuss later in this chapter.)

Unlike demand-driven assignments, learning-driven assignments require employees to build cross-cultural competencies and gain international experience as part of a succession plan or talent management program for career development.[8] Within this broad category of learning-driven assignments, there are two types of assignees, *developmental assignees* and *strategic assignees*. Developmental assignees are often junior in the organization and part of its global rotational program. The assignments for these developmental assignees have demand-driven performance goals—or, if they don't, then they almost certainly should be cut from budgets—but they allow room for growth, coaching, and experiential gains through "stretch" assignments.

Compared to developmental assignees, strategic assignees have less "wiggle room" for possible slipups, regardless of how powerful the lesson may be; their roles are critical to the organization's competitive success, and in their case, mistakes would be more costly. Strategic assignments are learning driven in the sense that these assignees should be building cross-cultural competencies while on assignment as part of an organizational succession plan. More precisely, they should be *building on* preexisting cross-cultural competencies; these critical roles, ideally, should not be employees' first foray into developing cultural agility.

Distinguishing among these assignments is not an academic exercise. It has strategic importance for the type of *global mobility practices* your organization should be offering. Global mobility practices will help manage international assignees as they relocate from one country to another. Global mobility professionals (within a global mobility function in most organizations) manage a myriad of complexities (and vendors)—everything from international assignees' taxes and visas to the movement of their household goods and enrollment of the assignees' children into international schools. Global mobility practices ease the transition for the relocation, help employees remain in compliance with tax and immigration laws, and encourage professional development.

Global mobility practices offered to demand-driven assignees should maximize their effectiveness in their role (as quickly as possible). The purpose of global mobility practices offered to learning-driven assignees is different. Of course, they should maximize the assignees' effectiveness in their role, but equally important, they should foster opportunities for development and growth. Helping assignees become *increasingly* more effective in their meaningful collaborations with host nationals is of paramount importance within this category. Figure 8.1 offers a closer look at the performance goals of international assignments and the corresponding global mobility practices that would best support those goals.

FIGURE 8.1.   *Getting It Right with Assignment Support*

International Assignment Performance Goals	Type of Global Mobility Practices Needed
Technical Assignments Performance goals are demand driven. These international assignees are sent solely to complete a given job, usually to fill a skill gap in a host country, and return home (generally to their home location). To accomplish their task-driven goals, they will not have meaningful collaborations with host nationals. They are interacting primarily with systems or machines or providing technical expertise as individual contributors.	**Support-Based Global Mobility Practices** The goal of global mobility practices is to enhance the assignees' abilities to do their jobs effectively. Support practices should, ideally, ease the transition as much as possible to reduce the time it takes to adjust to living and working in the host country. Living in compatriot communities, spending time in compatriot social clubs, using translators, and so on will enhance the outcome of the assignment because they would ease the adjustment process.
Functional Assignments Performance goals are primarily demand driven. These international assignees are similar to technical assignees, with one key difference: in order to succeed in their demand-driven goals, they are likely to need to engage in significant, meaningful interactions. Their assignments will therefore have more developmental properties even if development is not a stated goal.	**Mostly Support-Based with Some Strategic Development Global Mobility Practices** The goal of global mobility practices is to enhance the assignees' abilities to do their jobs effectively. As with technical assignments, support practices should, ideally, ease the transition as much as possible to reduce the time it takes to adjust to living and working in the host country. At the same time, collaborating effectively with host nationals is also critical to achieving performance goals. Thus practices to improve these collaborations (e.g., cross-cultural training, language training, and cultural coaching) are important.

(Continued)

FIGURE 8.1. *Getting It Right with Assignment Support (Continued)*

International Assignment Performance Goals	Type of Global Mobility Practices Needed
Developmental Assignments Performance goals are primarily learning driven. Although these international assignees are sent to fill a role, the primary purpose is for them to develop functional and cross-cultural competencies.	**Mostly Strategic Development with Targeted Support-Based Global Mobility Practices** The goal of global mobility practices is to both enhance and facilitate the assignees' development. A focus on candidate selection is critical, along with selecting locations to maximize peer-level interactions with host nationals. Practices to facilitate collaboration with host nationals (e.g., cross-cultural training, language training, and cultural coaching) and to evaluate development (e.g., performance measurement) are important.
Strategic Assignments Performance goals are both demand driven and learning driven. These international assignees hold critical roles and are often being groomed as part of a succession plan.	**Both Support-Based and Strategic Development Global Mobility Practices** Given the criticality of these assignments, the goal of global mobility practices is to manage the risk of failure and enhance the assignees' abilities to do their jobs effectively. At the same time, these assignees should be building on their cross-cultural competencies through cultural coaching, language training, and senior-level networking groups in the host country.

USING STRATEGIC GLOBAL MOBILITY PRACTICES TO BUILD CULTURAL AGILITY

Learning-driven international assignments need the right people in the right opportunities, without question. They also require *strategic global mobility practices* to support the effort. Compared to the global mobility practices offered in many organizations today, strategic global mobility practices are different because

- They are fully integrated with talent development practices.

- They focus on selection for personality characteristics that foster development.

- They involve crafting assignments with broader developmental goals in mind.

- They include more tailored support practices to retain the developmental components of the assignments.

- They focus on measuring, coaching, and leveraging cross-cultural competencies in subsequent roles within the organization.

To design a strategic global mobility program and help assignees achieve their learning-driven goals, your organization will need to reframe some key practices. Five practices, in particular, are especially critical to developing cultural agility:

1. Self-assessment

2. Selection

3. Appropriate support practices

4. Performance management

5. Repatriation

Let's look more closely at each of these.

Self-Assessment

Regardless of the type of assignment, accepting an international assignment is a major life decision, one that will affect the lives of employees and their families permanently. Many who accept international assignments have found their lives enriched, and report personal satisfaction in having spent time living and working in another country. However, as we have discussed in this book, international assignments are not right for everyone or every family. Given that families are pulled, roots and all, for the purpose of an international assignment, it is important for professionals to consider all the issues affecting them and their families before relocating to a host country.

Organizations offer employees and their families self-assessment tools with which to explore important personal issues confidentially before making a decision to accept an international assignment. According to Brookfield's recent study of global relocations trends, 25 percent of the organizations surveyed use international assignee self-assessment tools, such as the industry-leading Self-Assessment for Global Endeavors (The SAGE).[9] This rate of usage of self-assessment tools has been steadily increasing each year as the stakes for international effectiveness have become more critical. (See "The Critical First Step" for a brief overview of The SAGE.)

The Critical First Step: The Self-Assessment for Global Endeavors (The SAGE)

The SAGE was developed to help employees decide whether an international assignment is really right for them and their families. The SAGE considers three important areas:

1. Personality characteristics
2. Family and personal life
3. Career and professional development

The SAGE provides an interpretive feedback report. Employees are encouraged to discuss the results, when appropriate, with their spouse, family members, global mobility manager, and sending manager. For more information about The SAGE, please visit www.culturalagility.com.

Jean Phillips and I conducted an experimental research study to assess the effectiveness of international assignment self-assessment tools for employees. Sixty employees who were interested in prospective international assignments were surveyed on their level of self-efficacy (their belief that they "have what it takes") for success during an international assignment and their ability to make a thoroughly informed decision.[10] After they completed this survey, we randomly assigned them into two groups; one group had access to The SAGE, and the other did not. One month later, the two groups were surveyed again, using the same survey as before. The results were clear. The group that took The SAGE had a greater ability to make an informed decision and also had higher self-efficacy for success in the assignment.

Taken together, these results show that self-assessment tools, and The SAGE specifically, play an important role in the strategic global assignment process. First, they give prospective employees a chance to learn, in a nonevaluative way, about their personality characteristics relative to the demands of international assignments. This helps build efficacy for the assignment because employees understand their strengths that will help them succeed. Second, these tools structure a way to foster a discussion with family members and proactively identify solutions regarding what would be needed to foster cross-cultural adjustment and assignment success.

Among demand-driven assignees, these tools can be used to identify and remove any barriers to adjustment. For example, if the self-assessment reveals a less than ideal set of personality characteristics, then additional support practices can be crafted to smooth the adjustment for the duration of the assignment. Among learning-driven assignees, self-assessment can be used to identify if, when, and under what conditions the developmental international assignment should occur.

Selection

Offer the *right* international assignments to the *right* people, and development will occur. Learning-driven assignees with key personality traits, such as openness and extroversion, are more likely to gain cultural agility from the international assignment experience. As discussed in Chapter Five, personality traits are not likely to change with experience; in the case of learning-driven assignees, it is better to select employees who exhibit the key traits. In the case of demand-driven assignees, knowing the various levels of these traits will enable global mobility professionals to target support practices so as to facilitate adjustment.

Offer the right international assignments to the right people, and development will occur.

Consider the following Big Five personality traits and how they affect development and success during international assignments:

1. *Sociability and openness to people*. These characteristics directly affect assignees' ability to initiate contact with others from different cultures. These interactions, as we know, are critical for development.

2. *Tolerance and flexibility*. These characteristics directly affect assignees' ability to develop positive relationships with colleagues from different cultures. Deeper, more meaningful relationships with host nationals will foster more naturally occurring feedback and support.

3. *Emotional strength and self-efficacy*. These characteristics directly affect assignees' ability to feel comfortable in new and unfamiliar situations. Being confident and comfortable in these settings will encourage assignees to seek out cross-cultural experiences. These characteristics also facilitate greater resiliency when an experience is negative, embarrassing, or unsuccessful, making such negative experiences less likely to derail the employee.

4. *Curiosity and openness to experience*. These characteristics directly affect assignees' ability to embrace new cross-cultural experiences and accelerate their learning in the host country.

5. *Reliability and resourcefulness*. These characteristics directly affect assignees' ability to perform well during the cross-cultural experience. Successful assignees will be given increasingly challenging international and cross-cultural roles.

Given the effort and time it takes to develop a pipeline of culturally agile professionals, it is important to select for these characteristics, especially when selecting those international assignees who will be in roles requiring a significant amount of collaboration with host-country nationals. Personality can be evaluated by tests, a structured interview, or direct observations of behaviors. The box "Assessing Extroversion" provides an example of a structured interview protocol and behaviorally

Assessing Extroversion: Sample Interview Protocol

Instructions: This interview protocol directly assesses the Big Five personality characteristics. [The sample provided here assesses the dimension of extroversion.] In this structured interview protocol, there are some suggested questions for each personality characteristic. There are probably more questions than you will be able to use in a typical interview. Select or draft questions most appropriate for your candidate's or interviewee's level and target position. It is most important to standardize the questions within a target group (for example, new hires, high-potential leaders) at various stages in your talent pipeline.

Each personality characteristic has a behaviorally anchored rating scale (BARS) listing behaviors as examples that would justify a high score (5), a low score (1), and so on. *The listed behaviors are only examples.* You may find that no one example perfectly fits the individual you are assessing. It is up to you to judge where the individual falls on the scale after listening to his or her responses. *The examples are only there to help you make that judgment.*

Extroversion: Sociability and Openness to People

Definition: Extroverted people enjoy interacting with others and often seek social stimulation. They enjoy meeting people for the first time and are genuinely interested in and open to others.

Sample Interview Questions

1. What is your strategy for building and maintaining relationships with colleagues at work? How do you know whether this approach is effective?

2. Describe a situation where your ability to network in a professional context resulted in a positive outcome. What did you do to network professionally, and what was the outcome?

3. If given the choice, would you rather work on an individual project or a team project? Please explain your preference.

4. If I asked your colleagues to describe your level of extroversion or openness to people, what would they say? What would they describe in order to justify their answer?

Rating Scale for Sociability and Openness to People (Extroversion)

	1 Poor	2 Fair	3 Good	4 Very Good	5 Excellent
Behavioral Examples	*Rarely* engages others in conversation; *rarely* is the first to introduce self; more often takes a passive approach to meeting others, *OR* avoids meeting new people; demonstrates *little* effort to make others feel welcome and comfortable.	Is *minimally* proactive in engaging others in conversation; *rarely* the first to introduce self; more often takes a passive approach to meeting others; discusses *few minimally* effective strategies for making others feel welcome and comfortable (many strategies may be vague or ineffective).	Is *somewhat* proactive in engaging others in conversation; is *sometimes* the first to introduce self, but more often takes a passive approach to meeting others; discusses a *few moderately* effective strategies for making others feel welcome and comfortable (but some strategies may be vague or ineffective).	Is *often* proactive in engaging others in conversation; is generally the first to introduce self; discusses generally effective strategies for making others feel welcome and comfortable.	Is proactive in engaging others in conversation; is the first to introduce self; easily discusses several effective strategies for making others feel welcome and comfortable.
	Avoids or clearly dislikes working in teams; prefers to work independently; lets others take the lead in group projects and only does what is assigned to him or her by others; shows *minimal* effort to encourage others to participate to the extent that his or her behavior may actually discourage others from contributing.	Conveys *minimal* enthusiasm for working with others and generally prefers to work independently; demonstrates *minimal* effort in taking an active role when working in teams (e.g., vocalizes ideas, helps solidify plans), but will *often* let others take the lead; shows *minimal* effort to encourage others to participate (i.e., draws out quieter members of the team).	Conveys *some* enthusiasm for working with others; demonstrates *some* effort in taking an active role when working in teams (e.g., vocalizes ideas, helps solidify plans), but also lets others take the lead at times; shows *some* effort to encourage others to participate (i.e., draws out quieter members of the team).	Conveys *much* enthusiasm for working with others; generally takes an active role when working in teams (e.g., vocalizes ideas, helps solidify plans), *but may* also let others take the lead at times; *often* encourages others to participate (i.e., draws out quieter members of the team).	Conveys enthusiasm for working with others; takes an active role when working in teams (e.g., vocalizes ideas, helps solidify plans); knows how to effectively encourage others to participate (i.e., draws out quieter members of the team).

(Continued)

Rating Scale for Sociability and Openness to People (Extroversion) (Continued)

	1 Poor	2 Fair	3 Good	4 Very Good	5 Excellent
Behavioral Examples	Expresses *minimal* interest in maintaining connections with others and may even avoid relationships with peers; generally does not make an effort to maintain relationships with others; interaction style is generally unapproachable and discourages conversation with others.	Expresses *minimal* interest in maintaining connections with others; describes a *few minimally* effective methods for maintaining relationships with others, but strategies are not always proactive or effective; makes *minimal* effort to remain approachable (may welcome conversation and has an open-door policy with *select* colleagues).	Expresses *some* interest in maintaining connections with others; describes a *few moderately* effective methods for maintaining relationships with others, but strategies are not always proactive or effective; makes *some* effort to remain approachable (*may welcome* conversation and has an open-door policy with *some* colleagues).	Expresses an interest in maintaining connections with others; describes proactive and effective methods for maintaining relationships with others; remains approachable (welcomes conversation and has an open-door policy with *most* colleagues).	Expresses a genuine interest in maintaining connections with others; describes several proactive and effective methods for maintaining relationships with others; remains approachable (welcomes conversation and has an open-door policy).

anchored rating scales (BARS) for one of the five personality characteristics, extroversion (focusing on sociability and openness to people). In the example provided, you can see how the BARS could also be used by managers as a way to rate their observations of prospective international assignment candidates. For more information about the full structured interview and scoring BARS for selecting international assignees, please visit www.culturalagility.com.

Selection for international work starts where other systems stop, in that only those individuals who have a demonstrated competence for the tasks and duties of the job are considered. In essence, international assignment selection attempts to take a group of "qualified individuals" and determine which of these individuals can effectively deal with the challenges inherent in working with people and organizations that may approach work in a very different way. Not everyone with a proven record of professional success in a domestic context for a given job title will have what it takes to be successful in an international context—even doing the same job with the same job title.

It should also be noted that those assignments that are technical in nature, those with very little interaction with host nationals or significant adjustment required to the host country, might not require as much strength in these personality characteristics. For example, if your international assignees will not be interacting with host nationals, then extroversion might be somewhat less important. For most organizations, however, this is unlikely to be the case. Almost all international assignees will have necessary interactions with host nationals and will need to adjust to living and working in the host countries. In fact, Stefan Mol, Marise Born, Madde Willemsen, and Henk Van Der Molen conducted a large-scale meta-analysis (a study that combined the results of thirty studies) examining over four thousand international assignees and found that personality characteristics were predictive of international assignees' job performance.[11] Clearly, it is safe to say that most international assignments will require these most critical personality traits.

If you are in doubt, I recommend conducting a validation study for the personality tests you plan to use. You should conduct this research under the guidance of HR professionals or industrial and organizational psychologists who understand the technical aspects of conducting validation studies. In brief, they would likely conduct a concurrent validation study by assessing your current international assignees for their personality characteristics and relating those scores with their performance on the global components of their jobs. As with all employment testing, it is important to ensure that the tests you are using meet accepted scientific standards of reliability (measuring what they should be measuring and relatively free of measurement error) and validity (that is, appropriate inferences can be made from the test to job performance).

In international assignee selection, the most critical stage is selecting candidates for the personality characteristics needed for adjustment to living in the host country, performance while working in the host country, and, most important for this book, accelerated development of cultural agility from cross-cultural experiences. The Selection Test for

Selection Test for International Assignees (STIA)

The STIA assesses the most critical personality traits relating to development, cross-cultural adjustment, and performance during international assignments:

- Sociability

- Openness to people

- Tolerance

- Flexibility

- Emotional strength

- Self-efficacy

- Curiosity

- Openness to experience

- Reliability

- Resourcefulness

If assignments are learning driven, the STIA can identify candidates who do not have the requisite personality traits to develop cross-cultural competencies. If assignments are demand driven, the STIA will help identify the support that can be offered in the host country to foster task success, as needed and where practical.

For more information about the STIA, please visit www.culturalagility.com.

International Assignees (see box) is one recommended instrument that may help organizations avoid costly mistakes in selecting international assignees or failing to provide assignees with the support they need to succeed.

In concluding this discussion of selection, I summarize four best practices that are used in the most effective international assignment selection systems. These high-value-added practices build on each other and begin before assignments even become available or need to be filled. Although much of this material has been mentioned in previous sections, it is important to highlight the practices in the context of selecting for international assignments. Ignoring these steps can result in organizations' coming up short without enough available candidates in the talent pipeline when the need arises to fill international assignments.

Offer a Self-Assessment Tool for Decision Making   Start the selection process well in advance of international assignments' becoming available. Offer a private and confidential self-assessment decision-making tool (for example, The SAGE) to all or a targeted group of employees, giving employees and their families the chance to consider a prospective international assignment before one becomes available. Ignoring this step often leaves organizations with their most desired candidates refusing the assignment for family or other personal reasons.

Create a Database   A database of candidates can be created through self-assessment and self-nomination (possibly combined with managers' nominations). The database can also include information about individuals' technical skills, experience, countries of interest, languages spoken, time of availability, and the like. Ignoring this step will often result in few, if any, options for candidates. Ideally, the database is robust enough to have more than one candidate from which to choose for each international assignment.

Select for Technical Skills and Experience   Once a database is created, it can be used to screen for technical skills and experiences to create a short list of candidates. These candidates would be prescreened on the technical skills needed to successfully accomplish the international assignments' task goals. Those on the short list would also fit with your organization's succession plan, when relevant.

Select for Personality Characteristics   You should now look at the short list of candidates who match the technical and experiential needs for the assignment and assess these candidates for the appropriate personality characteristics (using, for example, observation, interview, and testing). If assignments are learning driven, screen out candidates who do not have the requisite traits for development of cross-cultural competencies. If assignments are demand driven, identify the support that can be offered in the host country to foster task success, as needed and where practical.

Appropriate Support Practices

In August 1996, fifty-seven-year-old Japanese native Mamoru Konno, the president of Sanyo Video Component Corporation in Tijuana, Mexico, was kidnapped after attending a baseball game. It is suggested that Konno became a target because he was too "predictable in his actions, particularly when attending ballgames."[12] Sanyo paid the $2 million in ransom, and Konno was released unharmed. Not all such incidents have happy endings. On November 12, 1997, four American auditors working in Pakistan for Union Texas Petroleum were killed by armed gunmen as they traveled their typical morning route.[13] Experts suggest that these men might have been saved had they varied their route, time of travel, and so on. Paul Johnson, an American working for Lockheed Martin, was also abducted and killed in Saudi Arabia. A senior U.S. State Department official commented that "Johnson lived away from the heavily fortified expatriate compounds," suggesting that Johnson might have been saved had he lived (and remained) within the gated expatriate community provided by his organization.[14]

Without question, organizations should be deeply involved in protecting the safety and security of their international assignees. When there are credible risks in the host countries, most organizations do, in fact, take tremendous tangible precautions (providing armed guards, drivers, gated accommodations, and so on). The risky alternative is not an option. Compared to demand-driven assignments that are generally location bound, learning-driven assignments can, in many organizations, occur almost anywhere. I strongly recommend that you offer learning-driven developmental assignments in host-country locations where armed guards and gated compound environments are not the norm for international assignees. By necessary design, these safety practices will limit interactions with host nationals.

Safety-related practices are among the most extreme examples of the possible support offered to international assignees. For decades, global mobility professionals and managers have been mitigating the maladjustment risks and facilitating smooth relocation to the host country by crafting support practices for international assignees, their spouses, children, and pets. As noted elsewhere, these support practices and destination services are designed to reduce the challenges of the relocation by smoothing the lifestyle transitions that the international assignee will experience. The support practices have become quite sophisticated: finding comparable accommodations in an expatriate community with fellow compatriots as neighbors, offering memberships to international clubs to facilitate social support and friendships among international assignees, providing market-basket pay differentials for international assignees to purchase their favorite home-country foods in the host country (usually accompanied by directions on where to find them), finding international schools for children (where their children's first language is spoken), and the like.

Whereas support practices are certainly appropriate for those with demand-driven assignment goals, they need to be designed more cautiously for those assignees with learning-driven assignment goals. Unwittingly, some support practices designed to facilitate adjustment have impeded the fulfillment of learning-driven goals. For international assignments with learning-driven goals, support practices should not wring the experience dry of authentic cross-cultural interactions with host nationals in the nonwork context (for example, neighborhoods, clubs, and associations). To facilitate development, offer support practices more judiciously when they impede meaningful interactions with host nationals—for example, possibly avoiding compatriot neighborhoods or memberships in social clubs designed for international assignees. To facilitate adjustment, offer support practices more liberally when they do not impede possible opportunities for meaningful host national interactions. It is also appropriate to offer support for accompanying family members of international assignees (for example, career assistance for the spouse, education assistance for children, a driver who knows the local streets and traffic patterns). Please read "Rule Number One Is to Support the Family" for more information about these important support practices.

Rule Number One Is to Support the Family

International assignees' lives are enmeshed with those of their partners, children, parents, and other loved ones. Partners and children, who usually accompany them to the host country, have their lives disrupted for the sake of the assignee's job. Family members' adjustment has been found to spill over and affect international assignees' performance.* For this reason, it behooves companies to support not only the individual worker but also his or her family as they make a cross-cultural adjustment. Brookfield's survey of global relocation trends provides a list of support practices that employers offer to family members, including**

- Cross-cultural training for the entire family: 49 percent offer

- Language training for spouses: 75 percent offer

- Education or training assistance for spouse: 32 percent offer

- Employment search assistance for spouse: 32 percent offer

- Sponsored work permits for spouse: 32 percent offer

- Career planning assistance for spouse: 30 percent offer

- Assistance with elderly family members: 6 percent offer

*Paula M. Caligiuri, MaryAnne Hyland, Aparna Joshi, and Allon Bross, "A Theoretical Framework for Examining the Relationship Between Family Adjustment and Expatriate Adjustment to Working in the Host Country," *Journal of Applied Psychology* 83, no. 4 (1998): 598–614.

**Brookfield Global Relocation Services, *Global Relocation Trends: 2011 Survey Report* (Woodridge, IL: Brookfield, 2011).

Some support practices fulfill a dual purpose in helping improve performance in both demand-driven and learning-driven assignments. Cross-cultural training, language training, and cultural coaching, as described in detail in Chapter Six, positively influence assignees' performance. Our research found that when offering cross-cultural and language training to international assignees, it is best to offer predeparture orientation (most often, Web based) on the basics of culture and on the practical issues expatriates might encounter from day one, such as safety, currency, travel, and etiquette. This training should be followed by in-country cross-cultural training or cultural coaching once the international assignees are in their host country and really "feeling" the differences.

Performance Management

The assignment's performance dimensions, whether demand driven, learning driven, or both, should determine the type of performance assessment needed. Identifying performance goals prior to an assignment is the prerequisite, a critical first step. At this stage, it is necessary for the key stakeholders—for example, the sending and receiving managers, the assignee, and the head of the rotational program or business unit—to reach agreement as to these goals for the given international assignment. There are likely to be different stakeholders for different assignments or groups of assignments, each of whom will have a somewhat different view of what should be accomplished and developed.

Anyone who has ever tried to gain this stakeholder agreement is smiling right now at the challenge inherent in my recommendation. Unless your organization has a history of aligning international assignees' performance goals across stakeholders, you might be surprised to see a lack of agreement among them, especially at first. This is a challenging step. Challenging, but not impossible, and the task is becoming easier as talent management programs have become more globally integrated in many organizations.

Stakeholder Alignment of International Assignees' Performance Goals

Instructions: At the point when an employee is identified for an international assignment, use this exercise to ensure alignment of performance goals and agreement on how they will be measured. Each key stakeholder in the international assignment (for example, the employee, sending manager, receiving manager, and talent management director) should complete this exercise. Ask each stakeholder to identify performance goals, the behavioral or observable indices of them, resources needed to achieve them, and the most appropriate rater or raters of each key goal. After the exercise is completed, have a goal alignment meeting. Discuss and agree on each category.

Top Three Performance Goals	Behavioral or Observable Indicators of Whether This Goal Is Achieved	Resources Needed to Achieve This Goal	Most Appropriate Rater or Raters of This Goal
1			
2			
3			
Top Three Development Goals (if relevant)			
1			
2			
3			

See "Stakeholder Alignment of International Assignees' Performance Goals" for an approach to help stakeholders identify performance goals and their behavioral indices, resources needed to achieve them, and who the most appropriate raters would be for each key goal.

Different Performance Goals   With respect to measuring against demand-driven performance goals, it is important to decide on the lens through which international assignees' performance should be evaluated. Within demand-driven goals, some assignees (typically those whose assignments are need-driven or technical) have more tasks involving cultural minimization. They are expected to become tacit transmitters of the corporate culture, upholding corporate norms for behaviors (for example, quality assurance, safety). Other international assignees with demand-driven goals are expected to adapt to the norms of the host country (for example, sales, marketing). Likewise, an international assignee's demand-driven performance might be evaluated differently depending on whether performance is being evaluated by a host-country manager or a home-country manager. (Cultural differences might change the subjective interpretation of the organization's performance indicators.)

With respect to measuring performance on learning-driven goals, organizations commonly will identify given international assignments as "developmental" without a structured method for evaluating whether developmental goals have been met. More often, their performance on learning-driven goals is *inferred* based on their performance on demand-driven goals. It is important to have clarity on just what it is that learning-driven international assignees are being asked to gain—whether cross-cultural competencies (for example, tolerance of ambiguity) or international business skills (language fluency, an understanding of the host national market). The box "Assessing Cross-Cultural Competencies" offers a sample performance measurement for assessing competencies as desirable learning-driven goals for international assignees to develop.

Different Raters   Brookfield's study found that 45 percent of international assignees are rated by host-country managers, whereas 9 percent are rated by home-country managers; 26 percent are rated by both.[15] In a research study, David Day and I found that international assignees' performance ratings are affected by the nationality of the supervisor making the rating, especially when the dimensions are more subjective.[16] Subjective performance dimensions can be culturally bound and might lack conceptual equivalence. For example, Asian managers might emphasize cooperation and teamwork when rating the performance dimension "leadership," whereas American managers might emphasize assertiveness and independence when evaluating the same dimension. Thus the same manager may be rated as highly effective on a leadership dimension by the host-country manager, but highly ineffective by the manager in the home country. This is one example of a key strategic decision: whether a company-wide or country-specific set of metrics and standards will be used. To facilitate making this decision, refer to "Stakeholder Alignment of International Assignees' Performance Goals" (on previous page), which encourages you to identify the behavioral indices and most appropriate raters for each key goal.

Assessing Cross-Cultural Competencies: An Example of a Performance Assessment for International Assignees

If international assignees are expected to develop cross-cultural competencies as part of their performance goals, then their development of those competencies should be assessed and coached. You should select the cross-cultural competencies most relevant for your organization, your business unit, the assignment, and so on. [This performance assessment is a sample for three of the twelve cross-cultural competencies.] For more information about the full performance assessment, or the 360° version of this assessment, please visit www.culturalagility.com.

Instructions for Evaluating the Three Cross-Cultural Competencies Affecting Responses: Consider the extent to which this international assignee has bridged the home- and host-country locations, keeping in mind that there are times when holding a standard or cultural minimization is needed, when adaptation to the host-country approach is needed, and when compromise or integration is needed. The key point of evaluation is whether the international assignee, in your opinion, adopts the correct approach in given professional situations. Use the following scale to rate [*Name*] on his or her behavioral responses during this international assignment. Add behavioral examples to justify your ratings of this international assignee.

Competency	Always Inappropriate	Usually Inappropriate	Sometimes Appropriate	Usually Appropriate	Always Appropriate
Cultural Minimization					
Cultural Adaptation					
Cultural Integration					
Comments to Justify Ratings:					

Repatriation

Thus far, this chapter has been dedicated to understanding the best way to manage international assignments for developmental purposes. However, a successfully completed international assignment is not the end of the story: assignees eventually come home. It is important to realize that using international assignments as a method to develop cultural agility will be effective only if this homecoming, or *repatriation*, is also managed well. If it is not, the organization risks losing the professionals in whom it has invested the cost and energy of the international assignment.

On the face of it, the retention of repatriates might not seem to be a concern, given that the annual attrition rate of repatriates is at 8 percent, the same attrition rate for employees generally across organizations.[17] For most organizations, however, an 8 percent attrition rate is high, given that the organization has spent valuable resources in selecting, training, and supporting international assignees with the goal of, in turn, competitively benefiting from their increased cultural agility. Thus repatriate retention, and the methods to increase repatriate retention, are paramount when building the pipeline of culturally agile professionals.

Among the repatriates who leave their organizations, roughly one-third of them leave within one year after repatriation.[18] The way in which your organization manages your repatriates' careers is critical for retention. Maria Kraimer, Margaret Shaffer, and Mark Bolino conducted a study with recently returned repatriates and found that lower levels of organizational career support led to greater turnover intentions.[19] Using the four goal categories (technical, functional, developmental, and strategic) that were listed in Figure 8.1, they found that repatriates who had been on strategic or developmental (learning-driven) assignments were more likely to advance with their organizations upon repatriation, compared to those on functional or technical (demand-driven) assignments. On the surface, this might make sense: those who were sent to develop career-enhancing cross-cultural competencies were rewarded for gaining them. Unfortunately, this is not the case. This study found no relationship between the acquisition of cultural skills and subsequent career advancement. The difference in attrition was related to career advancement opportunities, and there were more opportunities for career advancement among those in learning-driven assignments.

The picture is even more fine-grained. Although strategic and developmental repatriates both generally have their next move preplanned as a part of a talent management system, they have different levels of likely attrition. Strategic executive assignees are managed in the context of their cultural skills. For example, a product marketing leader might move from running a smaller regional market to a larger one. A finance leader might move from working in a stable, mature market to a high-growth market in a developing country. An operations leader might move from running the functional area in a region or country to a globally integrated role within headquarters upon repatriation. In the case of these high-level strategic assignees, their careers are planned in such a way that their cross-cultural skills are rewarded and utilized with subsequent career advancement. Their cross-cultural competencies were not just desirable but necessary for their subsequent roles within the organization's succession plan, a trend that has been found in companies headquartered in multiple countries. As a part of a five-person and five-country research team, colleagues and I conducted a study of over sixteen hundred international assignees to examine their career-related perceptions.[20] A dive into the data found that senior strategic assignees had the fewest concerns regarding their careers after repatriation, and reported the lowest intention of leaving their current employer to work for another organization.

Developmental assignees, usually more junior and often part of a rotational program, have a somewhat different pattern. Like strategic assignees, the developmental assignees have a desirable gain in cross-cultural competencies, but, unlike those of strategic assignees, those competencies might not be immediately necessary for their subsequent rotation. In their case, a problem for retention is that organizations are not using (or, in some cases, not even acknowledging) the assignees' gains in their cross-cultural competencies. Technical and functional (demand-driven) assignees have the same retention concern, but for a somewhat different reason. Unlike those of their learning-driven counterparts, their careers are being managed based on their functional, not cross-cultural, competencies. The cross-cultural competencies they have gained during an international assignment are oftentimes disregarded upon repatriation. In our five-country study, both they and the developmental assignees reported the highest intentions to leave the organization upon repatriation.[21]

This is where the problem lies. Whether their assignment was intended to be learning driven or not, repatriates might have gained (or believe they have gained) cross-cultural competencies during their international assignments. If they have that belief (whether justified or not), they will, quite understandably, expect to be recognized, rewarded, and promoted accordingly. Organizations that do not appropriately acknowledge the experience and that underutilize (or fully ignore) the newly developed cross-cultural competencies are at risk for higher repatriate attrition.

Some organizations view repatriation attrition as a competitive risk: they invest in the development of cross-cultural competencies, only to have another organization—or, even worse, a direct competitor— realize the human capital gain.

Some organizations view repatriation attrition as a competitive risk: they invest in the development of cross-cultural competencies, only to have another organization—or, even worse, a direct competitor— realize the human capital gain from their investment. Other organizations view repatriation attrition as generally expected turnover, a cost of doing business. From this human capital perspective, they believe that some repatriates' skills are not needed beyond the assignment. Most companies align more closely with the former view. Organizations holding the latter view tend to hire contractors or deploy employees who accept international assignments as their last position before retirement. These contractors and employees are able to manage their expectations accordingly; neither expect to stay with the organization upon repatriation.

Over the past decade, Mila Lazarova and I have studied the practices designed to lower unwanted repatriate attrition.[22] Here are five recommendations you should consider for your organization:

1. *Manage expectations.* As discussed in the Performance Management section of this chapter, it is important for stakeholders to agree on the performance goals for the assignment. Too often, employees are sent the message, "This experience is a developmental opportunity" when, in fact, they are on technical or functional assignments. They expect to be recognized and rewarded for their developed or honed cross-cultural competencies and are disappointed when they are not. At a minimum, do not raise your employees' expectations. If there are to be "no promises" of a global role that will utilize cross-cultural competencies, it is appropriate to manage this expectation prior to the start of the assignment.

2. *Structure networking opportunities.* More than one-third of organizations rely on informal networking to find suitable positions for their international assignees upon repatriation. You can help your international assignees create a robust informal network by structuring ways for them to stay professionally connected within the organization, business unit, or department while on their international assignments (especially the unit to which they plan to return). For example, you can structure mentoring programs for international assignees in which the mentors are asked to look out for suitable next opportunities for their mentees. When it is practical to do so, encourage your international assignees to schedule business trips to coincide with major meetings and important events where networking can occur easily.

3. *Provide career counseling.* Almost all organizations have discussions with their international assignees regarding their next steps upon repatriation. The question is when those discussions should occur. Roughly 20 percent of organizations have the career discussion before the international assignees leave for the assignment, and almost half wait until the assignees are less than six months away from repatriation.[23] There really should be a combination. It is important from the onset that the international assignees take some ownership for their careers and agree to stay networked. Depending on the organization, career planning discussions should be more formal and integrated into performance management sessions, just as they would for other professionals in the organization.

4. *Send credible messages.* If employees regularly observe their repatriated colleagues struggling to find appropriate placements in the organization after their assignment, then your organization's actions will speak much louder than its words regarding the extent to which international experience is valued. To reinforce credible messages regarding the value of international experience for one's career, it is important for senior leaders in the organization to have international experience and for key promotions to be awarded as a result of international assignment experience. These send a strong message about company values.

5. *Match goal fulfillment and rewards.* Be certain to reward the articulated performance goals. When assignments are demand driven, measure and reward the accomplishment of the tasks. When assignments are learning driven, reward the acquisition of cross-cultural competencies, in addition to the completion of tasks. Your organization will be sending the wrong message if it awards promotions to learning-driven expatriates who are no more culturally agile than they were before the assignment.

TAKE ACTION

Based on information presented in Chapter Eight, the following is a list of specific actions you can take to make your organization's international assignments more developmental and more successful in building cultural agility.

- Offer a private and confidential self-assessment tool well in advance of employees' needing to make a decision about a possible international assignment. This tool can help employees determine whether an international assignment is really right for them and their families, and can be used in conjunction with a self-nomination process and as a way to tailor support practices for the assignees.

- Select for personality traits. Especially for learning-driven (that is, developmental and strategic) international assignees, assess candidates for the personality characteristics discussed in this chapter. Use tests, a structured interview, direct observations of behaviors—or, ideally, all three.

- Follow the guidelines in this chapter to tailor the level of support to the developmental nature of the assignment. For learning-driven assignments, increase support practices that foster learning (for example, cross-cultural training) and decrease support practices that inhibit learning (for example, memberships to international clubs).

- Align performance management systems. Before the start of an international assignment, be certain that all key stakeholders have agreed on the goals of the assignment. Also align behavioral indicators and identify who will be evaluating performance for each of the key goals of the assignment.

- Leverage competencies gained during repatriation by improving retention. Increase repatriate retention by affording better networking opportunities, offering career counseling, managing expectations, and the like. Measure and manage these practices by tracking your organization's repatriate retention rate and adjusting retention practices as needed.

PART

5

CONCLUSION: LEADERSHIP AND ORGANIZATIONAL FACTORS

Reflect for a moment on what you have read in this book so far. We have covered a lot of ground, that's for sure. If you have put all of the recommendations in place, you should have the best possible talent ready to fill your pipeline. These individuals were attracted to your organization and applied to work there. The best of the best received your offer and happily accepted it, excited about the global growth opportunities with your organization. Thanks to your efforts, your organization now has the best possible learning system for them—cross-cultural training, developmental experiences, and international assignments—to build their cultural agility.

Does this sound like a desirable goal—or a wild fantasy? Is your organization ready for all this? Will your corporate culture and HR systems be able to sustain these practices? If not, you need to start somewhere—and probably not by plunging into the deep end of the pool. You will need to implement these practices to build cultural agility at the level and pace that is right for your organization. Your last and final step is to assess your organizational readiness—this is stepping into the wading pool for some and taking the high dive for others.

Here in the conclusion of the book, Chapter Nine, I will describe the ways in which leadership, organizational culture, and HR systems can be leveraged to create and sustain a pipeline of culturally agile professionals.

CHAPTER

9

MANAGING AND LEADING TO BUILD CULTURAL AGILITY IN THE WORKFORCE

Now based in Singapore, American-born Randall Bradford is currently on his *sixth* international assignment. Having worked nearly nineteen years for Merck & Co., a leading global health care company, and now three years for the world's largest medical technology company, Medtronic, Randall has had—and continues to have—an impressive international career. In addition to his current international assignment, Randall and his family have lived in Hong Kong, Germany, Austria, Norway, and France. He has also spent significant time working in the United Kingdom, Italy, Spain, Switzerland, Sweden, Denmark, Finland, Turkey, Africa (North, South, and Sub-Saharan), Pakistan, Egypt, Saudi Arabia, Cyprus, Lebanon, the United Arab Emirates, Japan, China, India, Korea, Thailand, Australia, Brazil, and Mexico. He speaks, reads, and writes four languages (English, German, Norwegian, and French).

In an excellent role for such a skilled culturally agile professional, Randall is currently responsible for leading the HR function for all of Medtronic's geography outside the United States (over one hundred developed and emerging markets). Randall leads his multicultural team of more than two hundred HR professionals from many countries around the world.

When Randall was in his twenties, he was offered sage advice about the important role of cultural and functional diversity in teams in encouraging knowledge creation and innovation. As a recent university graduate who had already lived internationally, Randall understood the advice deeply and was able to apply it inwardly, sharing that "the diversity of perspectives—which is so helpful for knowledge creation in teams— is also the key to one's own leadership development." For more than twenty years, this perspective has propelled Randall to seek out—and excel in—international assignments and progressively more challenging global leadership roles.

With each international assignment, Randall and his family have avoided expatriate enclaves, preferring to live in host national neighborhoods. True to this perspective, Randall and his wife, Melissa, have sent their children either to local host national schools or to international schools with strong concentrations of host national students, and provided them with additional language training to support their educational success. Between local schools and local neighborhoods, Randall has had many opportunities to grow his circle of host national friends along with his language and cultural skills. He underscores that "language is critical because it is the key to integration in the host community," adding that "it is also important to have a comfortable environment where you can practice the language and culture." Randall highlights how this is critical for developing cultural agility, stating that "it's a humbling experience making your way up the learning curve—you make a lot of mistakes and necessarily show your vulnerabilities, which is especially challenging when you're in a senior leadership role. Still, the benefits are worth all the discomfort, and it is a lot easier to make mistakes around host national friends."

Randall also effectively uses his business travel for professional development. Traveling extensively for his job, he asks his host national colleagues in advance of a planned trip to "build some time into the agenda—say, a morning or an afternoon" for his colleagues to share something about their culture. "I am not looking for a visit to a tourist site," he explains, but "rather, something that visitors don't often see but would help me understand the culture better." Without question, being intellectually curious and having a great respect for the hosts' cultures is a best practice for all international business travelers.

On a business trip in Saudi Arabia one summer, with the temperature soaring above 120°F (approximately 50°C), Randall asked a colleague (a Pakistani national who was working in Saudi Arabia) what the local Saudis do to escape the summer heat. The colleague gave an unexpected answer: they go to the mall to enjoy the air conditioning, he said, adding that his wife was probably there today. For a local experience (and to escape the heat), Randall and his colleague went to the mall to walk and talk. As the colleague predicted, they did run into his wife, who was there with a friend, enjoying a climate-controlled respite from the heat. As would be appropriate in this public place, both women were fully covered in long black *abayas*. When the colleague introduced his wife (also Pakistani and accustomed to greeting Westerners) to Randall, she extended her hand for a handshake. Next, Randall naturally extended his hand to the wife's friend—but she immediately jumped back, looking over her shoulder, fearing the *mutaween*, the Saudi religious police, who would view this interaction as a serious offense.

Although it was only a brief encounter, the woman's forceful reaction provided Randall with a powerful business lesson. "That moment taught me to never underestimate the depth of religious conviction when working in Saudi Arabia," Randall recalled. This lesson he later applied when staffing two highly qualified Saudi women for positions with Medtronic to interface with the company's clients in the Saudi government's health care facilities (some of the few locations where women were allowed to work). It took three years to hire these women legally, but "with time—and an abundance of sensitivity to religious convictions—we hired our first two Saudi female colleagues, who are both excellent."

As a senior executive, Randall can lead by example thanks to his years of immersing himself in, and excelling in, cross-cultural professional experiences. Organizations striving to build cultural agility into their talent pipeline will benefit from having more culturally agile leaders like Randall on board. These leaders will have a more intuitive sense for which candidates should be selected and which experiences they should be offered to build their cultural agility.

In addition to culturally agile leadership, there are other organizational factors that will also accelerate the creation of a culturally agile workforce. We will talk about them in this concluding chapter. The suggestions in this book (however interesting) are valuable only when they can be adapted for use in your organization and if, when implemented, they can help your organization become more globally competitive. In this chapter we focus on the implementation of the recommended practices and what they mean for you as you manage and lead to build a culturally agile workforce. We will target three levels: the organization's readiness for cultural agility practices, the leadership practices to foster cultural agility, and HR's role in building a culturally agile workforce.

YOUR ORGANIZATION'S READINESS FOR CULTURAL AGILITY PRACTICES

Cultural agility in the workforce will neither be created with a single practice nor disconnected from the reality of the organization. When considering whether your organization can implement cultural agility practices, which ones are most important, and how difficult they will be to implement, you will need to understand where your organization stands in regard to two salient issues. The first is the extent to which your HR and talent management functions are *already* strategically aligned and managed to be consistent with the global goals of the organization. The second is the extent to which cultural agility is a competitive necessity for your organization. Organizations with the most strategic HR and talent management practices *and* the most pressing needs will have the best preconditions to adopt these practices. At the other extreme, organizations with more administrative HR and with no immediate competitive need for a culturally agile workforce will be less likely to adopt these practices.

Strategic Versus Administrative HR Management

We know that it is generally popular for CEOs to describe their talent management practices as being one of their organizations' most critical vehicles for implementing global business growth strategies.[1] However, we also know that not all organizations have strategic talent management practices. Does yours? Ask yourself the following five questions:

1. Do your organization's HR management practices align with the goals of the business? Does your organization know, specifically, how to gain competitive advantage based on the competencies of its key employees in the organization's most critical roles?

2. Is your organization's culture performance driven—motivating and engaging to drive business results?

3. Do your organization's HR management practices, particularly its rewards and recognition programs, align employee behaviors to foster business results?

4. Does your organization have a robust performance management system that takes succession planning, development, and bench strength for key positions very seriously?

5. Does the senior HR leader in your organization report directly to your CEO?

If you answered yes to most of these questions, your organization has a more strategic HR function. This is great news. It will be easier to implement the cultural agility practices recommended in this book. Coming from Medtronic, an organization known for innovative talent management strategies, Randall Bradford knows that building a pipeline of cultural agile professionals will be "a deep conscious effort for the organization." Underscoring the need to integrate practices to build cultural agility into development plans for individuals in key positions, he noted that "companies need to build the development of cultural agility into their talent management systems and not hope that it will happen on their own." Organizations with strategic talent management systems will not leave this critical employee development to chance.

I recommend that you use the topics raised in this book as points of departure to stimulate thought on ways to improve on your organization's already existing talent management system. The book can help guide an assessment of your current practices, and I hope it will spark ideas to integrate some new practices with your current talent management system.

If you answered no to most of the questions here, your organization has a more administrative HR function. Administrative HR is involved in supporting the organization from the perspective of managing payroll, filling open positions, administering employee benefits, developing policies, ensuring legal compliance, planning company events, and the like. In organizations with a more administrative HR function,

"The shareholders want more cultural diversity. Choose a si-man, hai-man, and ja-man to replace three yes-men."

implementing cultural agility practices will need to occur within the context of a broader change management initiative to align talent management with the organization's strategic business goals. If this is your organization's starting point, you might need to invest some resources (for outside consultants, development for current HR managers, or both) to integrate cultural agility practices into a broader strategic talent management initiative.

You should also examine the extent to which your organization values cultural diversity. As the cartoon satirically illustrates, sometimes leaders don't fully appreciate that the organization's future success depends on diverse perspectives. This is a nonstarter. If the senior leaders do not respect, appreciate, and value diverse perspectives, they will not appreciate the practices that enable employees to be effective in cross-cultural situations. We can hope that this is not the case in your organization.

How Important Is Cultural Agility for Your Organization?

We need to recognize that not all organizations are on a burning platform when it comes to global competitiveness. Some organizations have an urgent competitive need

Organizations are more motivated to adopt these practices because of their urgent competitive demand for a culturally agile workforce to respond to key business challenges.

for global business growth, greater international market share, and a more globally integrated supply chain. These organizations are more motivated to adopt these practices because of their urgent competitive demand for a culturally agile workforce to respond to key business challenges. Is yours one of these? Think about the following five questions:

1. Does your organization's growth and expansion strategy include foreign markets?

2. Is there more international integration of your organization's supply chain or service providers?

3. Is the number of foreign employees in subsidiaries growing at a faster rate than the number of domestic employees?

4. Is your organization experiencing increasing competition from foreign organizations?

5. Is your organization's foreign market share growing faster than its domestic market? Are your goods or services being sold in a greater number of foreign markets compared to past years?

If you answered yes to most of these questions, your organization has a more critical need for cultural agility practices. These practices will be viewed as being consistent with business necessity and crucial for your organization's strategic growth. If you are responsible for implementing these cultural agility practices, you will likely have a sense of strategic urgency, greater support from senior leadership, the attention from line managers, and more tangible resources (for example, headcount, expert support, technology). Their implementation will not be put on the back burner because they are too important for the future of your organization. The spotlight will be on.

If you answered no to most of the questions here, then your organization has a less urgent need for cultural agility practices—at least for now. Organizations with a less critical need are still growing their domestic market share and do not yet feel competitive pressure to become more global. The advantage for such organizations is that they can get an early start and make long-term plans to build cultural agility in their workforce. If you would like to initiate a long-term cultural agility plan, you might need to garner some support from the business units with the greatest global activity. For example, if your organization has started exporting some products, you might suggest cross-cultural training for those professionals who will be working with global customers, probably business travelers or international assignees. Keep your ear to the ground for the early rumblings of global expansion and growth. If the need starts to intensify, you will be well positioned to encourage your organization to build cultural agility in the workforce so that the talent is ready for the global growth spurt.

LEADERSHIP PRACTICES TO FOSTER A CULTURALLY AGILE ORGANIZATIONAL CULTURE

Carlos Ghosn is, without question, one of the world's most respected CEOs.[2] Running two companies concurrently and successfully, Ghosn is at the helm of both the Japanese automaker Nissan (CEO since 2001) and French automaker Renault (since 2005). Ghosn has a Brazilian and French dual citizenship and a strong cultural connection to Lebanon. His parents immigrated to Brazil from Lebanon before he was born, and Ghosn spent ten years living in Lebanon in his youth.

As a Brazilian-Lebanese-Frenchman running a Japanese-French alliance (along with their separate companies, Nissan and Renault) who demonstrates every cross-cultural competency, Ghosn might be the world's most culturally agile professional. As we've discussed earlier in the book, the most culturally agile professionals are able to toggle among cultural minimization, cultural adaptation, and cultural integration. They know when to leverage each response—and knowing how to create the desired response given the cultural context is the key to cultural agility. In an interview for *Fortune* magazine, Ghosn, speaking about his first few years at Nissan in Japan, noted that he was "determined to become assimilated, without sacrificing my individuality or originality. I tried to be transparent to the people around me. Being observant, respectful, and willing to learn helped me overcome most cultural barriers. As an outsider arriving with a somewhat credible track record of performance, I was able to bring in new ideas and challenge the status quo. Results came quickly, skepticism was quieted, and the revival of Nissan justified our actions."[3]

In any setting, great business leaders like Ghosn inspire and motivate behavior. They provide a strategic vision and can articulate the plan for how to win the future. Great leaders can help shift the attitudes and behaviors of the workforce to align with the strategic needs of the organization. You and the entire team of your organization's leaders can have a powerful influence over the extent to which cultural agility is fostered in the workforce. As a management team, consider the following visible signs that will reinforce its importance:

- As leaders, are you measuring cultural agility and rewarding it through career advancement and promotions?

- As leaders, are you investing your organization's resources to build culturally agile talent?

- Do you lead by example, demonstrating the cross-cultural competencies of culturally agile professionals?

The following sections provide specific examples of ways leaders can signal to the workforce the importance of cultural agility.

Measure and Reward Cultural Agility

"What gets measured gets managed" is a well-known maxim often attributed to management guru Peter Drucker. The quotation holds sage advice, especially for organizations trying to move the needle on the cultural agility within their workforces. Cultural agility should be an important enough goal to be both measured and rewarded in performance management systems. Your organization needs to *measure* the extent to which cross-cultural experiences are developmental and the extent to which the development of cross-cultural competencies has occurred. It must also *reward* those who actively seek out cross-cultural experiences that are truly developmental and who gain cross-cultural competencies.

Measure and Reward Developmental Cross-Cultural Experiences We know that business trips, global project teams, international assignments, and the like *can* build cultural agility when structured with certain developmental qualities in mind. We also know that many of these purported developmental experiences fall short on these key qualities. As part of your development plans, assess key professionals on the experiences they have had throughout the year with respect to the developmental qualities of the experiences. (Return to Chapter Seven for the method to do this.)

Even if the method for assessing developmental qualities (found in Chapter Seven) is used only to start a conversation, it will begin to change the assumptions about experiences and begin the dialogue on *how* cross-cultural competencies are gained. Over time, assessing experiences for developmental properties and having these conversations will change the assumption that all cultural experience is cumulative. Ideally, employees should be rewarded for being proactive in self-initiating more developmental experiences (for example, engaging in peer-level interactions while on business trips or living in host national communities while on international assignments).

Measure and Reward the Acquisition of Cross-Cultural Competencies It will be most important for leaders to break any organizational habits of "anointing" professionals who have accumulated international experience as automatically possessing cross-cultural competencies. This bad habit produces succession plans in which talent is promoted for having cross-cultural competencies when, in fact, they might not exist. Change the assumption by changing the talent management approach to one that measures the acquisition of cross-cultural competencies directly.

Key times to conduct such evaluations are shortly before and shortly after a developmental cross-cultural experience, such as an international assignment, multicultural project, or global executive education program. This intervention is particularly powerful if the assessment is conducted with feedback from cross-national colleagues with whom your employees are working. Similar to receiving feedback on your language skills from a native language speaker, getting feedback from these colleagues can be an eye-opening activity as well as a useful one for identifying associates who deserve to be rewarded for building their cultural agility.

Measuring and rewarding cultural agility can also happen more organically when leaders provide informal support for the acquisition of cross-cultural competencies. Randall Bradford had a nice illustration of this from his own career when he was on an international assignment in Norway for Merck. His manager at the time sent Randall to a three-week intensive immersion program to learn the Norwegian language at the start of his assignment (all the more impressive to Randall, in that his manager had not learned Norwegian himself but understood the value it would bring to Randall and the organization). A few months after this intensive training, Randall was scheduled to make a presentation to his colleagues—in English. At the last minute, the country managing director encouraged Randall to give the presentation in Norwegian. Although he did not feel prepared and ready, Randall nervously gave the presentation in Norwegian as encouraged. Not only did it go much better than expected, but the experience became a positive tipping point for Randall's progression in the language and integration in the Scandinavian culture. The managing director informally rewarded Randall with a congratulatory email copied to more senior leaders in the organization, complimenting his presentation—and his skill with the Norwegian language. Everyone was impressed. Even today, Randall describes his personal standard and threshold for language acquisition as "whether I can give a professional presentation in the host national language."

Invest in Building Culturally Agile Talent

Leaders' decisions regarding the use of organizational resources can send salient messages within their organizations (and to shareholders and other stakeholders) about what is valued. Organizations that value cultural agility will invest in building cross-cultural competencies. They will "put their money where their mouth is" in terms of reinforcing cultural agility. Consider the implementation of these strategies and practices—and the positive message they are sending to your stakeholders regarding your organization's competitive edge in the global arena.

> *Organizations that value cultural agility will invest in building cross-cultural competencies.*

Invest in Experiences   When GlaxoSmithKline's CEO Andrew Witty championed the PULSE Volunteer Partnership (described in Chapter Seven), his support underscored his and the company's values for developing a global perspective and making a difference around the world. In a video interview on the GlaxoSmithKline Web site, Witty introduced the concept of PULSE, saying,

> *The PULSE initiative at GlaxoSmithKline is a really important program for us, this is all about really giving individuals inside GSK the opportunity to make a true contribution to communities in need around the world. And in the process not just help the communities they spend three or six months with but to come back a changed person. To come back somebody with a different worldview, a different view of*

being inside a corporation and to then bring that view to bring that change—and help change—the way this company thinks, to help change this company from the inside out. What PULSE is all about is saying to our employees who are motivated and want to volunteer that we'll give them the opportunity, we'll support their opportunity to go to a community anywhere in the world for three or six months to spend time typically with an NGO and to use their skills. So we don't ask accountants to go build buildings, we ask accountants to go help NGOs with their financial skills; we ask logistic experts to help with their ability to ensure materials can move around the world efficiently. We ask people to apply their skills in a way which add real value for the NGO . . . We can learn from some of the most challenged communities in the world, that actually we can do things a better way, we can be more focused, we can be simpler, we can take away a lot of the complexity that we've acquired over many, many years . . . And for that reason PULSE is one of the things I am most proud about inside GSK, and it's something that we're committed to continuing on an ongoing basis.[4]

Culturally agile organizations will invest in experiences like GlaxoSmithKline's PULSE Volunteer Partnership. They will encourage and continue to fund opportunities to develop meaningful relationships with colleagues from different cultures, such as international corporate volunteerism programs, global conferences, and global rotational programs. They will also maintain investment in learning-driven international assignments, even during periods of cost containment, because they are viewed as valuable for developing critical competencies in the organization.

Invest in Collaboration Although many firms have increased their investment in technology to facilitate the exchange of information electronically, the more culturally agile firms have gone further. They have, for example, invested in cross-cultural training programs for global team collaboration (see more about the Global Teams Tool in Chapter Seven). These organizations have also allocated travel budgets for these geographically distributed team members to meet face-to-face, especially at the onset of cross-border collaborations.

Lead by Example

Effective business leaders who value cultural agility are authentic and lead by example. Anyone working for Nissan or Renault can understand the behaviors of cultural agility by watching Carlos Ghosn in action. Leading by example is critical for creating cultural agility in the workforce. Consider the following leadership behaviors that will help create a culturally agile culture in your organization.

Lead with Cultural Humility Cultural humility is embedded into the leadership styles of the decision makers in culturally agile organizations. They are aware that in every cultural context, "the way that *has worked*" might not be "the way that it works *here*." In the interview with *Fortune* mentioned earlier, Ghosn described how he came in to Nissan as a cultural outsider, needing to turn a struggling organization around. In responding to how he made changes in this difficult situation, Ghosn pointed out that "people who try to impose one system onto another only wind up destroying it. Nissan had to be changed from the inside." It wasn't Ghosn's way that needed to be implemented; rather, what was needed was the right way for Nissan.

Leaders like Ghosn set an example by understanding the limits of their knowledge when it comes to how practices will work within a given cultural context. They make it acceptable and necessary to consider the context in every business decision.

Appreciate Real Cultural Expertise The people to whom leaders turn for advice send a powerful message to the organization. When it comes to seeking advice on cultural contexts, leaders can set a positive example by turning to those who have had the richest experience in a given country or firsthand knowledge of that country—not to those who have logged the most frequent-flier miles or the greatest number of years in expatriate housing. When leaders make so-called internal cultural experts of professionals who don't deserve the implicit title, they reinforce the value of superficial experience. Change this value by respecting and reinforcing those who are true cultural experts in the organization.

Engage in Developmental Cultural Experiences If leaders want to reinforce the value of cultural agility, they will encourage key professionals to have developmental cultural experiences. To make this a credible experience needed for career advancement, however, they themselves should also have such experiences. Examining the career paths of the Fortune 100 American organizations and FTSE 100 British organizations, Elisabeth Marx found that only 30 percent of the CEOs from American organizations have had international experience, compared to nearly 70 percent of the CEOs from the British organizations.[5] Given the United Kingdom's smaller domestic markets, it makes sense that British organizations would have a longer history of rewarding international experience. However, as we've discussed in this book, all international experience is not created equal. Leaders should be encouraged both to champion and to engage in truly developmental cross-cultural experiences, and to communicate the value of their experiences broadly across the organization.

HR'S ROLE IN BUILDING THE CULTURALLY AGILE WORKFORCE

The HR functional areas of recruitment, talent development, and global mobility need to be strategically integrated to develop a pipeline of culturally agile professionals in their organizations. HR professionals from these three functional areas are usually located down the same corridor in most corporate headquarters. When at their best, they work in a complementary way. At their worst, they work in silos with little collaboration. In either case, their functional activities tend to be separated, each affecting the employee at a different point in his or her employment life cycle. If you are not familiar with these different functional areas within HR, here is a broad-brush summary of their general activities:

- *Recruitment.* When new employees are needed, business units generally make their requisitions to staffing or recruiting professionals. These professionals support the business unit by helping source candidates using the employee recruitment and selection techniques that are most appropriate for the skill level needed, field, experience level, and so on. Depending on the organization, recruiting might be involved in on-boarding, campus recruitment, and activities to improve the company's employer image.

- *Talent development.* Working with the business units, talent development provides the structure to evaluate talent, usually through assessment of potential and performance, along with talent developmental and succession planning meetings to place associates in progressively developmental roles. Performance measurement systems are generally integrated with total rewards, and, ideally, strategically aligned learning systems are in place to ensure that the most necessary competencies are being developed.

- *Global mobility.* As described in the previous chapter, global mobility professionals manage the issues related to relocation for international assignments. This function works with candidates for international assignments to ease their transition before, during, and after the assignment. They are involved, either directly or through service providers, with taxes, visas, the movement of their household goods, the enrollment of the assignees' children into international schools, and many other issues.

The most effective way for HR functions to support their organizations in the development of culturally agile professionals is for these three key areas to work together in a more integrated way.

The most effective way for HR functions to support their organizations in the development of culturally agile professionals is for these three key areas to work together in a more integrated way, rather than the complementary way they are likely to be working today. *Recruiting* professionals will need to find those who are (or are likely to become) culturally agile. They will need to attract and select ideal talent who will potentially fill the pipeline of culturally agile professionals in the organization. They might also need to educate and persuade the line managers regarding the value of cross-cultural competencies above and beyond technical skills. Change is never easy, especially for a line manager with an open position requisition and the immediate need for certain technical skills.

If needed, *talent development* can be recruitment's ally in the education and persuasion of line managers, especially when it comes to encouraging them to assess and select talent for the critical immutable personality characteristics described in this book. They need to bring in those candidates who will be most likely to gain cultural agility.

Once employees are selected for the organization, the *talent development* professionals would then need to create the progressive cross-cultural experiences to reinforce cultural understanding and give employees learning systems to help build their cross-cultural competencies. The talent development professionals should provide some structured method for assessing performance from the perspective of cultural agility and work with line managers to identify who will be ready for increasingly more important global roles. At this point, managers might identify the need for international assignments.

In this more integrated approach, *talent development and global mobility professionals would work together* to determine when talent is ready for international assignments. Again, education and persuasion might be needed. Talent development professionals will need to persuade line managers of the importance of employees' readiness and appropriateness for international assignments, above and beyond their technical skills. With the assistance of global mobility, they will need to encourage self-assessment and candidate selection, which takes into account the immutable personality characteristics described in Chapter Eight.

Global mobility professionals have a unique lens through which talent development decisions should be made when the decisions involve international assignments. For example, global mobility professionals know that some of the predictors of international assignee success will not fit neatly into the organization's performance management systems. There are—thankfully!—no boxes to check off indicating the stability of the employee's marriage, the special needs of the employee's spouse or child, or the physical health of the employee's elderly parents. Nevertheless, global mobility professionals know that these are critical factors.

Global mobility professionals also know how to tailor support practices to increase the probability of the desired cross-cultural competencies' being gained. The final benefit of greater strategic integration between global mobility professionals and talent management is that, together, they can provide more accurate estimates of the return on investment (ROI) of international assignments (see box on next page). See "Assessment of Global Mobility Practices for Strategic Alignment" on page 199 for an evaluation that you can conduct with your HR function to assess whether the global mobility and the talent management functions are aligned.

The Case for ROI: The Return on Investment (ROI) of International Assignments

Every few years, the question of the ROI of international assignments surfaces as organizations struggle with the rising costs of their global mobility programs. The ROI issue returns in force during periods of organizational cost containment.

With little attention to the benefit of the assignments for growing cultural agility in the workforce, the debate generally follows a predictable pattern:

1. Senior executives call for the reduction of the number of international assignees, given their high cost.

2. Accounting firms are brought in as consultants to identify savings on tax equalization and other compensation issues.

3. Relocation service providers have their contracts squeezed or cut.

4. Global mobility professionals respond with documentation, reports, and advice on why it is fiscally unwise to break international assignees' leases (and personally unkind to remove children from their international schools midyear).

5. There is angst for a period, and, once the cost-containment beast has been placated, the need to demonstrate the benefits of international assignments is temporarily suspended.

6. Pause.

7. Repeat a few years later.

In truth, very few organizations *can* calculate the ROI of their international assignments and other cross-cultural initiatives; many wish they could.* The added benefit of strategically integrating HR practices in the fashion suggested in this chapter is that the collaboration between global mobility and talent management offers the foundation for ROI to be estimated. This would be a welcome change.

Collaboration between global mobility and talent management enables ROI to be estimated for international assignments. Working with the sending and receiving organizations, global mobility professionals can provide details on the investment side of the ROI equation. For the return side to be assessed, the talent management professionals can offer a system for managing the performance of assignees—for evaluating both the demand-driven and learning-driven goals. The ROI calculations would be estimations, at best, but they would get us closer than ever before to cracking this most challenging organizational code.

*Yvonne McNulty, *Measuring Expatriate Return on Investment in Global Firms: Industry Report for Participating Firms and Their Expatriates*, Technical Report, Monash University, Australia, 2009.

Assessment of Global Mobility Practices for Strategic Alignment

Instructions: Professionals involved in your organization's global mobility program (for example, members of the global mobility team, HR leaders) should complete this assessment. First, ask each person to complete the assessment separately. Then, after the assessment is completed individually, compile the results. Use the results to identify the "low-hanging fruit"—any global mobility practices that can be implemented easily, with relatively little cost. Then discuss a strategic plan for improving upon those practice areas most important for your organization.

	No, our organization does not do this.	Our organization does this to some extent, but we could do it better.	Yes, our organization does this well.
General *Our organization . . . .*			
1. Differentiates between demand-driven and learning-driven international assignments			
2. Identifies task-based performance goals for international assignees			
3. Identifies developmental performance goals for international assignees			
4. Is able to identify key stakeholders for each international assignment			
5. Has a method in place to ensure that there is agreement across stakeholders on performance goals for each assignment			

(Continued)

199

Self-Assessment *Our organization . . .*	No, our organization does not do this.	Our organization does this to some extent, but we could do it better.	Yes, our organization does this well.
1. Has a validated and comprehensive self-selection tool available to help international assignees make well-informed decisions			
2. Has an approach in place that encourages candidates for international assignments to speak with family members about the possibility of living in another country			
3. Has resources or a method in place for international assignment candidates to confidentially ask for more information regarding support-related issues affecting self, spouse/partner, and children			
4. Has resources or a method in place for international assignment candidates to have career-related questions answered			
5. Creates a database of self-nominated candidates for international assignments			

	No, our organization does not do this.	Our organization does this to some extent, but we could do it better.	Yes, our organization does this well.
Selection *Our organization . . . .*			
1. Uses a database from which to select international assignee candidates			
2. Selects candidates based on the technical and experiential requirements of the international assignment			
3. When appropriate, selects candidates based on the developmental goals of the candidates (e.g., necessary succession planning, competency development)			
4. Assesses for personality characteristics using a personality test			
5. Conducts interviews of prospective international assignees regarding their personality traits			

(Continued)

	No, our organization does not do this.	Our organization does this to some extent, but we could do it better.	Yes, our organization does this well.
Support Practices *Our organization . . .*			
1. Provides the best possible support practices in terms of safety and security			
2. Provides the best possible support practices for assignees' immediate family members (spouse/ partner and children)			
3. Offers general support practices to ensure performance success (for example, language and cross-cultural training) across all assignees			
4. Varies support practices depending on the goals of the assignment			
5. Tailors support practices to facilitate specific learning-driven goals			

	No, our organization does not do this.	Our organization does this to some extent, but we could do it better.	Yes, our organization does this well.
Performance Management *Our organization . . . .*			
1. Has gained agreement across stakeholders on performance goals			
2. Has established behavioral or observable indicators of key performance goals			
3. Has practices in place to provide international assignees with the resources needed to improve performance on an ongoing basis			
4. Has identified the most appropriate rater or raters to assess each performance goal			
5. Has the method to deliver feedback and coaching to international assignees based on performance assessment			

(Continued)

Repatriation Our organization . . .	No, our organization does not do this.	Our organization does this to some extent, but we could do it better.	Yes, our organization does this well.
1. Manages expectations of international assignees regarding the role of this assignment in possible career advancement			
2. Provides structured professional networking opportunities for international assignees during assignment			
3. Provides career counseling with international assignees well before repatriation			
4. Acknowledges and rewards the competencies gained during the international assignment			
5. Leverages the competencies gained from the international assignment in subsequent roles			

YOUR CULTURAL AGILITY

You are now at the end of a book fully dedicated to building cultural agility in others—the employees in your organization's workforce. There is still one more person we need to discuss when it comes to developing cultural agility. That person is *you*.

You've quite possibly done your own intuitive self-assessment as you read the book. You might have compared your own life experiences to the experiences of those profiled. You might have read the descriptions of cross-cultural competencies and personality traits and assessed yourself on these characteristics. Do you have a sense of your own level of cultural agility—or your own propensity to become culturally agile?

I invite you to conduct a deeper self-exploration and take the online Cultural Agility Self-Assessment (CASA), which was mentioned in Chapter Five. CASA is a private and confidential tool designed to help individuals gain insight into their cross-cultural competencies and offer guidance on how to develop those competencies. The CASA assesses all twelve dimensions in the Cultural Agility Competency Framework. The tool will give you feedback on the developmental propensity of your individual experiences. After taking the CASA, you will receive an interpretation of your results and some guidance for furthering the development of your cultural agility.

I wish you great success in your personal journey to gain cultural agility!

Cultural Agility Self-Assessment (CASA)

You can review the CASA for yourself as a single-use trial by following these instructions:

Visit www.culturalagility.com/user/register

Enter registration code: CulturalAgility-2013

You will be sent an email with a unique password.

This trial will be available through December 31, 2013. If you would like to try the CASA after December 31, 2013, please send a request for a code through the "contact" tab at www.culturalagility.com.

TAKE ACTION

Based on information presented in Chapter Nine, the following is a list of specific actions you can take to implement management and leadership practices that will help build your pipeline of culturally agile professionals:

- Assess for readiness. Work with other leaders in your organization to assess whether talent management is already strategically aligned and managed to be consistent with the global goals of the organization. Also assess whether cultural agility is a competitive necessity for your organization. You can use this diagnostic to have an honest discussion regarding your organization's level of commitment to building cultural agility.

- Encourage leadership behaviors to reinforce the importance of cultural agility. Along with other leaders in your organization, use the practices suggested in this chapter to brainstorm and agree on key leadership behaviors that will foster cultural agility in your workforce.

- Integrate the HR function. Meet with your HR leaders (especially recruiting, talent development, and global mobility) to discuss their respective roles in building a pipeline of culturally agile professionals. Agree on ways to work together in a more integrated way.

STAY CONNECTED TO LEARN MORE

Do you want to find additional resources and keep up with all the latest on cultural agility? For updates on the best practices, tools, company cases, and research findings, please visit www.culturalagility.com and sign up to stay connected via Facebook, LinkedIn, Twitter, or email.

I look forward to staying connected with you!

APPENDIX

LISTS TO ASSESS YOUR ORGANIZATION'S GLOBAL EMPLOYER IMAGE

The following is a list of Interbrand's 2011 Ranking of the 100 Most Recognizable Global Brands.[1] I have added the name of the parent company (or subsidiary) and the country where each company (or subsidiary) is headquartered.

Interbrand's 2011 Ranking of the 100 Most Recognizable Global Brands

1. Coca-Cola (The Coca-Cola Company) USA

2. IBM (IBM) USA

3. Microsoft (Microsoft Corporation) USA

4. Google (Google, Inc.) USA

5. GE (General Electric Company) USA

6. McDonald's (McDonald's Corporation) USA

7. Intel (Intel Corporation) USA

8. Apple (Apple Inc.) USA

9. Disney (The Walt Disney Company) USA

10. Hewlett-Packard (Hewlett-Packard Company) USA

11. Toyota (Toyota Motor Corporation) Japan

12. Mercedes-Benz (Daimler AG) Germany

13. Cisco (Cisco Systems, Inc.) USA

14.   Nokia (Nokia Corporation) Finland

15.   BMW (Bayerische Motoren Werke AG) Germany

16.   Gillette (Procter & Gamble) USA

17.   Samsung (Samsung Group) South Korea

18.   Louis Vuitton (LVMH Moët Hennessy • Louis Vuitton S.A.) France

19.   Honda (Honda Motor Company) Japan

20.   Oracle (Oracle Corporation) USA

21.   H&M (H & M Hennes & Mauritz AB) Sweden

22.   Pepsi (PepsiCo Inc.) USA

23.   American Express (American Express Company) USA

24.   SAP (SAP AG) Germany

25.   Nike (Nike, Inc.) USA

26.   Amazon.com (Amazon.com, Inc.) USA

27.   UPS (United Parcel Service, Inc.) USA

28.   J.P. Morgan (JPMorgan Chase & Company) USA

29.   Budweiser (Anheuser-Busch) USA

30.   Nescafé (Nestlé SA) Switzerland

31.   IKEA (IKEA International Group) Sweden

32.   HSBC (HSBC Holdings) UK

33.   Canon (Canon Inc.) Japan

34.   Kellogg's (Kellogg Company) USA

35.   Sony (Sony Corporation) Japan

36.   eBay (eBay, Inc.) USA

37.   Thomson Reuters (Thomson Reuters Corporation) Canada

38.   Goldman Sachs (The Goldman Sachs Group, Inc.) USA

39.   Gucci (PPR SA) Italy

40.   L'Oréal (L'Oréal SA) France

41.   Philips (Koninklijke Philips Electronics N.V.) The Netherlands

42.   Citi (Citigroup Inc.) USA

43. Dell (Dell Inc.) USA

44. Zara (Inditex) Spain

45. Accenture (Accenture) USA

46. Siemens (Siemens AG) Germany

47. Volkswagen (Volkswagen Group) Germany

48. Nintendo (Nintendo Company, Ltd.) Japan

49. Heinz (H.J. Heinz Company) USA

50. Ford (Ford Motor Company) USA

51. Colgate (Colgate-Palmolive Company) USA

52. Danone (Groupe Danone SA) France

53. AXA (AXA SA) France

54. Morgan Stanley (Morgan Stanley Smith Barney) USA

55. Nestlé (Nestlé SA) Switzerland

56. BlackBerry (Research In Motion Limited) Canada

57. Xerox (Xerox Corporation) USA

58. MTV (Viacom, Inc.) USA

59. Audi (Audi AG) Germany

60. Adidas (adidas AG) Germany

61. Hyundai (Hyundai Motor Group) South Korea

62. KFC (Yum! Brands, Inc.) USA

63. Sprite (The Coca-Cola Company) USA

64. Caterpillar (Caterpillar Inc.) USA

65. Avon (Avon Products) USA

66. Hermès (Hermès International SA) France

67. Allianz (Allianz SE) Germany

68. Santander (Grupo Santander) Spain

69. Panasonic (Panasonic Corporation) Japan

70. Cartier (Compagnie Financière Richemont SA) France

71. Kleenex (Kimberly-Clark Corporation) USA

72. Porsche (Porsche Automobile Holding) Germany

73. Tiffany & Co. (Tiffany & Co.) USA

74. Shell (Royal Dutch Shell plc) The Netherlands

75. Visa (Visa Inc.) USA

76. Yahoo (Yahoo! Inc.) USA

77. Moët & Chandon (LVMH Moët Hennessy • Louis Vuitton S.A.) France

78. Jack Daniels (Brown-Forman Corporation) USA

79. Barclays (Barclays plc) UK

80. Adobe (Adobe Systems) USA

81. Pizza Hut (Yum! Brands, Inc.) USA

82. Credit Suisse (Credit Suisse Group AG) Switzerland

83. Johnson & Johnson (Johnson & Johnson) USA

84. Gap (The Gap) USA

85. 3M (3M Company) USA

86. Corona (Grupo Modelo SAB de CV) Mexico

87. Nivea (Beiersdorf AG) Germany

88. Johnnie Walker (Diageo) UK

89. Smirnoff (Diageo) UK

90. Nissan (Nissan Motor Company) Japan

91. Heineken (Heineken International NV) The Netherlands

92. UBS (UBS AG) Switzerland

93. Armani (Giorgio Armani S.p.a.) Italy

94. Zurich (Zurich Financial Services AG) Switzerland

95. Burberry (Burberry Group plc) UK

96. Starbucks (Starbucks Corporation) USA

97. John Deere (Deere and Company) USA

98. HTC (HTC Corporation) Taiwan, China

99. Ferrari (Fiat, S.p.a.) Italy

100. Harley-Davidson (Harley-Davidson Motor Company) USA

The following is a list of the Reputation Institute's 2011 List of the 100 Most Reputable Organizations.[2] I have added the country where each company is headquartered.

Reputation Institute's 2011 List of the 100 Most Reputable Organizations

1. Google (USA)

2. Apple (USA)

3. The Walt Disney Company (USA)

4. BMW (Germany)

5. LEGO (Denmark)

6. Sony (Japan)

7. Daimler (Germany)

8. Canon (Japan)

9. Intel (USA)

10. Volkswagen (Germany)

11. Microsoft (USA)

12. Nike, Inc. (USA)

13. Panasonic (Japan)

14. Johnson & Johnson (USA)

15. Nokia (Finland)

16. Nestlé (Switzerland)

17. Hewlett-Packard (USA)

18. Michelin (France)

19. L'Oréal (France)

20. Kellogg's (USA)

21. Goodyear (USA)

22. Ferrero (Italy)

23. Philips Electronics (The Netherlands)

24. 3M (USA)

25. Nintendo (Japan)

26. Colgate-Palmolive (USA)

27. IBM (USA)

28. The Coca-Cola Company (USA)

29. Honda Motor (Japan)

30. Danone (France)

31. Pirelli (Italy)

32. IKEA (Sweden)

33. Amazon.com (USA)

34. Dell (USA)

35. Sony Ericsson (UK)

36. Bridgestone (Japan)

37. Swatch Group (Switzerland)

38. Xerox (USA)

39. Marriott International (USA)

40. Cisco Systems (USA)

41. Eastman Kodak (USA)

42. Deutsche Lufthansa (Germany)

43. Samsung Electronics (South Korea)

44. Procter & Gamble (USA)

45. Toshiba (Japan)

46. FedEx (USA)

47. Fujifilm (Japan)

48. Siemens (Germany)

49. UPS (USA)

50. Hilton Worldwide (USA)

51. LVMH Group (France)

52. Barilla (Italy)

53. DuPont (USA)

54. Sharp (Japan)

55. Singapore Airlines (Singapore)

56. Boeing (USA)

57. HJ Heinz (USA)

58. Electrolux (Sweden)

59. Unilever (The Netherlands/UK)

60. Toyota (Japan)

61. Nissan Motor (Japan)

62. Roche (Switzerland)

63. Suzuki Motor (Japan)

64. General Electric (USA)

65. LG Corporation (South Korea)

66. Hitachi (Japan)

67. Heineken (The Netherlands)

68. Oracle (USA)

69. Marks & Spencer Group (UK)

70. Acer Inc. (Taiwan)

71. Kraft Foods Inc. (USA)

72. Virgin Group (UK)

73. Qantas Airways (Australia)

74. Airbus (France)

75. GlaxoSmithKline (UK)

76. PepsiCo (USA)

77. SAS (Sweden)

78. Fujitsu (Japan)

79. Starbucks Coffee Company (USA)

80. General Mills (USA)

81. Avon Products (USA)

82. Inditex (Spain)

83. Hyundai (South Korea)

84. Carlsberg (Denmark)

85. Lenovo Group (China)

86. Air France-KLM (France)

87. Motorola (USA)

88. Sara Lee (USA)

89. De Beers (South Africa)

90. Diageo (UK)

91. Anheuser-Busch InBev (Belgium)

92. Vodafone (UK)

93. Petrobas (Brazil)

94. Carnival (USA)

95. SABMiller (UK)

96. Carrefour (France)

97. Lockheed Martin (USA)

98. Tsingtao Beer (China)

99. Haier Group (China)

100. BHP Billiton (Australia/UK)

The following is a list of Universum's 2011 World's Most Attractive Employers.[3] This list is divided into two parts, one listing the most attractive for those in business and the other listing the most attractive for those in engineering. The numbers in parentheses represent last year's ranking.

Universum's 2011 Ranking of the World's Top 50 Most Attractive Employers for Those in Business

1. Google (1)

2. KPMG (2)

3. PwC (4)

4. Ernst & Young (3)

5.   Deloitte (5)

6.   Microsoft (7)

7.   Procter & Gamble (6)

8.   J.P. Morgan (9)

9.   Apple (18)

10. Goldman Sachs (10)

11. Sony (13)

12. The Coca-Cola Company (8)

13. L'Oréal (11)

14. BMW (12)

15. Johnson & Johnson (14)

16. IBM (19)

17. McKinsey & Company (16)

18. Morgan Stanley (17)

19. Nestlé (21)

20. IKEA (23)

21. Deutsche Bank (20)

22. The Boston Consulting Group (15)

23. adidas (24)

24. Bank of America / Merrill Lynch (22)

25. Unilever (26)

26. General Electric (27)

27. LVMH (incl. Louis Vuitton, Moët Hennessy, Dior, Sephora) (39)

28. Accenture (25)

29. Citi (29)

30. PepsiCo (28)

31. Kraft Foods (32)

32. Bain & Company (33)

33. Credit Suisse (31)

34. Hewlett-Packard (37)

35. UBS (30)

36. American Express (35)

37. Volkswagen (38)

38. Intel (44)

39. Siemens (new)

40. Heineken (34)

41. 3M (new)

42. Toyota (41)

43. Nokia (42)

44. Shell (40)

45. Esso / ExxonMobil (43)

46. Dell (45)

47. Ford Motor Company (47)

48. Pfizer (46)

49. Cisco (48)

50. Daimler (new)

Universum's 2011 Ranking of the World's Top 50 Most Attractive Employers for Those in Engineering

1. Google (1)

2. IBM (3)

3. Microsoft (2)

4. BMW (5)

5. Intel (6)

6. Sony (4)

7. Apple (10)

8. General Electric (7)

9. Siemens (8)

10. Procter & Gamble (9)

11. Johnson & Johnson (12)

12. Hewlett-Packard (13)

13. Cisco (11)

14. Volkswagen (17)

15. The Coca-Cola Company (15)

16. Shell (14)

17. Ford Motor Company (20)

18. Toyota (18)

19. Esso / ExxonMobil (16)

20. General Motors (23)

21. Accenture (24)

22. L'Oréal (29)

23. McKinsey & Company (26)

24. Oracle (31)

25. Nokia (27)

26. 3M (21)

27. Nestlé (19)

28. BP (28)

29. Schlumberger (30)

30. Goldman Sachs (34)

31. Dell (22)

32. Daimler (new)

33. IKEA (35)

34. Philips (25)

35. Bayer (39)

36. J.P. Morgan (41)

37. Pfizer (32)

38. Deloitte (40)

39. Bosch (33)

40. Kraft Foods (38)

41. Unilever (42)

42. The Boston Consulting Group (36)

43. adidas (43)

44. Lenovo (44)

45. BASF (45)

46. Morgan Stanley (50)

47. PepsiCo (new)

48. Ericsson (new)

49. ABB (new)

50. Heineken (48)

NOTES

CHAPTER 1: WHAT IS CULTURAL AGILITY—AND WHY IS IT SO CRUCIAL TODAY?

1. PwC, *10th Annual Global CEO Survey*, January 2007, http://www.pwc.com/extweb/insights.nsf/docid/46BC27700D2C1D18852572600015D61B (accessed September 7, 2007; URL is no longer available).
2. The Conference Board, *The Conference Board CEO Challenge 2011: Fueling Business Growth with Innovation and Talent Development*, Research Report TCB-R-1474-11-RR (New York: The Conference Board, April 12, 2011).
3. PwC, *14th Annual Global CEO Survey*, January 2011, www.pwc.com/gx/en/ceo-survey/download.jhtml.
4. Percentages from the following sources: Associated Press, "Latin American Market Lifts Profit at Avon," *New York Times*, May 4, 2011, B6, http://www.nytimes.com/2011/05/04/business/04avon.html; Indra K. Nooyi, "Is Good for All," letter to shareholders, PepsiCo, 2010, http://www.pepsico.com/annual10/downloads/PepsiCo_Annual_Report_2010_Letter_to_Shareholders.pdf; and Jack Kaskey, "McDonald's, Verizon Mark U.S. Profit Slowdown on Consumer Woes," *Bloomberg Businessweek*, October 6, 2010, http://www.businessweek.com/news/2010–10–06/mcdonald-s-verizon-mark-u-s-profit-slowdown-on-consumer-woes.html.
5. Ernst & Young, *The Ernst & Young Business Risk Report 2010: The Top 10 Risks for Business: A Sector-Wide View of the Risks Facing Businesses Across the Globe*, EYG no. AU0583 (December 17, 2010), http://www.ey.com/Publication/vwLUAssets/Business_risk_report_2010/$FILE/EY_Business_risk_report_2010.pdf.
6. Ibid., 19.
7. U.S. Army, *Army Culture and Foreign Language Strategy* (Washington, DC: Headquarters, Office of the Army, December 1, 2009).
8. Mariama Diallo, "International Players' Impact on NBA Grows in Past Two Decades," *Voice of America News*, February 17, 2011, http://www.voanews.com/english/news/sports/International-Players-Impact-on-NBA-Grows-in-Past-Two-Decades-116426514.html; Reuters, "Players Born Outside the United States Made up 28 Percent of Major League Baseball's Opening Day Rosters,"

April 1, 2008, http://www.reuters.com/article/2008/04/02/us-baseball-international-idUSSP8408520080402.

9. Ernst & Young, "Act Differently: Sponsor People Who Are Not Like You," http://www.ey.com/GL/en/Issues/Business-environment/Leading-across-borders--inclusive-thinking-in-an-interconnected-world---Act-differently--sponsor-people-who-are-not-like-you.

10. Paula M. Caligiuri, Mila Lazarova, and Stephan Zehetbauer, "Top Managers' National Diversity and Boundary Spanning: Attitudinal Indicators of a Firm's Internationalization," *Journal of Management Development* 23, no. 9 (2005): 848–859.

11. U.S. Census Bureau, "Nation's Foreign-Born Population Nears 37 Million," press release, October 19, 2010, http://www.census.gov/newsroom/releases/archives/foreignborn_population/cb10-159.html.

12. For world population, see Population Reference Bureau, *2005 World Population Data Sheet* (Washington, DC: Population Reference Bureau, 2005), http://www.prb.org/pdf05/05WorldDataSheet_Eng.pdf. See also United Nations, Department of Economic and Social Affairs, Population Division, *Migration Report 2006: A Global Assessment: Part 1. International Migration Levels, Trends and Policies* (New York: United Nations, 2009), http://www.un.org/esa/population/publications/2006_MigrationRep/part_one.pdf.

13. Brookfield Global Relocation Services, *2011 Global Relocation Trends Survey* (Woodridge, IL: Brookfield, 2011).

14. Egencia, *2011 Global Supply Benchmarking Research and Analysis* (Bellevue, WA: Egencia, 2011).

15. Financial Times, *Business School Rankings 2011* (London: Financial Times, 2011), http://rankings.ft.com/businessschoolrankings/global-mba-rankings-2011.

16. Paula M. Caligiuri and Victoria DiSanto, "Global Competence: What Is It—and Can It Be Developed Through Global Assignments?" *Human Resource Planning Journal* 24, no. 3 (2001): 27–38.

17. Jan Selmer and Corinna de Leon, "Parent Cultural Control Through Organizational Acculturation: HCN Employees Learning New Work Values in Foreign Business Subsidiaries," *Journal of Organizational Behavior* 17 (1996): 557–572.

18. Frost & Sullivan, *Meetings Around the World II: Charting the Course of Advanced Collaboration*, white paper sponsored by Verizon and Cisco, October 2009. http://newscenter.verizon.com/kit/collaboration/MAW_WP.pdf.

19. Cristina B. Gibson and Jennifer Gibbs, "Unpacking the Concept of Virtuality: The Effects of Geographic Dispersion, Electronic Dependence, Dynamic Structure and National Diversity on Team Innovation," *Administrative Science Quarterly* 51, no. 3 (2006): 451–495.

20. Pnina Shachaf, "Cultural Diversity and Information and Communication Technology Impacts on Global Virtual Teams: An Exploratory Study," *Information and Management* 45 (2008): 131–142.

CHAPTER 2: THREE CROSS-CULTURAL COMPETENCIES AFFECTING CULTURALLY AGILE RESPONSES

1. Patrick J. Kiger, "Corporate Crunch," *Workforce Management*, April 2005, 32–38.

2. Ben & Jerry's, "Scrapbook," http://www.benjerry.com/company/history/; "Ben & Jerry," *Biography*, DVD (New York: A&E Home Video, 2008).

3. For more on Ben and Jerry's continued corporate social responsibility, see http://www.unileverusa.com/brands/foodbrands/benandjerrys/.

4. Kiger, "Corporate Crunch."

5. The Economist Intelligence Unit, *The Global Talent Index Report: The Outlook to 2015* (Chicago: Heidrick & Struggles, 2011), 14.

6. Chantihika Pornpitakpan, "The Effects of Cultural Adaptation on Business Relationships: Americans Selling to Japanese and Thais," *Journal of International Business Studies* 30, no. 2 (1999), 317–337.

7. "Rankings," Darla Moore School of Business, http://mooreschool.sc.edu/about/rankings.aspx; see also *U.S. News & World Report*, "International: Best Business Schools," 2011, http://grad-schools.usnews.rankingsandreviews.com/best-graduate-schools/top-business-schools/international-business-rankings.

8. Giles Hirst and others, "Cross-Cultural Variations in Climate for Autonomy, Stress and Organizational Productivity Relationships: A Comparison of Chinese and UK Manufacturing Organizations," *Journal of International Business Studies* 39, no. 8 (2008): 1343–1358.

9. My analysis was based on data from the following study: Paula M. Caligiuri and Ibraiz Tarique, *Dynamic Competencies and Performance in Global Leaders: Role of Personality and Developmental Experiences* (Alexandria, Virginia: SHRM Foundation, 2011), http://www.shrm.org/about/foundation/research/Pages/SHRMFoundationResearchCaligiuri.aspx.

10. Shung J. Shin, Frederick P. Morgeson, and Michael A. Campion, "What You Do Depends on Where You Are: Understanding How Domestic and Expatriate Work Requirements Depend Upon Cultural Context," *Journal of International Business Studies* 38, no. 1 (January 2007): 64–83.

11. Andrew Spicer, Thomas Dunfee, and Wendy Bailey, "Does National Context Matter in Ethical Decision Making? An Empirical Test of Integrative Social Contracts Theory," *Academy of Management Journal* 47, no. 4 (2004): 610–620.

12. Maddy Janssens, Jeanne Brett, and Frank Smith, "Confirmatory Cross-Cultural Research Testing the Viability of a Corporation-Wide Safety Policy," *Academy of Management Journal* 38, no. 2 (1995): 364–382.

13. T. Hidayat, "Darwin Silalahi: Aiming to Become a Memorable Leader," *Jakarta Post*, August 22, 2007, http://www.thejakartapost.com/news/2007/08/22/darwin-silalahi-aiming-become-memorable-leader.html

14. Ping Ping Fu and others, "The Impact of Societal Cultural Values and Individual Social Beliefs on the Perceived Effectiveness of Managerial Influence Strategies: A Meso Approach," *Journal of International Business Studies* 35 (2004): 284–305.

15. P. Christopher Earley and Elaine Mosakowski, "Creating Hybrid Team Cultures: An Empirical Test of Transnational Team Functioning," *Academy of Management Journal* 43, no. 1 (2000): 26–49.

16. Tyrone S. Pitsis and others, "Constructing the Olympic Dream: A Future Perfect Strategy of Project Management," *Organization Science* 14, no. 5 (2003): 574–590.

17. Ibid., 577.

18. Ibid., 585–586.

19. Pitsis and others, "Constructing the Olympic Dream."

20. Chuan Zhi Liu, "Lenovo: An Example of Globalization of Chinese Enterprises," *Journal of International Business Studies* 38 (2007): 573–577.

21. Ibid., 576.

CHAPTER 3: NINE CROSS-CULTURAL COMPETENCIES AFFECTING SUCCESS OF CULTURALLY AGILE PROFESSIONALS

1. Ingrid Anderzén and Bengt Arnetz, "Psychophysiological Reactions to International Adjustment," *Psychotherapy and Psychosomatics* 68, no. 2 (1999): 67–75.

2. Paula M. Caligiuri and Ibraiz Tarique, *Dynamic Competencies and Performance in Global Leaders: Role of Personality and Developmental Experiences* (Alexandria, VA: SHRM Foundation, 2011), http://www.shrm.org/about/foundation/research/Pages/SHRMFoundationResearchCaligiuri.aspx.

3. Stefan Mol and others, "Predicting Expatriate Performance for Selection Purposes: A Quantitative Review," *Journal of Cross-Cultural Psychology* 36, no. 5 (2005): 590–620.

4. Michael McCloskey and others, *A Developmental Model of Cross-Cultural Competence at the Tactical Level*, Technical Report 1278 (Arlington, VA: U.S. Army Research Institute for the Behavioral and Social Sciences, 2010).

5. Michael Frone, "Intolerance of Ambiguity as a Moderator of the Occupational Role Stress-Strain Relationship: A Meta-Analysis," *Journal of Organizational Behavior* 11, no. 4 (1990): 309–320.

6. Nehemia Friedland, Giora Keinan, and Talia Tytiun, "The Effect of Psychological Stress and Tolerance of Ambiguity on Stereotypic Attributions," *Anxiety, Stress, and Coping* 12, no. 4 (1999): 397–410.

7. The relationship between self-efficacy and job performance has been established in a variety of job categories. Among creative professionals, for example, see Pamela Tierney and Steven M. Farmer, "Creative Self-Efficacy: Its Potential Antecedents and Relationship to Creative Performance," *Academy of Management Journal* 45, no. 6 (2002): 1137–1148.

8. A number of studies have demonstrated the role of self-efficacy in predicting adjustment in international assignments. See, for example, AAhad M. Osman-Gani and Thomas Rockstuhl, "Cross-Cultural Training, Expatriate Self-Efficacy,

and Adjustments to Overseas Assignments: An Empirical Investigation of Managers in Asia," *International Journal of Intercultural Relations* 33, no. 4 (2009): 277–290. See also Margaret Shaffer, David Harrison, and K. Matthew Gilley, "Dimensions, Determinants, and Differences in the Expatriate Adjustment Process," *Journal of International Business Studies* 30, no. 3 (1999): 557–581.

9. Purnima Bhaskar-Shrinivas and others, "Input-Based and Time-Based Models of International Adjustment: Meta-Analytic Evidence and Theoretical Extensions," *Academy of Management Journal* 48, no. 2 (2005): 257–281.

10. *Curiosity* is a term that has a variety of close correlates, such as *need for cognition, learning orientation*, and *intellectual curiosity*. For one study linking curiosity with job performance, see Thomas Reio and Jamie Callahan, "Affect, Curiosity and Socialization-Related Learning," *Journal of Business and Psychology* 19, no. 1 (2004): 3–23.

11. Margaret Shaffer and others, "You Can Take It with You: Individual Differences and Expatriate Effectiveness," *Journal of Applied Psychology* 91, no. 1 (2006): 109–125.

12. Paula M. Caligiuri and Ibraiz Tarique, "Predicting Effectiveness in Global Leadership Activities," *Journal of World Business* 44, no. 3 (2009): 336–346.

13. McCloskey and others, *A Developmental Model*.

14. Caligiuri and Tarique, *Dynamic Competencies and Performance in Global Leaders*.

15. Jon Shapiro, Julie Ozanne, and Bige Saatcioglu, "An Interpretive Examination of the Development of Cultural Sensitivity in International Business," *Journal of International Business Studies* 39, no. 1 (2008): 71–87. (Quotation is from p. 82.)

16. Orly Levy and others, "What We Talk About When We Talk About 'Global Mindset': Managerial Cognition in Multinational Corporations," *Journal of International Business Studies* 38, no. 2 (2007): 231–258.

17. Nigel Andrews and Laura D'Andrea Tyson. "The Upwardly Global MBA," *Strategy + Business*, no. 36 (Fall 2004), http://www.strategy-business.com/media/file/sb36_04306.pdf.

18. Shapiro, Ozanne, and Saatcioglu, "An Interpretive Examination."

19. Sources of material regarding Walmart in Germany: Andreas Knorr and Andreas Arndt, "Why Did Wal-Mart Fail in Germany?" *Materialien des Wissenschaftsschwerpunktes "Globalisierung der Weltwirtschaft,"* vol. 24 (Bremen, Germany: Institute for World Economics and International Management, published by Andreas Knorr, Alfons Lemper, Axel Sell, and Karl Wohlmuth, University of Bremen, June 2003), http://www.iwim.uni-bremen.de/publikationen/pdf/w024.pdf; Don B. Bradley III and Bettina Urban, "Wal-Mart's Learning Curve in the German Market," *Proceedings of the Academy for Studies in International Business* 4, no. 1 (New Orleans: Allied Academics International Conference, 2004), http://www.sbaer.uca.edu/research/allied/2004/internationalBusiness/pdf/

12.pdf; Louisa Schaefer, "World's Biggest Retailer Wal-Mart Closes Up Shop in Germany," *Deutsche Welle*, July 28, 2006, http://www.dw-world.de/dw/article/0,2144,2112746,00.html; and Mark Landler and Michael Barbaro, "Wal-Mart's Overseas Push Can Be Lost in Translation—Business—International Herald Tribune," *New York Times*, August 2, 2006, http://www.iht.com/articles/2006/08/02/business/walmart.php.

20. Paula M. Caligiuri and Ibraiz Tarique, *Dynamic Competencies and Performance in Global Leaders.*

21. Eric Goosby, "Peace Corps Volunteers Are Leaders in the Fight Against HIV/AIDS," *DipNote* (U.S. Department of State's official blog), March 31, 2011, http://blogs.state.gov/index.php/site/entry/peace_corps_pepfar.

CHAPTER 4: ATTRACTING AND RECRUITING FOR CULTURAL AGILITY

1. Vesa Suutari and Milla Taka, "Career Anchors of Managers with Global Careers," *Journal of Management Development* 23, no. 9 (2004): 833–847.

2. Edgar H. Schein, *Career Anchors: Discovering Your Real Values* (San Francisco: Pfeiffer, 1996).

3. Vesa Suutari, "Global Managers: Career Orientation, Career Tracks, Life-Style Implications and Career Commitment," *Journal of Managerial Psychology* 18, no. 3 (2003): 185–207; Suutari and Taka, "Career Anchors."

4. Erin Burnett and Michelle Lodge, "Mormons Wield Influence in Business," CNBC, June 23, 2010, http://www.cnbc.com/id/37872991/Mormons_Wield_Influence_in_Business; *U.S. News & World Report*, "Best Business Schools," 2011, http://grad-schools.usnews.rankingsandreviews.com/best-graduate-schools/top-business-schools/mba-rankings.

5. Burnett and Lodge, "Mormons Wield Influence in Business."

6. Mattias Parey and Fabian Waldinger, "Studying Abroad and the Effect on International Labor Market Mobility: Evidence from the Introduction of ERASMUS," *Economic Journal* 121, no. 551 (March 2011): 194–222.

7. Christof Van Mol, "The Influence of European Student Mobility on Migration Aspirations" (paper presented at the British Educational Research Association conference, Warwick, England, 2010).

8. Christof Van Mol, "The Influence of Student Mobility on Future Migration Aspirations. Empirical Evidence from Europe and Recommendations to Study the Impact of International Exchange Programmes," *Canadian Diversity* 8, no. 5 (2011): 105–108.

9. *U.S. News & World Report*, "Study Abroad," Spring 2011, http://colleges.usnews.rankingsandreviews.com/best-colleges/rankings/study-abroad-programs.

10. Education and Culture DG, "Youth in Action Programme, Overview of Activities 2007–2010," http://ec.europa.eu/youth/glance/doc/youth_in_action_figures/overview_2007_2010.pdf.

11. The Economist Intelligence Unit, *The Global Talent Index Report: The Outlook to 2015* (Chicago: Heidrick & Struggles, 2011).

12. Universum, "Big 4 Challenge Google's Position as the World's Most Attractive Employer," press release, September 28, 2010, 2.

13. The Economist Intelligence Unit, *Global Talent Index Report*.

14. United Nations Conference on Trade and Development, *The Universe of the Largest Transnational Corporations* (New York: United Nations, 2007), http://www.unctad.org/en/docs/iteiia20072_en.pdf.

15. Nestlé, "About Us: Quick Facts," 2010, http://www.nestle.com/Common/Nestle Documents/Documents/Library/Documents/About_Us/Quick-Facts-2010-EN.pdf.

16. Nestlé, "Careers," http://www.careers.nestle.com/meet/Welcome.htm.

17. Shelba Devendorf and Scott Highhouse, "Applicant-Employee Similarity and Attraction to an Employer," *Journal of Occupational and Organizational Psychology* 81, no. 4 (2008): 607–617.

18. Greet Van Hoye and Filip Lieven, "Investigating Web-Based Recruitment Sources: Employee Testimonials vs Word-of-Mouse," *International Journal of Selection and Assessment* 15, no. 4 (December 2007): 372–383, http://users.ugent.be/~flievens/mouse.pdf.

19. Maryann Stump, "How Do Strong Brands Affect Talent Recruitment? Top Brands Attract Top Candidates," Interbrand, 2010, http://issuu.com/interbrand/docs/interbrand_strong_brands_and_recruitment?viewMode=presentation&mode=embed.

CHAPTER 5: ASSESSING AND SELECTING FOR CULTURAL AGILITY

1. TalentDrive, "Annual Labor Market Survey Finds Rise in Companies Planning to Increase Recruitment Spend in 2011," January 27, 2011, http://www.amerisurv.com/content/view/8300/2/.

2. Zofia Wodniecka and others, "Does Bilingualism Help Memory? Competing Effects of Verbal Ability and Executive Control," *International Journal of Bilingual Education and Bilingualism* 13, no. 5 (2010): 575–595; Ellen Bialystok, "Cognitive Effects of Bilingualism: How Linguistic Experience Leads to Cognitive Change," *International Journal of Bilingual Education and Bilingualism* 10, no. 3 (2007): 210–223.

3. Ellen Bialystok and Dana Shapero, "Ambiguous Benefits: The Effect of Bilingualism on Reversing Ambiguous Figures," *Developmental Science* 8, no. 6 (2005): 595–604.

4. Numerous scholars have written on the Five Factor model of personality. See, for example, Paul Costa and Robert McCrae, "Normal Personality Assessment in Clinical Practice: The NEO Personality Inventory," *Psychological Assessment* 4, no. 1 (1992): 5–13; Robert McCrae and Paul Costa, "More Reasons to Adopt the Five-Factor Model," *American Psychologist* 44, no. 2 (1989): 451–452; Robert McCrae and Paul Costa, "Validation of the Five-Factor Model of Personality Across Instruments and Observers," *Journal of Personality and Social Psychology* 52, no. 1 (1978): 81–90; Robert McCrae and Oliver John, "An Introduction to the Five-Factor Model and Its Applications," *Journal of Personality* 60, no. 2 (1992): 175–216.

5. Paula M. Caligiuri, "The Big Five Personality Characteristics as Predictors of Expatriate Success," *Personnel Psychology* 53, no. 1 (2000): 67–88; Paula M. Caligiuri, Ibraiz Tarique, and Rick Jacobs, "Selection for International Assignments," *Human Resource Management Review* 19, no. 3 (2009): 251–262; Stefan T. Mol and others, "Predicting Expatriate Job Performance for Selection Purposes: A Quantitative Review," *Journal of Cross-Cultural Psychology* 36, no. 5 (2005): 590–620.

6. Paula M. Caligiuri, "Selecting Expatriates for Personality Characteristics: A Moderating Effect of Personality on the Relationship Between Host National Contact and Cross-Cultural Adjustment," *Management International Review* 40, no. 1 (2000): 61–80.

7. Caligiuri, "Big Five Personality Characteristics."

8. Timothy Judge and Remus Ilies, "Relationship of Personality to Performance Motivation: A Meta-Analytic Review," *Journal of Applied Psychology* 87, no. 4 (2002): 797–807.

9. Robert Hogan, Gordon J. Curphy, and Joyce Hogan, "What We Know About Leadership: Effectiveness and Personality," *American Psychologist* 49, no. 6 (1994): 493–504; Timothy Judge and others, "Personality and Leadership: A Qualitative and Quantitative Review," *Journal of Applied Psychology* 87, no. 4 (2002): 765–780.

10. "Executive Sweet," *Goldsea: Asian American Wonder Women*, n.d., http://www.goldsea.com/WW/Jungandrea/jungandrea.html.

11. "Andrea Jung," *Encyclopedia of Business*, 2nd ed., Reference for Business, http://www.referenceforbusiness.com/businesses/A-F/Jung-Andrea.html.

CHAPTER 6: BUILDING THE FOUNDATION FOR CULTURAL AGILITY WITH CROSS-CULTURAL TRAINING

1. Brookfield Global Relocation Services, *Global Relocation Trends: 2011 Survey Report* (Woodridge, IL: Brookfield, 2011).

2. Jared Sandberg, "Cubicle Culture: It Says Press Any Key. Where's the Any Key? India's Call-Center Workers Get Pounded, Pampered," *Wall Street*

Journal, February 20, 2007, B1, http://online.wsj.com/public/article_print/SB117193317217413139.html.

3. P. Christopher Earley and Soon Ang, *Cultural Intelligence: Individual Interactions Across Cultures* (Stanford, CA: Stanford Business Books, 2003). For a nice summary, you should also read P. Christopher Earley and Elaine Mosakowski, "Cultural Intelligence," *Harvard Business Review*, October 2004, 139–146.

4. Brookfield Global Relocation Services, *Global Relocation Trends*.

5. Ibid.

6. RW³ LLC, "Case Study: Global and Virtual Team Effectiveness," http://rw-3.com/tools-and-courses/tools-for-global-team-members/.

7. *Wall Street Journal-Japan*, "English 101, Courtesy of Rakuten," August 6, 2010, http://blogs.wsj.com/japanrealtime/2010/08/06/english-101-courtesy-of-rakuten/. Other details about the Rakuten language policy can be found at http://www.live-english.net/blog/business-english/all-english-business-meetings-are-coming/.

8. Ibraiz Tarique and Paula Caligiuri, "Effectiveness of In-Country Cross Cultural Training: Role of Cross-Cultural Absorptive Capacity," *International Journal of Training and Development* 13, no. 3 (2009): 148–164.

9. Brookfield Global Relocation Services, *Global Relocation Trends: 2011 Survey Report* (Woodridge, IL: Brookfield, 2011).

10. Filip Lievens, Michael Harris, Etienne Van Keer, and Claire Bisqueret found that those trainees who were lower in openness were also lower in cross-cultural training performance. See Filip Lievens and others, "Predicting Cross-Cultural Training Performance: The Validity of Personality, Cognitive Ability, and Dimensions Measured by an Assessment Center and a Behavior Description Interview," *Journal of Applied Psychology* 88, no. 3 (2003), 476–489.

CHAPTER 7: CRAFTING DEVELOPMENTAL CROSS-CULTURAL EXPERIENCES TO INCREASE CULTURAL AGILITY

1. Paula M. Caligiuri and Ibraiz Tarique, "Predicting Effectiveness in Global Leadership Activities," *Journal of World Business* 44, no. 3 (2009): 336–346.

2. Shawn Carraher, Sherry E. Sullivan, and Madeline Crocitto, "Mentoring Across Global Boundaries: An Empirical Examination of Home and Host Country Mentors on Expatriate Career Outcomes," *International Journal of Business Studies* 39, no. 8 (2008): 1310–1326.

3. Steve Hamm, "IBM's Global Mentoring Program," Globespotting, March 2009, http://www.businessweek.com/blogs/globespotting/archives/2009/03/ibms_global_men.html.

4. Matthew Gitsham, Mark Pegg, and Vicki Culpin, "The Shifting Landscape of Global Challenges in the 21st Century: What This Means for What Businesses Want from Tomorrow's Leaders, and the Implications for Management Learning," *Business Leadership Review* 8, no. 2 (April 2011): 1–15.

5. Deloitte, *2010 Executive Summary: Deloitte Volunteer Impact Survey* (New York: Deloitte Development LLC, 2010).

6. Paula M. Caligiuri, Ahsiya Mencin, and Kaifeng Jiang, "Win-Win-Win: The Long-Term Influence of Company-Sponsored Volunteerism Programs," *Personnel Psychology* (under review).

7. Joyce Osland, *The Adventure of Working Abroad: Hero Tales from the Global Frontier* (San Francisco: Jossey-Bass, 1995).

8. Paula M. Caligiuri and Victoria DiSanto, "Global Competence: What Is It—and Can It Be Developed Through Global Assignments?" *Human Resource Planning Journal* 24, no. 3 (2001): 27–38.

CHAPTER 8: DEVELOPING CULTURAL AGILITY THROUGH INTERNATIONAL ASSIGNMENTS

1. Paula M. Caligiuri and others, "A Theoretical Framework for Examining the Relationship Between Family Adjustment and Expatriate Adjustment to Working in the Host Country," *Journal of Applied Psychology* 83, no. 4 (1998): 598–614.

2. Günter Stahl and Paula M. Caligiuri, "The Relationship Between Expatriate Coping Strategies and Expatriate Adjustment," *Journal of Applied Psychology* 90, no. 4 (2005): 603–616; Paula M. Caligiuri and Mila Lazarova, "The Influence of Social Interaction and Social Support on Female Expatriates' Cross-Cultural Adjustment," *International Journal of Human Resource Management* 13, no. 5 (2002): 1–12.

3. Paula M. Caligiuri and Saba Colakoglu, "A Strategic Contingency Approach to Expatriate Assignment Management," *Human Resource Management Journal* 17, no. 4 (2007): 393–410.

4. Ibid.

5. TraQs Consulting, *Global Talent Pipeline: Critical Metrics, Effective Strategies* (Henley-on-Thames, England: TraQs Consulting, 2011).

6. Colleagues and I have written extensively on this topic. See, for example, Günter Stahl and others, "Predictors of Turnover Intentions in Learning-Driven and Demand-Driven International Assignments: The Role of Repatriation Concerns, Satisfaction with Company Support, and Perceived Career Advancement Opportunities," *Human Resource Management* 48, no. 1 (2009): 89–109; Caligiuri and Colakoglu, "A Strategic Contingency Approach"; Paula M. Caligiuri and Mila Lazarova, "Strategic Repatriation Policies to Enhance Global Leadership Development," in *Developing Global Business Leaders: Policies, Processes, and Innovations*, ed. Mark Mendenhall, Torsten Kuehlmann, and Günter Stahl (Westport, CT: Quorum Books, 2001), 243–256.

7. Vladimir Pucik, "Globalization and Human Resource Management," in *Globalizing Management: Creating and Leading the Competitive Organization*, ed.

Vladimir Pucik, Noel M. Tichy, and Carole K. Barnett (Hoboken, NJ: Wiley, 1992), 61–84.

8. Ibid.

9. Brookfield Global Relocation Services, *Global Relocation Trends: 2011 Survey Report* (Woodridge, IL: Brookfield, 2011).

10. Paula M. Caligiuri and Jean M. Phillips, "An Application of Self-Assessment Realistic Job Previews to Expatriate Assignments," *International Journal of Human Resource Management* 14, no. 7 (2003): 1102–1116.

11. Stefan Mol and others, "Predicting Expatriate Job Performance for Selection Purposes: A Quantitative Review," *Journal of Cross-Cultural Psychology* 36, no. 5 (2005): 590–620.

12. Samuel Greengard, "Mission Possible: Protecting Employees Abroad," *Workforce* 76, no. 8 (August 1997): 30–36. I have also conducted research with Jean-Luc Cerdin on this topic. Please visit www.culturalagility.com for updates on our research related to security issues and international assignments.

13. John Burns, "Four Americans Slain in Pakistan: Link to Killing at C.I.A. Is Seen," *New York Times*, November 13, 1997, http://www.nytimes.com/1997/11/13/world/4-americans-slain-in-pakistan-link-to-killing-at-cia-is-seen.html?pagewanted=all&src=pm.

14. Elise Labott, "U.S. Warns of More Attacks in Saudi Arabia," CNN, June 18, 2004, http://articles.cnn.com/2004–06–18/world/saudi.arabia.warning_1_saudi-arabia-islamist-web-travel-warning?_s=PM:WORLD.

15. Brookfield Global Relocation Services, *Global Relocation Trends*.

16. Paula M. Caligiuri and David V. Day, "Effects of Self-Monitoring on Technical, Contextual, and Assignment-Specific Performance: A Study of Cross-National Work Performance Ratings," *Group and Organization Management* 25, no. 2 (2000): 154–175.

17. Brookfield Global Relocation Services, *Global Relocation Trends*.

18. Ibid.

19. Maria Kraimer, Margaret Shaffer, and Mark Bolino, "The Influence of Expatriate and Repatriate Experiences on Career Advancement and Repatriate Retention," *Human Resource Management* 48, no. 1 (2009): 27–47.

20. Stahl and others, "Predictors of Turnover Intentions."

21. Ibid.

22. Mila Lazarova and I have written several articles on the topic of repatriate retention: Mila Lazarova and Paula M. Caligiuri, "Psychological Contract and Repatriate Intentions to Turnover," *Journal of World Business* 36, no. 4 (2001): 389–402; Mila Lazarova and Paula M. Caligiuri, "Repatriation and Knowledge Management," in *International Human Resource Management*, ed. Anne-Wil Harzing and Joris Van Ruysseveldt (Thousand Oaks, CA: Sage, 2004); and Caligiuri and Lazarova, "Strategic Repatriation Policies."

23. Brookfield Global Relocation Services, *Global Relocation Trends*.

CHAPTER 9: MANAGING AND LEADING TO BUILD CULTURAL AGILITY IN THE WORKFORCE

1. The Conference Board, *CEO Challenge 2011: Fueling Business Growth with Innovation and Talent Development*, Report R-1474-11-RR (New York: The Conference Board, April 12, 2011).
2. "CEO Profile: Carlos Ghosn—CEO of Nissan-Renault," *CEO Quarterly*, 2010, http://www.ceoqmagazine.com/mostrespectedceos/ceo_nissan_carlosghosn .htm.
3. Alex Taylor, "Advice from a Fellow Outsider: Nissan CEO and Sony Board Member Carlos Ghosn on Making an Impact on an Old-Line Japanese Company," *Fortune*, April 4, 2005, http://money.cnn.com/magazines/fortune/fortune_archive/ 2005/04/04/8255919/index.htm.
4. "GSK: CEO Andrew Witty Describes PULSE" [video], December 11, 2008, http://www.gsk.com/community/pulse/index.htm.
5. Elisabeth Marx, *Route to the Top: A Transatlantic Comparison of Top Business Leaders* (London: Heidrick & Struggles, 2008).

APPENDIX: LISTS TO ASSESS YOUR ORGANIZATION'S GLOBAL EMPLOYER IMAGE

1. Interbrand, *Best Global Brands 2011: The Definitive Guide to the Most Valuable Brands* (London and New York: Interbrand, 2011), http://www.interbrand.com/ en/best-global-brands/Best-Global-Brands-2011.aspx. Reprinted by permission of Interbrand.
2. Reputation Institute, "The Global RepTrak™ 100: The World's Most Reputable Companies," 2011, http://www.reputationinstitute.com/events/2011_Global_ RepTrak_100_Release_08june2011.pdf. © Copyright 2011. Reputation Institute. All Rights Reserved.
3. Universum, "The World's Most Attractive Employers 2011," http://www .universumglobal.com/IDEAL-Employer-Rankings/Global-Top-50. Reprinted with permission from Universum.

ABOUT
THE AUTHOR

Paula Caligiuri, Ph.D., is a professor in the Human Resource Management Department at Rutgers University, where she was the director of the Center for Human Resource Strategy (CHRS) from 2001 until 2010. Paula is a leading expert in strategic human resource management with a focus on global leadership development, international assignee management, and cultural agility. She has been recognized as one of the most prolific authors in the field of international business for her work in these areas.

Paula is the president of Caligiuri and Associates, Inc., a consulting firm specializing in selection, performance management, and development of culturally agile professionals. Across a wide range of industries, her clients include private sector, military, and nonprofit organizations in the United States, Asia, Australia, and Europe. Paula is a frequent keynote speaker for industry conferences and company meetings and is an expert guest on CNN and CNN International.

Paula's academic publications include several articles in the *International Journal of Human Resource Management, Journal of World Business, Journal of Applied Psychology, Personnel Psychology*, and *International Journal of Intercultural Relations*, and she currently serves as the HR area editor for the prestigious *Journal of International Business Studies*. Paula has written *Managing the Global Workforce* (Wiley, 2010) with Dave Lepak and Jaime Bonache and *Get a Life, Not a Job: Do What You Love and Let Your Talents Work for You* (FT Press, 2010).

Paula holds a Ph.D. from Penn State University in industrial and organizational psychology.

INDEX

Page references followed by *fig* indicate an illustrated figure.

DATE DUE

BRODART, CO.   Cat. No. 23-221